STEPHANIE HARVEY & ANNIE WARD

From Striving to Thriving

How to Grow Confident, Capable Readers

■SCHOLASTIC

Photos ©: cover: Sasiistock/iStockphoto; 51: Craig Froehle; 53: Courtesy of GE Healthcare; 59 top: Dennis Ku/Shutterstock; 135: Nathaniel Minor/Colorado Public Radio; 198: wavebreakmedia/Shutterstock; 255 top: Valentin Armianu/Dreamstime. Additional classroom photography courtesy of Richard Freeda, Ehren Joseph, Annie Ward, Stephanie Harvey, Margaret Hoddinott, Ken Broda-Bahm, Katrina Reda, Simone Westergard, Laurie Pastore, Supamas Lertrungruengrul, and Maria Lilja. Illustrations by Aleksey Ivanov and Sarah Morrow.

CONTENTS

A NOTE FROM THE AUTHORS

How many authors have a bona fide superhero introduce their book? We thanked our lucky stars when Dav Pilkey agreed to write and illustrate this foreword to our book. Dav's superpowers come neither from a cape nor a pair of tighty-whities, but rather from his mighty pen. Through 70+ million copies of Captain Underpants books published in 20 languages, Dav has led numerous kids gleefully to literacy, especially countless striving readers who discovered the joy of reading through the humor and mischief that is Dav and his Tilt-a-Whirl of images and words.

Although we knew Dav's own path to reading was complicated, we were deeply saddened at the graphic but honest depiction of his painful school journey, marked by labeling, ridicule, and exclusion. Thankfully, the experience Dav Pilkey endured is no longer acceptable. But it is a stark reminder of the impact we can have on kids, positively or otherwise. Unfortunately, more subtle forms of discouragement persist. We continue to label kids, and in spite of our good intentions and best efforts, striving readers are still apt to internalize messages that erode confidence and motivation.

More than 40 years after Dav's experience, we know what works and what doesn't. We have decades of indisputable research and field-testing of superb, high-quality teaching. We understand that children learn to read by reading. We know that kids need access to books they want to read; time to read; and loving, knowledgeable teachers who trust them as powerful learners and know how to build on their strengths. Thank heavens Dav's mother intuited that an affirming approach rooted in love would yield powerful results.

We have championed teachers throughout our careers. In this book, we invite you to channel Barbara Pilkey by meeting each child with positive expectancy and nurturing approval. We encourage you to introduce strivers to the widest, wildest array of texts and endorse their choices without judgment; to let go of labels; and, above all, to believe wholeheartedly in every child. In these conditions, reading growth isn't merely possible; it's inevitable.

Steph Harvey   *Annie Ward*

From Striving to Thriving
One Reader's Story
By Dav Pilkey

I never needed anybody to tell me I had reading problems.

I figured that out on my own.

MAYBE I SHOULD SEND YOU BACK TO KINDERGARTEN!!!

My teacher helped.

I never needed an assortment of Labels to Zap my confidence, either.

Dyslexic
Challenged Reader
Reluctant Reader
Slow Reader

I Learned to hate books all by myself.

On the rare occasions when I **DID** find something I wanted to read...

...it seemed as if my choices were never good enough for my teacher.

THAT'S NOT YOUR READING Level!!!

CAN'T YOU find Something More SUBSTANTIAL?

You've ALREADY READ THAT BOOK A HUNDRED TIMES!

THAT'S NOT A REAL BOOK!

But just when everything seemed hopeless, my mom came up with a GREAT idea:

Instead of focusing on WHAT I was reading...

...She made sure THAT I was Reading.

So she got me a library card...

...and let me choose Whatever I wanted to read— with NO Judgment.

It didn't matter if it was a magazine...

...or if it was below my reading Level...

...or if I'd already read it a Hundred Times.

My mom believed that if I read what I Loved...

...I might develop a LOVE for Reading.

And She was RIGHT!

LOVE was the key.

Love Led to habits...

...and habits Led to Skills.

Skills that Continue to this day.

I am a reader Today because of one GREAT idea...

...and a lot of LOVE.

The book you are about to read is filled with GREAT IDEAS!

All you need to do is add the LOVE!

Dav Pilkey 2017

"Children should see the point of reading, and come to know that it can be an intrinsically pleasurable and engaging activity—not just a school exercise where the point lies only in getting every word right."

—Henrietta Dombey, Margaret Moustafa & CLPE Staff

The Best Intervention Is a Good Book

One of Annie's favorite fall rituals is going to the New York City Marathon and watching the parade of runners enter Central Park at East 90th Street for the final stretch to the finish line at Tavern on the Green. While the elite runners dazzle with their flashing speed and impeccable form, the hordes of amateurs are equally amazing—firefighters, costumed Tinkerbells and Batmen, and septuagenarians who invite encouragement by Magic-Markering first names on their jerseys. While marathoners' endurance is awe-inspiring, it's not mysterious. It's obvious that their powerful legs, efficient strides, and mental discipline have developed through thousands of steps over time. There is simply no other route to this level of fitness.

It should be just as obvious that readers, too, develop through practice—by turning page after page in books that they love. Not only is this common sense, but also, four decades of research have established that voluminous, pleasurable reading is key to literacy development. Ask successful adults about their childhood reading habits, and you'll hear about flashlights under the covers, comic books, magazine subscriptions, quickly devoured series, dog-eared rereads, tattered library cards . . . in short: steady consumption of vast amounts of appealing reading material.

It follows that striving readers are inexperienced readers. They simply haven't read enough *yet*. They haven't taken enough steps inside books that grab their hearts or pique their curiosity. They haven't learned the ways books work.

Striving readers typically lack positive experiences with reading; in fact, they are likely to have had many negative interactions with unappealing and difficult material. Children's author Jon Scieszka has called this the reading "death spiral." "It's where kids aren't reading and then are worse at reading because they aren't reading, and then they read less because it is hard and they get worse, and then they see themselves as non-readers, and it's such a shame" (Strauss, 2008).

Research on volume gives us a clear and empowering professional mandate. We have an opportunity to change kids' lives by putting them on an upward reading spiral. The first step is to trust that through experience with appealing books—through a high volume of pleasurable reading—these readers will thrive. We replace the dooming label "struggling reader" with the dynamic, effort-based term "striving reader" because it connotes energy, action, and progress. We feel urgency and agency about matching striving readers with compelling reading material, arranging time and space to read a lot, and providing expert instruction.

WHAT DOES SUCCESS LOOK LIKE?

With the right books in their hands and our close monitoring, teaching, and support, strivers will:

- enter the world of reading with anticipation, rather than dread.
- marshal the full force of language—speaking, listening, reading, and writing, as well as multimedia and the visual and dramatic arts—to make sense of text.
- participate in lively book talks and discussions about "their" books.
- learn that reading is personal, social and cultural, engages minds and hearts, and sounds like language, which it is.
- recognize that reading is about thinking, understanding, learning, and building knowledge.
- develop identities as readers with personal reading tastes and inclinations (e.g., discover favorite authors, topics, and genres—plus, learn where, when, and how to read).
- gain self-confidence.

All of which add up eventually, over time, to a vibrant and deeply fulfilling reading life.

About Our Book

From Striving to Thriving grew out of a shared and evolving recognition that far too many striving readers are suffering unproductive and unintended consequences of the very instructional tools and approaches designed to support their growth. Systems of text-gradient leveling may stamp strivers with the label of a level. Remedial programs often separate strivers from their classroom peers and deprive them of the voluminous reading experiences necessary for growth. Additionally, strivers may miss out on the classroom community building that stems from a shared reading experience. Our mission is to guide children to active literacy. To make sense of their ever-changing world, develop informed positions, and take principled action, children need the technical skills to access print and the comprehension strategies to make meaning and think critically about it.

Children also need to understand that reading is thinking and should sound like language. If it doesn't, and the text becomes a grab bag of words on a page, that's a signal that something has gone awry, and they need to call up their strategies to regain meaning. This ability to self-monitor for meaning is the hallmark of a thriving reader.

In our work, we feel a particular sense of urgency for striving readers—those children who have not yet developed the robust literacies they need and deserve. Like you, we feel an affinity and affection for these kids; we are intrigued by their interests and curious to know what gets in the way of their reading. For a few children—perhaps five percent of the population—learning differences or disabilities prevent them from learning to read as readily as their peers do. For the vast majority, it's more external—lack of access to compelling reading material, for example, and well-intentioned but theoretically unsound interventions that actually confuse kids and interfere with the reading process.

> **The ability to self-monitor for meaning is the hallmark of a thriving reader.**

This book aims to change all that, beginning with the most important step of all: showing strivers that they *are* readers who, with informed and thoughtful instructional support that honors what we know about language and language acquisition, can read their way into a robust and deeply meaningful reading life.

In short, with this book, we seek to close a massive "knowing-doing gap" by doing the best of what's been known for decades: providing all children with daily access to books that jolt their hearts and turbocharge their minds, abundant time to read, and sound instruction in essential skills and strategies grounded in close observation and conversation. What's more, we immerse our students in an inclusive classroom environment that honors their culture, language, and interests, stimulates their curiosity, and provides the time and resources to ask questions and search for answers.

We Stand With You

As you read *From Striving to Thriving*, please know that we empathize with you and stand with you. We know that you may be required to use your district's intervention program. We recognize that you may live in a test-driven pressure cooker. We're simply asking that you think beyond your students' scores and any

labels they've been given, and get to know them as multidimensional people. We bet you'll find strivers who know how to read and love reading in ways that intervention data may not reflect. We also know that, most likely, you already view your kids in holistic ways—in ways that can't be measured by test scores. You are closer to your kids than almost anyone. We wrote this book to support you as you advocate for them, particularly your striving readers. For the sake of equity, as well as sheer love, they deserve nothing less.

About the Framework: Trust, Teach, Transform

We have divided the book into three parts, reflecting the mindset and spirit we think is needed to help turn strivers into thrivers.

TRUST

We recommend that you claim your rightful role as a professional decision-maker. Study the research, gather the data, and trust yourself to make wise and informed instructional decisions for your strivers every day.

At the same time, trust your strivers—trust that with access to abundant books, time to read books they choose, expert instruction, and a chance to learn what reading is and how it works, they will become confident, capable readers because you've ignited a spark that will burn bright.

TEACH

Recognize as well the critical role of sensitive, thoughtful teaching that is informed continuously by research and assessment. Remember, we are always teaching the striver—not a program.

TRANSFORM

And finally, transform. We're firm believers that to fall in love with reading forever, all it takes is getting lost in one good book. When that happens, we discover that reading is one of life's greatest pleasures. An entire generation became readers inside the pages of Harry Potter books. We advocate for our strivers every day so they, too, will experience nothing short of the transformative joy and power of reading.

What's Inside Each Chapter

Our chapters are organized around a clear, easy-to-navigate template. Here's what you'll find.

CHAPTER 1

Table the Labels

To this day Steph is guided by the *aha* moment of a striving for reader named Anthony. This high-spirited, inquisitive boy felt reading as any child she had ever met. He was convinced he could out during reading workshop daily for a special reading class whe on nonsense words for 30 minutes among other meaningless activ floundered. He got far less reading time than the other kids. Each the room, he felt the sting of their stares, whether real or imagine benchmark testing showed little or no growth. And all the while, tl animated boy slipped deeper into a sense of assumed disability and lonely isolation.

Steph pleaded with the administrators to let Anthony stay in class during reading workshop time, and they agreed once they understood her argument. Seated near the front of the whole class bunched on the floor, Anthony participated in the daily shared ...teractive comprehension ...re central to literacy ...his classroom. The kids turned ...oughout and jotted their ...tions, and new learning on

PRACTICES AND LESSONS

In the back of the book you will find Practices and Lessons for each chapter. These are also available for downloading at scholastic.com/ThriveResources.

See the following Practices and Lessons for this chapter:

These sheets are also available at scholastic.com/ThriveResources.

VIGNETTE

We open each chapter with a classroom- or home-based story that captures the point of the chapter.

Striving to Thriving © 2017 by Stephanie Harvey & Annie Ward, Scholastic Inc.   31

RESEARCHERS ON TABLING THE

1. Peter Johnston's wise words have guided us for over a decad
   a reservoir of research, his books, *Choice Words* and *Openin*
   the power of language to build agency, lift kids up, and make
   asserts, "In productive classrooms, teachers don't just teach
   build emotionally and relationally healthy learning communiti
   that lead to more successful learning outcomes. In *Choice W*
   suggests language for us to use with kids to build confidence
   of agency. For instance, telling kids they are *so smart* is finite
   learning potential, whereas telling them they are *so thoughtf*
   to continue to think deeply and engage in learning. He reveals the impact of
   our words—the power of what we say and what we don't say—to shape literate,
   empathetic, efficacious human beings.

2. In *Closing the Achievem*
   words about the inequit
   bilingual and multilingua
   and a deficit-laden appr
   that focuses on what stu
   students' lives and send

   - Limited English Pro
   - Language Minority
   - Auditory Processin
   - Intellectually Hand
   - Special Needs
   - Attention Deficit D
   - At Risk
   - Hearing Impaired

   While some students
   too many, particularly t
   English, become their d
   innocuous label such as
   attribute that most chall
   we mean well, tagging s

   - exacerbate their fe
     linguistic differenc

36   *From Striving to Thrivi*

RESEARCHERS: THREE TO KNOW

We highlight pivotal literacy researchers you'll want to know. We make it easy for you to remember them by showcasing three seminal studies and/or bodies of work related to the chapter topic that every teacher should know, presented in a succinct, compelling way.

TAKE ACTION

What You Can Do to Table the Labels and Grow Confident, Capable Readers

To table the labels and build confident, capable readers, we recommend taking these five actions:

1. Let go of labeling kids.
2. Champion a true growth mindset.
3. Encourage empathy.
4. Get to know your kids ASAP.
5. Create conditions for interaction and boundless reading.

1. Let go of labeling kids.

In 1977, Steph was teaching second grade using a basal reading program. Her class was divided into four ability groups—high, medium-high, medium-low, and low—all practicing round robin reading. Shocking, right? And more than a little embarrassing!

In the summer of that year, the first Star Wars movie premiered, and Steph stood in line for 12 hours to ensure a front-row seat and free t-shirt. The movie transformed her into an instant Star Wars geek. That September, she headed to Burger King to snag the first in a series of Star Wars character posters, which was free with the purchase of a Whopper. By the month's end (many Whoppers), she had posters of Luke Skywalker, R2-D2, Darth Vader, and Chewbacca. She decided to post them on the classroom bulletin board and name her reading groups after the characters. Guess which group was named after Luke Skywalker? The high group. And the low group? Chewbacca. Sheesh—a mortifying story for sure, and one that's painful to share. But we don't pop out of the womb knowing how to teach reading. Becoming a wise reading teacher takes time, thoughtfulness, deep study, and sheer effort. Teaching reading to striving readers is rocket science! Learning how to teach

ACTIONS

Professional moves that will help you make an immediate and tangible difference in your strivers' lives are presented in the imperative voice to inspire you to act!

38   *From Striving to Thriving © 2017 by Stephanie Harvey & Annie Ward, Scholastic Inc.*

ASSESSING READERS IN THE ROUND

TABLE THE LABELS

Use these questions to drive responsive, learner-focused teaching based on what kids *can* do.

Self-Questions

- Do I believe that an expert, caring teacher is superior to programmatic instruction?
- Do I believe that striving readers can become avid, proficient readers?
- What are some ways I can build confidence in my striving readers?
- Do I share my area of specialty with my kids and encourage them to share theirs?
- Do I share with my kids times I have made mistakes or experienced frustration?
- Do I share stories that show how effort and hard work eventually lead to success?
- Have I designed and created comfortable learning spaces in my classroom? Spaces that make reading more desirable?

Kidwatching Questions

- Does the student believe that he can become a good reader?
- Does the student believe that reading will help her grow more knowledgeable?
- Does the student become frustrated when he loses meaning while reading?
- Is the student willing to try again?
- Does the student easily find reading materials she is interested in?
- What does the student know and care about?
- Are there spots in the room where the student knows he can work most easily and productively?

Conferring Questions

- Do you want to try that again? What will you try differently in the next attempt?
- Did you learn anything you would like to explore further?
- What do you care about most in life?
- What topics do you like to read about most?
- Do you need a more comfortable space to do this work?

ASSESSING READERS IN THE ROUND (ARR)
Integrated throughout the book, the ARR helps guide your kidwatching, conferring, and data collection across a spectrum of reading behaviors, attitudes, and understandings.

Annie Ward, Scholastic Inc.   69

From Striving to Thriving © 2017 by Stephanie Harvey & Annie Ward, Scholastic Inc.

What We Know About Reading

Taking our lead from literary researcher Louise Rosenblatt (1938), we believe that reading is a meaning-charged transaction between the reader and the text. For that reason, the meaning you take away from a book may vary from the meaning somebody else takes away. For example, Annie recently paused outside the high school band room to talk with Addie, a ninth grader, who was reading *Wild*, Cheryl Strayed's memoir of her solo hike on the Pacific Crest Trail. Having recently finished the book herself, Annie was eager to talk to someone about it, particularly about Strayed's grief over the loss of her mother. Annie's own mother was in the final stage of a long battle with lung cancer, and Strayed's writing moved her viscerally.

"What do you think so far?" Annie asked. Addie replied, "You know how Cheryl names her backpack Monster because it's so enormous and heavy? Well, this is my Monster because it's a big hardcover nonfiction book, and I don't usually read nonfiction. I'm challenging myself to read the whole thing, and I'm getting inspired because if Cheryl can keep hiking, I can keep reading and finish this Monster." When Annie mentioned that she was devastated by Strayed's loss, Addie politely acknowledged, "Yeah, for sure—but I'm really drawn to her perseverance along the trail."

When Annie told Steph about the exchange, Steph shared that, although she is an avid hiker and mountain woman, she would never attempt the Pacific Crest Trail alone. *Wild* made her reflect on the challenges of growing older, but also helped her come to terms with it. Three readers, three different, meaningful "mosaics of thought" (Keene & Zimmermann, 2007). Which interpretation is "right"? Of course, they all are—and, undoubtedly, they are not the only ones. There are unlimited ways to read and interpret the book. The writer Annie Proulx says simply, "The reader writes the story."

How We Define Reading

And that brings us to our definition of reading. We believe that reading is a personal process, a social/cultural process, thinking, and language.

- **A Personal Process** To every text we read, we bring our life experiences (including those with other books), values, perspectives, and cultural and linguistic backgrounds (Smith, 2011; Goodman et al., 2016). Thus, the book you read is not exactly the same book your best friend reads. Reading should change us (Harvey & Goudvis, 2017; Beers & Probst, 2017)—enrich and enchant us, anger, delight, or move us—and that change is always shaped by our own life experiences and personal values and beliefs.

- **A Social/Cultural Process** "Literacy floats on a sea of talk" (Britton, 1970). Oral and written language are always learned in a social/cultural context (International Reading Association et al., 2010)—we learn to talk, read, and write through our interactions with others. And the meaning that we take away from a book may shift as we discuss that book with others and learn what they think. Nothing engages us and enhances our comprehension more than our own cultural perspectives and talking to others about what we've read, whether in partnerships, book clubs, or conferences.

● **Thinking** Always, at its core, reading is thinking and serves multiple purposes—to inform and instruct, narrate and delight, question and challenge, and regulate and guide (Halliday, 1973). Thoughtful readers pay attention to their inner conversation as they read, listen, or view. They develop an awareness of their thinking, monitor for understanding, learn to think strategically, and actively use knowledge. As a knowledge-building activity, reading shapes and changes thinking. We want readers, particularly striving readers, to recognize the power of their own thinking when reading. Few things will give striving readers more confidence than knowing they can turn information into knowledge by thinking about it (Harvey & Goudvis, 2017).

Nothing engages us and enhances our comprehension more than talking to others about what we've read, whether in partnerships, book clubs, or conferences.

- **Finally, We Believe That Reading Is Language** We think Peter Johnston (2010) explains it best: "Language is very much like a living organism. It cannot be put together from parts like a machine, and it is constantly changing." The more we learn about written language, what it is, and how it works, the more effective we'll become as teachers. As Peter notes, "Instructional outcomes in the language arts and assessment policies and practices should reflect what we know about language and its acquisition."

In general, children learn best when they are working with real, complete texts and applying all language cuing systems—graphophonic, syntactic, and semantic—to create a rich network of meaning. The more text children have at their disposal, the more meaning support they have and, therefore, the easier it is for them to make sense of that text (Goodman et al., 2016).

Oral Language Is the Foundation of Literacy

Children are powerful language learners. At a very young age, they arrive to school with noteworthy control of oral language, the foundation of written language. The instructional strategies we provide scaffold children to cross the bridge from oral to written language. With shared reading, for example, students observe an expert reading a text with fluency and expression, enabling them to learn critical concepts such as the alphabetic principle, phonemic awareness, vocabulary, and spelling while also learning how to orient themselves on a page, starting at the top and working their way down, left to right (Fountas & Pinnell, 2017). (See page 296 for more on shared reading.)

The key is to give our strivers access to the full force of language: reading, writing, speaking, and listening.

The Reading-Writing Connection

Additionally, children may learn the intricacies of written language—sounds, letters, words, and the like—when they create texts themselves, using "invented spelling." (See page 298 for more on invented spelling.) In other words, there is ample evidence (Ouellette & Sénéchal, 2017; Feldgus et al., 2017) that children drill themselves on sound/letter relationships as they write their own meaningful stories, essays, and the like. As Donald Graves observed way back in 1983, for some children, writing—which gives them active control of written language—is an easier, more meaningful entry into reading. Always, the key is to give our strivers access to the full force of language: reading, writing, speaking, and listening.

What We Understand About Reading Drives Our Teaching and Assessment

Because of what we understand about reading, we refer to certain practices repeatedly throughout this book. Those practices propel our cycle of teaching and assessing. Always, we:

- **Keep reading instruction and practice embedded in real texts** that quicken the pulse and engage minds and hearts. Learning to read is easier when kids love what they're reading. So, we build robust classroom libraries; surround our students with engaging texts in a range of topics, genres, and formats, written for various purposes; and invite students to choose texts—with thoughtful assistance from us—that pique their interest and that they are able to read.

- **Immerse students in the richest curriculum possible,** driven by their own curiosity and questions about the world. We believe that kids need multiple ways to enter reading—and multiple ways to show what they know about reading. So, while Darius may not enjoy reading a novel yet, he comes to life when our digital projector is on the blink, and we encourage him to jump online to try to figure out why. Strivers need a constellation of entry points into information and ideas.

- **Understand that the most effective teaching is responsive;** we respond best to kids when we get to know them well by listening to them, talking with them, watching them in action in our classrooms, and analyzing the products of their learning. For that reason, we rely on multifaceted assessment that helps us capture a wide spectrum of information that reveals students' strengths. We learn what they *can* do and build from there.

- **Understand that the most effective assessment is inquiry driven.** To understand our students as readers, we engage in a process of inquiry. We ask ourselves, what support do they need to become confident, capable readers who understand that reading should be meaningful and pleasurable? How do we help them develop the skills and know-how to monitor their own reading for meaning, and, when they become lost and confused, use the fix-up strategies to regain meaning? What kinds of evidence can we collect that will demonstrate what our strivers already know about reading, which we can then use to help them thrive?

- **Engage our students in self-reflection.** Striving readers in particular lose confidence in themselves as readers. To regain and build their confidence, they need to see evidence of their reading strengths. The best way to do that is to show them everything that they are doing that's productive, such as self-monitoring for meaning, and help them move past the behaviors, attitudes, and understandings that are interfering with their reading, such as using only one reading strategy (e.g., "sound it out") to the exclusion of others. This kind of self-reflection is critical to their growth as readers.

- **Balance one-shot summative assessments with more nuanced, child-centered formative assessments.** We need multiple indicators of reading growth and success! A single measure, such as a reading achievement test, fails to deliver the rich sampling of data we need for triangulation and problem solving, a key part of our inquiry-driven assessment process. For too long, we have assessed children's reading based on one vertical measure: reading level. We deem readers strong or weak based simply on the level at which they read.

A reading level certainly indicates to some degree a reader's proficiency. But reading is about much more than levels. For example, although Ollie and Cassidy are both reading at level Q, they have markedly different reading profiles. Ollie is a third grader with a challenging home life, whose demeanor changes from combative to calm when he escapes into fantasy fiction. Cassidy is a fourth grader who has shown tremendous growth reading graphic novels, most notably the *Lumberjanes* series, and is now willing to explore other genres. We maintain that assessment is best when it is holistic and multidimensional. The chart below shows a child's reading level as derived from a software leveling program, but offers no more information about the child as a reader. The diagram on the next page shows a sampling of some of the many behaviors, attitudes, and understandings that make up the dynamic, robust process known as reading.

↑	↑	↑	↑
K	7–8	2	451–550
J	6–8	1	451–500
I	6–7	1	80–450
H	6–7	1	80–450
G	6–7	1	80–450
F	6–7	1	80–450
E	6–7	1	80–450
D	4–7	1	80–450
C	4–6	K	BR–70
B	4–6	K	BR–70
A	4–6	K	BR–70
Level	**Age**	**Grade**	**LEXILE®**

SPECTRUM OF THRIVING READER BEHAVIORS, ATTITUDES, AND UNDERSTANDINGS

A sampling of some of the behaviors, attitudes, and understandings you might monitor, document, and analyze.

Surface Structure

- Matches letters and sounds
- Develops phonemic awareness
- Uses the graphophonic cuing system to help construct meaning from print

Language

- Uses entire linguistic repertoire for meaning-making
- Uses integrated cueing system—syntactic, semantic, and graphophonic—to make sense of print
- Self-monitors miscues
- Regards home language as a resource across all content areas
- Recognizes bilingualism as an asset

Volume

- Reads extensively at school and at home
- Settles into personal, comfortable reading rhythm and routine
- Develops identity as a reader
- Builds empathy
- Enjoys discussing books with teacher and peers

Knowledge Acquisition

- Activates and builds background knowledge
- Merges thinking with text to turn information into knowledge
- Reads, writes, talks, and thinks across the curriculum (content literacy)
- Researches questions; follows a line of inquiry
- Comes to care and take action

Spectrum of Reading Behaviors

Comprehension

- Engages in a dynamic thinking process to construct meaning from print
- Grasps literal meaning of text
- Reflects understanding through retelling
- Uses comprehension strategies flexibly to enhance understanding. Specifically:
  » Connects new to known
  » Asks questions
  » Infers and visualizes meaning
  » Determines importance
  » Summarizes and synthesizes
- Monitors for meaning and applies fix-up strategies for clarification
- Reads critically with a thoughtful eye and a skeptical stance

[See Comprehension Continuum on p. 26.]

Genre & Format Knowledge

- Navigates nonfiction text features, text structures, graphic features, and infographics.
- Recognizes different nonfiction text types—essay, biography, feature writing, procedural—and fiction—realistic, historic, mystery, fantasy, sci-fi, etc.
- Distinguishes formats—series books, graphic novels, picture books, joke books, etc.
- Attends to the form, structure, white space, and figurative language of poetry
- Navigates and researches digital text online and develops digital citizenship

Fluency

- Reads orally with expression
- Reads at a pace that sounds like conversation
- Reflects the elements of prosody—the music of language

Vocabulary Development

- Builds word knowledge through voluminous reading
- Uses context clues to infer the meaning of unfamiliar words and ideas
- Recognizes appropriate grammatical syntax
- Stops to figure out words when meaning breaks down
- Skips unfamiliar words when they do not disrupt meaning
- Understands parts of speech and their purposes
- Uses prefixes and suffixes to crack open meaning

Text Selection

- Considers interest
- Explores genre
- Searches for text worth thinking and talking about
- Follows teacher/peer recommendations
- Peruses front and back covers; flips through book
- Chooses appropriate reading level

THE ILA/NCTE READING AND WRITING ASSESSMENT STANDARDS

In addition to what we've discussed thus far, we take our cues from the ILA/NCTE Task Force on Standards for the Assessment of Reading and Writing (2010), which guide our assessment, and therefore, our teaching.

- The interests of the student are paramount in assessment.

- The teacher is the most important agent of assessment.

- The primary purpose of assessment is to improve teaching and learning.

- Assessment must reflect and allow for critical inquiry into curriculum and instruction.

- Assessment must recognize and reflect the intellectually and socially complex nature of reading and writing and the important roles of school, home, and society in literacy development.

- Assessment must be fair and equitable.

- The consequences of an assessment procedure are the first and most important consideration in establishing the validity of the assessment.

- The assessment process should involve multiple perspectives and sources of data.

- Assessment must be based in the local school learning community, including active and essential participation of families and community members.

- All stakeholders in the educational community—students, families, teachers, administrators, policymakers, and the public—must have an equal voice in the development, interpretation, and reporting of assessment information.

Standards for the Assessment of Reading and Writing Joint Task Force IRA & NCTE, 2010.

COMPREHENSION CONTINUUM

Answers Literal Questions	Retells	Merges Thinking With Content	Acquires Knowledge	Actively Uses Knowledge
Answering literal questions shows that learners can skim and scan for answers, pick one out that matches the questions, and have short-term recall. *Only demonstrates surface understanding.*	Retelling shows that learners can organize thoughts sequentially and put them into their own words. Shows short-term recall of events in a narrative and bits of information in nonfiction. *Does not, in and of itself, demonstrate understanding.*	Real understanding takes root when learners merge their thinking with the content by connecting, inferring, questioning, determining importance, synthesizing, and reacting to information. *Understanding begins here.*	Once learners have merged their thinking with the content, they can begin to acquire knowledge and insight. They can learn, understand, and remember. *Shows more robust understanding.*	With new insights and understandings, learners can actively use knowledge and apply what they have learned to the experiences, situations, and circumstances at hand to expand understanding and even take action. *Understanding is used for problem solving and acting.*
TEACHER LANGUAGE	**TEACHER LANGUAGE**	**TEACHER LANGUAGE**	**TEACHER LANGUAGE**	**TEACHER LANGUAGE**
What is . . . ? *Where did . . . ?* *Who was . . . ?* *How did . . . ?* *How many . . . ?*	*What has happened thus far?* *What was this about?* *Retell what you read.* *What comes first, second, and third?* *When did . . . ?*	*What do you think?* *What did you learn?* *What does this remind you of?* *What do you wonder?* *What do you visualize?* *What do you infer?* *What is this mostly about?* *What makes you say/think that?* *How did you come up with that?* *What, if anything, confuses you?*	*What did you learn that you think is important to remember?* *Why does it matter?* *What do you think the author most wants you to get out of this?* *What evidence can you cite to make your claim?* *What do you think are some big ideas here?* *What difference does it make?* *Say more about that.*	*What do you want to do about this?* *Why do you want to take action?* *Is there a way you can get involved?* *How do you think you can help?* *How would you convince others of your point of view?* *What is your plan?* *How might you engage the help of others?*

From *Comprehension & Collaboration: Inquiry Circles in Action* by Stephanie Harvey and Harvey Daniels. Copyright © 2009 by Stephanie Harvey and Harvey Daniels. Published by Heinemann. Used by permission.

From Striving to Thriving © 2017 by Stephanie Harvey & Annie Ward, Scholastic Inc.

The Comprehension Continuum on the previous page shares five comprehension processes and the matching teacher language. The continuum is not sequential in nature, but rather a continuum of understanding that increases in sophistication from literal comprehension to the active use of knowledge. While all processes are important, we hope you pay particular attention to the last three columns to help kids think strategically and critically to build knowledge and actively use it.

Assessing Readers in the Round (ARR) helps you put into action what we've discussed in this introduction. It appears on the gatefold of this book's cover, as well as throughout the book at the end of each chapter where you'll find questions that serve three purposes:

1. self-reflection

2. kidwatching

3. conferring

The questions are organized according to the four principles that define reading for us: reading as a personal process, a social/cultural process, thinking, and language. For a complete overview, see Chapter 7: Assess Readers in the Round.

Closing Thoughts

Our students live rich and varied literacy lives. In their own homes, no one thinks of them or refers to them as "struggling readers." Our goal is to make sure that our students remain students and don't become labels. Additionally, we aim to expand their literacy repertoires as we guide them toward capable, confident independent reading. In supportive, literate classroom communities, let's make sure that all our students, with our thoughtful guidance, develop strong identities and competencies as successful readers, thinkers, and learners.

Part I: Trust

"Teachers need to trust in children's learning and in their own ability to learn along with their children. When teachers believe in their own professional judgments and respect children's abilities, success occurs as a part of curricular experience."

—*Yetta Goodman*

 scholastic.com/ThriveResources

"A child is, in essence, what Shefali Tsabary describes as a 'spirit throbbing with its own signature.' We have the opportunity, as teachers, with the power of our position to accept and name those signatures in appreciative ways rather than as failures."

—Katherine Bomer

Table the Labels

To this day, Steph is guided by the "aha" moment of a striving fourth-grade reader named Anthony. This high-spirited, inquisitive boy felt as defeated by reading as any child she had ever met. He was convinced he couldn't read. Pulled out during reading workshop daily for a special reading class where he was timed on nonsense words for 30 minutes among other meaningless activities, Anthony floundered. He got far less reading time than the other kids. Each time he left the room, he felt the sting of their stares, whether real or imagined. Continual benchmark testing showed little or no growth. And all the while, the once animated boy slipped deeper into a sense of assumed disability and lonely isolation.

Steph pleaded with the administrators to let Anthony stay in class during reading workshop time, and they agreed once they understood her argument. Seated near the front of the whole class bunched on the floor, Anthony participated in the daily shared reading and interactive comprehension lessons that were central to literacy instruction in this classroom. The kids turned and talked throughout and jotted their thoughts, questions, and new learning on

See the following Practices and Lessons for this chapter:

PRACTICES

LESSON

These sheets are also available at scholastic.com/ThriveResources.

sticky notes. Steph emphasized that nothing was more important than their thinking. This shared reading experience built community. Kids got to know each other. Through these rich conversations, Anthony heard from the other kids and they heard from him.

After these lessons, Steph conferred with him about book choice and helped him find books he wanted to and was able to read. He read independently every day for a good deal of the workshop time, met regularly with Steph and his teacher in conferences, and occasionally joined a needs-based, temporary small group where he got support in reading skills and strategies.

A month or so in, he spotted a copy of Chris Van Allsburg's *The Polar Express*, a book he recognized, and pulled it off the shelf. Steph was skeptical; she knew the text was beyond his reading level. But as she watched him, she could see that he was able to read some of it and to make sense of most by using the strategies he had learned. One morning, as Steph conferred with another student across the room, Anthony's classmates almost fell off their chairs when he blurted out, "Reading is thinking!" At that moment, he got it—he understood that reading is about more than simply calling words. Over the course of that year, he grew into an avid reader who believed he was a capable learner. As Anthony changed his reading, reading changed Anthony.

From Striving to Thriving © 2017 by Stephanie Harvey & Annie Ward, Scholastic Inc.

Joyful Reading and Expert Instruction for *All* Children

Every teacher has an Anthony story. Too many kids are languishing in skills-based interventions, missing out on the joys of meaningful reading and suffering from a lack of confidence. In the many years that Steph and Annie have spent working with teachers, few of them have felt the need to seek extra help for the kids who are rocking it in reading! Not surprisingly, the vast majority of teachers seek help for the readers for whom they have concerns, the striving readers we address in this book.

> *"Reading is thinking!" At that moment, Anthony got it— he understood that reading is about more than simply calling words.*

We have seen many kids learn to read and have witnessed many paths to getting there. We've seen kids who seem to learn by osmosis. They come into kindergarten reading, or at least close to reading, and most of their parents, although delighted, have no clue why. Steph remembers taking her four-year-old son Alex and his pre-school friend Max to the pool many years ago. As they walked along the edge, Max queried, "What is horseplay?"

"What an interesting question, Max. What makes you ask it?"

Max pointed, "That sign says no running, no splashing, no jumping, no horseplay." Steph was slack-jawed. The boys were barely out of diapers, and Max was reading words like "horseplay."

For other kids, explicit instruction in reading strategies, combined with plenty of time to read, puts them on a path to active, voracious reading in the expected time frame.

Then there are kids like Anthony and Dav, kids for whom learning to read is a puzzle and a source of much consternation and sadness for them and those who love them. They struggle mightily. Reading is unpleasant and even painful rather than what it ought to be: compelling and joyful. Let's be clear, human beings move toward pleasure and away from pain. If reading is painful, why would anyone do it? We need to do everything in our power to help our striving readers see reading as a meaningful act that will bring them pleasure and pride. They need to view themselves as meaning makers—as capable, confident readers. This is tough when a striver like Anthony ends up sitting next to a fluent reader like Max on the first day of school. But that should not stop us. In fact, it should make us more determined to help them.

Reading researcher Dick Allington says that, of all the things he has learned over the years, one of the most important ideas is simply that children differ. We wholeheartedly concur. But although children differ, after many years of teaching reading and studying the teaching of reading, we do not advocate differentiating instruction. We can practically hear the gasps of many of you! But the truth is, good instruction is good instruction for all kids. Too often, striving readers like Anthony and Dav are given a label,—"disabled learner," "struggling reader," "at-risk student"—shipped off to one programmatic intervention after another, and, as such, deprived of the potent, meaningful literacy experiences that spring from a robust classroom community. Devastatingly, they are stripped of confidence, reading choice, and reading volume, the very things that would most accelerate their growth.

Why are the kids who feel the most stigmatized shifted out of the classroom and into a "special room"? Why are the kids who need the most time to read getting the least time to read? In the classrooms where we work, striving readers are not pulled out during reading time—not for whole-group instruction time, small-group time, or independent reading time. We view reading time as sacred. But please don't misunderstand. We absolutely differentiate, but in our own way. While some children may require more intense reading interventions, focused instruction in English, and/or special education services, *all* children need and deserve an active reading life fueled by caring teachers. We must ensure, foremost and forever, that striving readers have abundant daily access to compelling books, a choice of what to read, and copious time to read in school and at home. And we must make sure that access, choice, and time to read are firmly in place before we make decisions to send kids off for special services.

What Our Strivers Need

We individuate for our striving readers every day and scaffold their learning by:

- engaging them in community-building classroom interactions.
- encouraging them to read extensively from a vast array of texts they can and want to read—we flood the room with compelling books at every level.
- building in time for them to read, write, talk, and inquire every day.
- providing them with a wide range of entry points into literacy.
- teaching a repertoire of comprehension strategies to construct meaning.
- meeting with them in reader-to-reader, heart-to-heart conferences.
- teaching them in flexible, temporary, needs-based small groups.

As such, readers like Anthony begin to feel as confident as readers like Max. (Oh, and in case you are wondering, some 32 years later, Anthony and Max are reading at the same level!)

Look, if you are a good reader, school, not to mention life beyond school, is likely productive and rewarding. In fact, reading well correlates with just about everything in life that matters, including happiness and longevity (British Institute of Education, 1970). So, with that in mind, we write this book because we want every single child on earth to read well and love to read, with a particular bias towards those

children for whom reading is tough. We know that if we can help them find their way into reading, they will exceed our expectations, which are already sky high. And that begins with tabling the labels.

RESEARCHERS ON TABLING THE LABELS

1. Peter Johnston's wise words have guided us for over a decade. Grounded in a reservoir of research, his books, *Choice Words* and *Opening Minds*, extol the power of language to build agency, lift kids up, and make them whole. He asserts, "In productive classrooms, teachers don't just teach children skills, they build emotionally and relationally healthy learning communities"—communities that lead to more successful learning outcomes. In *Choice Words* (2004), he suggests language for us to use with kids to build confidence and instill a sense of agency. For instance, telling kids they are *so smart* is finite and can limit their learning potential, whereas telling them they are *so thoughtful* encourages them to continue to think deeply and engage in learning. He reveals the impact of our words—the power of what we say and what we don't say—to shape literate, empathetic, efficacious human beings.

2. In *Closing the Achievement Gap* (2008), Noah Borrero and Shawn Bird mince no words about the inequity too many of our students encounter, particularly our bilingual and multilingual students, when they enter classrooms driven by testing and a deficit-laden approach to teaching and learning—in short, on instruction that focuses on what students can't do. They point to labels that may define these students' lives and send them on a downward spiral:

   - Limited English Proficient
   - Language Minority
   - Auditory Processing Deficit
   - Intellectually Handicapped
   - Special Needs
   - Attention Deficit Disorder
   - At Risk
   - Hearing Impaired

   While some students do face real challenges that require specialized support, too many, particularly those who enter school with a heritage language other than English, become their deficit label. As Borrero and Bird point out, even a seemingly innocuous label such as *English language learner* "defines students by the very attribute that most challenges (and often intimidates) them." Sadly, even though we mean well, tagging students "ELL" may serve to:

   - exacerbate their feelings of inadequacy by labeling them by their linguistic difference.

- isolate them in "ELL Ghettos" (Valdés, 2001), where students who speak a language other than English are often at the bottom of the achievement track.
- ignore their bilingualism or multilingualism—which is a tremendous asset!

For this reason, language researchers such as Ofelia García and Li Wei recommend that we acknowledge students' language heritage and refer to them as "emerging bilinguals"—in other words, they already have one language and they are acquiring another—a strength!

Those who work with emerging bilinguals would do well to investigate the developing research about *translanguaging*. Within a translanguaging framework, language learning is understood as a dynamic and social process rather than a linear and individual one—and the student's home language is regarded as an essential resource across literacy, math, and other content areas. When we accept reading as thinking and meaning making, it makes sense that emerging bilingual students should have access to their entire linguistic repertoire to make sense of text (2014).

3. The Department of Education reports that about five percent of all kids, due to extreme cognitive or processing deficits, are likely to need more intense intervention than we offer in this book. But currently, as many as 13 percent of kids are identified for special ed—and many thousands more are slotted into Response to Intervention groups (2016). RTI, a ubiquitous framework for teaching reading in elementary schools, is a multi-tier approach to early identification and support for students with learning needs. Like so many initiatives, RTI grew out of a well-meaning desire to reduce the number of children in special ed classes and help them become grade-level readers. But the unintended consequence of RTI is that even more children are being deficit-labeled in reading and landing in an array of decontextualized, unhelpful interventions.

Unfortunately, RTI has had disappointing results when it comes to literacy achievement. According to a comprehensive federal evaluation of the framework involving more than 20,000 students in 13 states, first graders who received RTI interventions performed "worse than their virtually identical peers . . . and second and third graders who were identified for Tier 2 had no significant reading benefits either" (2015).

Karen Wixon, a literacy professor and dean of education at the University of North Carolina at Greensboro, notes that the study found that RTI interventions were more likely to focus on phonics instruction than on comprehension, a serious problem if our intent is to grow proficient, lifelong readers. According to Wixon, "Students are missing a lot of broader things that are going to make a difference in their ability to put it all together in functional reading" (2015).

1. Let go of labeling kids.

In 1977, Steph was teaching second grade using a basal reading program. Her class was divided into four ability groups—high, medium-high, medium-low, and low—all practicing round robin reading. Shocking, right? And more than a little embarrassing!

In the summer of that year, the first Star Wars movie premiered, and Steph stood in line for 12 hours to ensure a front-row seat and free t-shirt. The movie transformed her into an instant Star Wars geek. That September, she headed to Burger King to snag the first in a series of Star Wars character posters, which was free with the purchase of a Whopper. By the month's end (and after too many Whoppers), she had posters of Luke Skywalker, R2-D2, Darth Vader, and Chewbacca. She decided to post them on the classroom bulletin board and name her reading groups after the characters. Guess which group was named after Luke Skywalker? The high group. And the low group? Chewbacca. Sheesh—a mortifying story for sure, and one that's painful to share. But we don't pop out of the womb knowing how to teach reading. Becoming a wise reading teacher takes time, thoughtfulness, deep study, and sheer effort. Teaching reading to striving readers is rocket science! Learning how to teach

Becoming a wise reading teacher takes time, thoughtfulness, deep study, and sheer effort.

them to read is an ongoing, lifelong process. Few things matter more to striving readers than expert and caring teachers who help them to become thriving readers.

Although we don't call students "Bluebirds" or "Robins" anymore, labels persist. Kids view themselves as learners based on how we view them. They lose motivation to read if we label them "low," and they don't bust through the ceiling if we label them "high." In this era of increasingly demanding standards coupled with high-stakes testing, whenever a child scores below benchmark, we tend to slap an intervention on him or her, usually in the form of a published program. We are not the first to say it, but we'll say it anyway because it's so very true: *Programs don't teach kids, teachers do.* In fact, an extensive review of programs by the federal government's What Works Clearinghouse (2007) found that Reading Recovery was the only intervention that made a significant difference in reading achievement for young children and that few other comprehensive or supplemental published programs had any evidence of raising students' reading achievement. Sadly, none of the most popular interventions were backed by rigorous enough research to even be included in the review.

> **WATCH YOUR LANGUAGE!**
>
> Labeling is problematic beyond reading instruction. For instance, a child who loves singing may be labeled "the musician," which could discourage her from trying out for soccer. Child therapist Brenna Hicks suggests we exercise mindfulness when talking about children's traits. "If you must define certain things about kids to yourself or others, try to choose positive versions of the same trait, for example, *spirited* rather than *hyper, cautious* rather than *timid* . . . . Keeping focus on the child's positive attributes while avoiding labels can encourage children to become healthy and happy" (2008). Striving readers, in particular, are often referred to negatively: *wild, passive,* or *out of control.* How about *creative, sensitive,* or *energetic* instead?

An Intervention on Interventions

We need an intervention on interventions. Let's call it Intervention Prevention. And let's not forget, the best intervention is a good book—one a child can and wants to read (Bridges, 2010). Indeed, the milestone that lead to Anthony and Dav's breakthroughs was their desire to read the books they cared about most. Striving readers need access to terrific texts within their reach and of interest to them, targeted, explicit instruction, and plenty of time to read.

We need an intervention on interventions. Let's call it Intervention Prevention. And let's not forget, the best intervention is a good book—one a child can and wants to read.

In fact, they need more time to read than grade-level readers. Mary Howard reminds us that "successful interventions engage students in meaningful reading and writing activities using interesting texts and tasks that guarantee a high level of success while integrating discrete reading skills in context" (Howard, 2009).

As we drafted this book, we wrestled with how to refer to kids for whom reading is difficult. We settled on "striving" because we all strive in various ways every day of our lives. Steph is a full-on striving reader when it comes to tech manuals. Annie loathes even scanning health insurance forms, let alone reading them. And, like kids, we also thrive at times! Thus, the title: *From Striving to Thriving*. At the core of this book is the firm belief that we know that all readers can thrive if we view them as capable, give them time to read voluminously, and provide expert instruction.

Think "Reading Behaviors" Rather Than "Reading Abilities"

When presenting to educators, Steph sometimes conducts a thought experiment where she divides the whole into three smaller groups—high, medium, and low.

- She begins with the "high" group and pretends to pass out a copy of *From Striving to Thriving* to each participant. She suggests they grab a partner and a notebook, and take the book anywhere they choose, flip through it, talk about it, jot down their questions, and meet with her to debrief in an hour or so.

- She moves on to the "medium" group, explaining that she will pass out copies of the shrink-wrapped book, but participants shouldn't open it because she has to tend to the "low" group. So she encourages the "medium" group to check out the cover and read the blurb once and perhaps again since rereading never hurt anyone.

- She moves on to the "low" group and holds up a copy of the brand-new, shiny book, and tells participants that unfortunately they can't have it yet. Instead, she hands out a packet of worksheets and activities, and says that if they stay on task, she will hand out the book later, after she finishes working with the other groups.

A nervous chuckle always fills the room, because the audience recognizes that this is what happens to striving readers in school every single day. Steph's thought experiment illustrates the impact of teachers' expectations on students' performance, a phenomenon documented in Rosenthal and Jacobson's famous *Pygmalion in the Classroom* study (1968).

Good instruction is not merely about reading levels; it's about reading behaviors, attitudes, and understandings. Too often, though, we view instruction through an ability lens—a labeling lens where kids are measured on a vertical scale based simply on reading level. We judge them only on the basis of text complexity gradients. Sadly, kids follow suit. Steph recalls a time when she asked a young reader what she was reading only, to hear her answer "I'm an N." Somewhat taken aback, Steph queried her about how she chose the book. "From the N basket. That's how we get books." Of course, text level is one consideration when choosing books. But when kids refer to themselves as levels, Houston, we've got a problem!

Reading is a complex, dynamic process that involves comprehension, genre knowledge, fluency, and so many other factors (see the Spectrum on page 24). Juliana may be below benchmark based on her DRA results, but she might be the best inferential thinker in the room. If we equate reading competence simply to reading level, striving readers don't stand a chance. If we believe kids are low, and then call them low, our practice suffers, as Steph's thought experiment illustrates. Beliefs drive language and language drives practice. What we believe, say, and do matters. It's time to table the labels NOW!

> *Beliefs drive language and language drives practice. What we believe, say, and do matters. It's time to table the labels NOW!*

EYES AND EARS ON KIDS!

Anyone who has ever bought a bathing suit knows that labels are unreliable. Human size is multidimensional and cannot be captured accurately on a single tag—hence the need for fitting rooms! While it is widely accepted that clothing sizes are unreliable, text gradients as a means of labeling children's reading are, too.

Todd Rose, Director of the Mind, Brain, and Education Program at Harvard University, challenges the myth of norms in his book, *The End of Average* (2016). The book opens with a fascinating account of 1940s Air Force cockpit design, based on "average" human measurements. When an unacceptable number of crashes ensued, the Air Force measured thousands of individual pilots in 10 dimensions (e.g., arm length, torso length) and found that no single pilot was close to average on all 10 measurements. In other words, the carefully engineered cockpit suited no one, and Air Force engineers designed adjustable seats!

Rose outlines three principles of individuality:

- **Jaggedness:** All human characteristics are multidimensional; complex abilities require multiple descriptors.

- **Context-dependence:** Abilities vary with conditions; fixed traits don't exist.

- **Pathways:** Everyone takes the road less traveled; abilities develop along idiosyncratic routes and timelines.

We must attend to "a person's context-specific behavioral signature" and avoid "averagarian labels," Rose argues. All this has huge implications for reading assessment. We must make many observations of each child's reading behaviors over time and in different contexts to generate an accurate profile of him or her as a reader. "There are no fixed ladders of development in reading," Rose states. Irene Fountas and Gay Su Pinnell, the developers of the ubiquitous Fountas and Pinnell Text Level Gradient System, agree. They claim, "Trying to climb the text level ladder is not what reading is about" (2016).

By Assessing Readers in the Round, we create a profile of each child through close and continuous observation of his or her reading behaviors and reader-to-reader, heart-to-heart conferences.

2. Champion a true growth mindset.

Carol Dweck, professor at Stanford and author of the bestseller *Mindset: The New Psychology of Success* (2007), has spent over a decade investigating the difference between a fixed mindset and a growth mindset. She suggests, "In a fixed mindset, students believe their basic abilities, their intelligence, their talents, are just fixed traits. They have a certain amount and that's that, and then their goal becomes to look smart all the time and never look dumb. In a growth mindset, students understand that their talents and abilities can be developed through effort, good teaching, and persistence. They don't necessarily think everyone's the same or anyone can be Einstein, but they believe everyone can get smarter if they work at it" (2012).

Over time, the concept of mindset wended its way into mainstream culture. Parents and teachers read books on the subject, surfed related websites, watched Dweck's celebrated TED Talks, and invited mindset gurus to PTA meetings. Many teachers climbed aboard and attempted to create a classroom culture that fostered a growth mindset, believing it would benefit all kids. But recently, Professor Dweck began to notice a trend that she's labeled as "false growth mindset," where teachers and parents seem to believe that all they need to do is tell kids to work harder to be successful. Although effort clearly matters, success takes more than effort. So, Dweck encourages us to take a more nuanced view of mindset, explaining that when parents and teachers praise only the effort and not the outcome, kids view praise as "a consolation prize." Dweck suggests that to avoid false growth mindset, we should "praise the effort that led to the outcome or learning progress; and not just effort, but strategy... so support the student in finding another strategy" (2016).

> *Dweck suggests that to avoid false growth mindset, we should "praise the effort that led to the outcome or learning progress; and it's not just effort, but strategy... so support the student in finding another strategy" (2016).*

This is great news because it gives teachers a clear guideline for helping kids. Rather than simply telling kids to work harder, teachers can share strategies and resources that help kids engage in the learning process, believe in themselves, make progress, and come to understand that intelligence is not fixed and minds are malleable. Having a true growth mindset emboldens strivers with the sense of self-efficacy that they so desperately need.

Believe in Your Kids

We appreciate Dweck's latest thinking on growth mindset. From our standpoint, what matters is that all teachers believe, from the depth of their souls, that all striving readers are eminently capable. Jeff Howard, founder and president of the Efficacy Institute, says, "Smart is not something you are: Smart is something you get." And you get smart by reading, writing, thinking, discussing, working hard, and building knowledge. That doesn't mean having kids slog through tedious textbooks or repetitive test prep. Kids should not be working their tails off on monotonous, mind-numbing material.

If the curriculum doesn't intrigue, if it lacks challenging ideas and riveting controversies, why should kids put up with it? It is the content that is seductive. Interesting content motivates all of us, particularly striving readers. We need to

From Striving to Thriving © 2017 by Stephanie Harvey & Annie Ward, Scholastic Inc.

offer strivers content they simply can't resist. We need to provide them with accessible entry points to that content so they can build knowledge. When strivers dive deep into compelling content, they work hard and gain knowledge, which fosters a growth mindset. It is a reciprocal process: a win-win! They see evidence that they are, in fact, growing more knowledgeable—and that builds their confidence. Here are a few post-reading prompts that can encourage a growth mindset:

If the curriculum doesn't intrigue, if it lacks challenging ideas and riveting controversies, why should kids put up with it?

- What did you do to become a better reader today?
- How did that reading make you more knowledgeable?
- What did you learn?
- What new ideas do you have?
- What do you still wonder about?
- What do you need to help you grow more knowledgeable?
- What more do you want to learn about this?
- How do you plan to keep learning more about this?

We must believe in striving readers' infinite capacity to learn and go with what interests them. When strivers find the perfect nonfiction book on a subject that fascinates them or a story they can't resist, they begin to read their way out of trouble. How cool is that?

Help Kids Build Agency and Creative Confidence

Of course, the ability to think and work independently matters. But independence alone is not enough. We've all seen strivers during reading workshop who look as though they are working independently when they are simply running their eyes across the page, gaining little. Peter Johnston urges us to help kids develop a sense of agency. He explains, "Agency is simply the perception that the environment is responsive to our actions" (2004).

Kids with a sense of agency go beyond independence. They believe they are the kinds of kids who can figure things out. They have strategies to gain background knowledge, to solve a problem, and to work through something

OUR TAKE ON GRIT AND STAMINA

In her *New York Times* bestselling book and viral TED talk, psychologist Angela Duckworth defines grit as "passion and perseverance for long-term goals" and posits that grit is a better predictor of success than IQ or family income. "Grit" has become a nationwide buzzword; many schools have adopted or adapted Duckworth's "grit scale" as a means of measuring and increasing students' degrees of grittiness.

While it's hard to argue with "stick-to-itiveness" as an asset, a number of concerns have been raised about the application of Duckworth's theory.

First, a focus on grit discounts the crushing impact of poverty and woefully under-resourced schools by suggesting that disadvantaged children need to simply "pull themselves up by their bootstraps" to achieve success. In FAQs on her website, Duckworth acknowledges that grit is insufficient to mitigate the toxic stressors of poverty: "I know that a child who comes to school hungry, or scared, or without glasses to see the chalkboard is not ready to learn. Grit alone is not going to save anyone" (2017).

Second, a focus on grit places responsibility to persevere in the learner's court, regardless of the quality or worth of the assigned task. In a blog post entitled "The Problem with Grit," Harvard Graduate School of Education Professor Jal Mehta writes, "A focus on grit (takes) a heavily impoverished view of human motivation; in the long run, most people do not persevere at things because they are good at persevering; they persevere because they find things that are worth investing in" (2015). Mehta argues that schools should spend less time figuring out how to boost students' grit and more time ensuring that curriculum fosters purpose and passion. *New Yorker* critic David Denby puts it even more bluntly: "If grit mania really flowers, one can imagine a mass of grimly determined people exhausting themselves and everyone around them with obsessional devotion to semi-worthless tasks" (2016).

Annie has noticed this "grit mania" sometimes showing up in classrooms, focused on stamina, and measured in minutes read per day (see example below). In her own reading life, Annie knew that stamina was a non-issue when she was enthralled with what she was reading. After a major plot twist in the book *Gone Girl*, for example, she kept reading at the beach long past sunset and miss`ed dinner. The more we focus on engagement, the less we need to focus on grit and stamina. Change the book, change the reader!

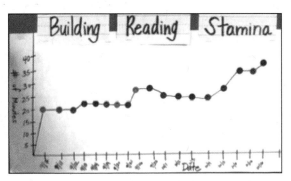

The more we focus on engagement, the less we need to focus on grit and stamina.

From Striving to Thriving © 2017 by Stephanie Harvey & Annie Ward, Scholastic Inc.

difficult when they are out on their own. You can't be agentive without being strategic, and no one needs a sense of agency and useful strategies more than striving readers.

David and Tom Kelley, authors of the book *Creative Confidence*, are leaders in the world of Design Thinking, the process that designers go through to solve complex problems and come up with innovative solutions. The Kelley brothers' notion of "creative confidence"—one's belief in him- or herself to change the world—is a central tenet of Design Thinking. People with creative confidence believe they can achieve what they have set out to do. Creative confidence flourishes when we recognize that our ideas matter and when we have the freedom to explore, take risks, fail, and try again (2013).

In his book *Creating Innovators* (2012), Tony Wagner explores three factors that drive people to innovate at work: passion, purpose, and play. He points out that passion matters, of course, but passion without purpose rarely goes far. The innovators he studied were passionate and had a purpose—and they were given time to play, meaning they were given time to explore and to try again and again. The combination of passion, purpose, and play was what led to extraordinary innovation.

Striving readers have experienced too many perceived failures along the way and haven't learned that these defeats are actually opportunities to innovate and learn. Whereas proficient readers are often encouraged to read about and investigate their passions, strivers are so overloaded with worksheets and assorted "edu-tasks" that they rarely get time to do that. In addition, they receive almost no time for free exploration, because they are so often given inconsequential assignments and practices that neither engage them nor build reading skill. Passion and inquisitiveness are on the back burner, if they are part of the recipe at all, not because strivers lack those traits but because too often in school they are denied the opportunity to pursue what they care most about and explore. We need to build in time every day for strivers to do that. We have to trust that the time we devote to exploration and inquiry offers strivers much more than test-prep worksheets and phonics drills. Peter Johnston says, "If nothing else, children should leave

school with a sense that if they act strategically, they can accomplish their goals" (2004). His books, *Choice Words* (2004) and *Opening Minds* (2012), have fueled us to better understand kids who lack agency and to help us do what we can to build it in our striving readers. Run, don't walk, to pick these up!

Embrace Mistakes as Learning Opportunities

We both remember coming of age in schools where teachers spent a good deal of time grading papers, red-marking errors, and jotting "AWK" in the margin when the writing was poorly composed. We felt the sting of those marks when we got our papers back. The main thing we learned was that mistakes were something to avoid like the plague. So we tried our darndest to make as few as possible.

If we want to table the labels and raise risk takers, we need to quit disparaging mistakes. This is particularly important for our striving readers—the kids who think they make the most mistakes and are castigated for them rather than commended. Neither of us can think of when we got something challenging right the very first time we tried it—or even the first few times, for that matter. Can you? We grow by trying something, working through it, and trying again, just as Anthony and Dav did as they came to read beloved books fluently. That's life in a nutshell. Sir Ken Robinson, a specialist in creativity, ingenuity, and education, says, "In schools, we stigmatize mistakes rather than value them. We now run educational systems where mistakes are the worst things you can make . . . . If you are not prepared for being wrong, you will never come up with anything original" (2006). Check out his TED Talk "Do Schools Kill Creativity?" With 47 million views and counting, it is the most widely watched TED Talk of all time.

> *"We don't grow into creativity. We grow out of it. Or rather, we get educated out of it."*
>
> **—SIR KEN ROBINSON**

From Striving to Thriving © 2017 by Stephanie Harvey & Annie Ward, Scholastic Inc.

Many great successes started out as failures. Post-it Notes are a classic example. Engineers at the 3M Company were attempting to make a super-strong adhesive, but kept failing. Five years into the process, one of the employees decided to cut some of the leftover paper with the low-tack adhesive into small pieces to use as bookmarks for his hymnbook. And, voilà, Post-it Notes!

Alina Tugend, an award-winning *New York Times* columnist and parent in Annie's school district, looks at how to transform mistakes into opportunities in her book *Better by Mistake: The Unexpected Benefits of Being Wrong* (2012). She explores the dichotomy that we need to make mistakes in order to learn, but that we generally loathe making them. She notes, "If we can all forgive our and others' errors more often, if we can acknowledge that perfection is a myth and human beings screw up on a regular basis—we can either simply feel bad about it and find someone to accuse or we can learn from it—then we are on the right track."

One idea. We've all been told, countless times, we should learn from our mistakes. But for striving readers, making mistakes too often only brings embarrassment and even shame. So, we have an idea: Why don't we call them "attempts" instead? Such as, "Savannah, clever attempt at that problem. Let's try another way and see how that works." We have found that referring to mistakes as attempts decreases kids' fear of being wrong and increases their desire to have a go. Give it a try and let us know what you find out. See the Practice entitled "Embracing Mistakes Through Story" on page 254.

Believe in the Power of "Yet"

In a TED Talk titled "The Power of Believing That You Can Improve" (2014), Carol Dweck shares the story of a high school in Chicago that doesn't use the word

"Fail" when kids don't master a task or pass a course. It uses "Not yet." When this grading system was implemented, rather than feeling wracked by failure, the students made progress and improved because they felt they were on a learning curve.

The right word matters! And one of the most powerful words in the English language when it comes to supporting and believing in striving readers (and all readers for that matter) is only three letters long: "yet," as in "Suzanna is not successful at inferring themes in fiction yet," and "Jake doesn't seem to grasp fractions yet." We need to move to a "yet sensibility." No more "Suzanna can't infer" or "Jake doesn't get fractions." Suzanna and Jake will get there if we trust them as learners and give them the right support.

MISCUES, NOT MISTAKES

Miscue analysis was originally developed by Ken Goodman for the purpose of understanding the reading process. Goodman used the term "miscue" to describe an observed response in a student's reading that does not match the expected response, based on what the text says. For example, the student who reads "pony" when the text says "horse." Goodman uses the term "miscue," rather than "error" or "mistake," to avoid negative value judgments. In other words, departures from the text, such as substitutions, omissions, or insertions that do not interfere with meaning, are not necessarily problematic, but rather "windows on the reading process," reflecting the reader's construction of meaning (1996; 2016).

What readers do as they read—including miscue—is neither accidental nor random. Reading is shaped by the readers' knowledge of language, their own personal and cultural experiences, values, perceptions of the world, and the like (Goodman, 2016). As such, high-quality miscues are not cause for concern (we all miscue while reading)—unless they interfere with meaning. In fact, miscues are just the opposite because typically they reveal the linguistic strengths that readers bring to the reading process as they construct meaning from a text. By analyzing miscues, we're able to determine which language cueing systems—graphophonic (letter/sound relationships), syntactical (word/structure relationships), and semantic (meaning)—readers are using to make sense of print. To learn more about this invaluable diagnostic tool, see Ken Goodman's *On Reading: A Common-Sense Look at the Nature of Language and the Science of Reading* (1996) and Sandra Wilde's *Miscue Analysis Made Easy: Building on Student Strengths* (2000).

From Striving to Thriving © 2017 by Stephanie Harvey & Annie Ward, Scholastic Inc.

BREAK DOWN BARRIERS TO EQUITY!

Treating every child exactly the same is not fair or equal, even though contemporary education seems to be based on the notion that it is. All kids take the third-grade reading test, regardless of their reading level. Since those tests don't measure growth, even striving readers who have made a great deal of progress often don't pass the test, thereby crushing the fragile confidence their teachers worked so hard to help them develop.

We want nothing more than for all kids to achieve at the highest levels, but to get them there, we must focus on how much they've grown as readers as opposed to how high they score as test takers. Hiebert and Martin have found that the "new standards . . . require fifth graders to read at a text complexity level previously expected of eighth graders" (2015). How unfair! They go on to say this is an epic shift. What does this mean for striving readers?

This book is about breaking down barriers to equity. Many of our kids grow up in high-poverty homes. They lack food, security, and proper medical care, and have limited access to books. We are with Neuman and Celano, authors of *Giving Our Children a Fighting Chance*, who suggest it's not about leveling the playing field, it's about tipping it toward the underdogs (2012). To do so, we need to identify and remove barriers.

EQUAL TREATMENT

EQUITABLE TREATMENT

Differentiation

EQUITY

Systematic barriers removed

But there's usually that one kid who we've taught "like our hair is on fire" since September who makes less progress than we hoped by June. Assuming we have worked our tails off to foster reading growth and build confidence and have adopted a true growth mindset all year yet still see disappointing results, we find solace in the wise words of our colleague Harvey "Smokey" Daniels: "They don't all bloom on our watch" (2017). So, rather than beat ourselves up, we delight in the progress the child eventually makes. If Curtis didn't blossom with us in third grade *YET*, we delight in the smile of his fourth-grade teacher when she shares how he has come into his own and is soaring in reading. We trust that with access to terrific books, plenty of time to read, and adept reading instruction, all strivers will become capable readers. It really does take a village.

We need to make sure our kids develop a "yet sensibility" as well. To help them do so, and have a little fun in the process, check out the "The Power of Yet" with Janelle Monáe on *Sesame Street*. Kids love this! (Zumic.com/music…/power-of-yet-janelle-monae-on-sesame-street-youtube-video-lyrics/.)

3. Encourage empathy.

In *Creative Confidence* (2013), Tom and David Kelley share the story of Doug Dietz, a veteran GE Healthcare designer of high-tech imaging and scanning devices. Doug led a team of engineers to design and create a revolutionary new CT scanner that was thought to be the best in the industry. Once it was installed and operational, Doug proudly visited a pediatric hospital to see it in action. As he was about to leave, he noticed a young girl sobbing as she held her mom's hand. Doug overheard the MRI technician call an anesthesiologist, only to discover that children were generally so frightened by the machine that most of them needed to be sedated to go through the procedure. Doug's pride turned to a sense of failure. But this nudged him to think about MRI design from an empathic stance, rather than a purely engineering one.

Ultimately, after much investigating, brainstorming, and putting himself in the pediatric patient's shoes, Doug had a simple but powerful and cost-effective idea: create an engaging, swashbuckling distraction! He and his team covered the scanner and the screening room walls with a pirate ship and ocean decals. They wrote an adventure story about a pirate ship on the high seas, which the technician read as kids entered the MRI. The number of pediatric patients who needed sedation dropped significantly. Doug's greatest thrill came when he witnessed a little girl, after having an MRI, ask her mom if she could have another one. Doug's MRI design is now the standard in children's hospitals across the country, and the lives of kids, parents, technicians, and the rest of us are better for it. This is what can happen when we add empathy to the creative, innovative mix.

Like Doug Dietz, we need to put ourselves in striving readers' shoes. We need to watch them carefully and do our best to get inside their heads. An empathetic classroom community ensures a more understanding, collaborative experience for all kids.

And research backs this up. Scientists at McGill University studied mother/baby interaction among rats and found that baby rats whose mothers nurtured them frequently, particularly in times of stress, were more confident and capable, and less frightened, than those whose mothers didn't. This applies to humans as well. Dr. Nadine Burke Harris found that children who have had four or more adverse childhood experiences are 32 times more likely to have learning difficulties in school than children who haven't. Poor kids are disproportionately affected by this, which doesn't surprise us teachers. We've all seen that too many impoverished children fall into the striving reader/learner category. According to John Converse Townsend, empathy reduces the negative effects of stress in children, just as it does in rats, which suggests that empathy has a positive social and academic impact on kids, in school and out. When kids and teachers develop empathy, everyone wins.

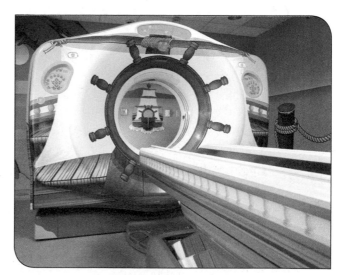

Doug Dietz's kid-friendly MRI machine

Teach Empathy Through Reading

A new body of research points to the power of reading literature to develop empathy in young readers. Maria Nikolajeva, education professor at Cambridge University, found that "reading fiction provides excellent training for young people in developing and practicing empathy and theory of mind, that is, the understanding of how other people feel and think." Researchers at Emory University found that "fiction tricks our brains into thinking that we are a part of the story." And scientists at Carnegie Mellon discovered that "when you get lost in a book, your brain lives through the characters at a neurological level" (2015).

By reading the books that Annie and her colleagues have gathered in rich classroom libraries, striving readers have made great gains and grown to better understand and care about themselves and those around them. One particularly powerful book is Jacqueline Woodson's *Each Kindness*, which includes themes of exclusion, regret, and the ripple effect of our behaviors and actions. In Mamaroneck, Karin Harris shared it with her fourth graders on the first day of school to encourage empathy all year. After the read-aloud and discussion, Karin invited each child to choose a pebble to cast into a makeshift pond to signify the "positive ripples" he or she pledged to make every day in the classroom community.

EmpathyLab's mission is to use story to build empathy and make the world a better place. Its website is a treasure trove of all things related to developing empathy through reading: teaching ideas, regularly updated lists of books, and so forth. Those who maintain the site keep up with the most recent research and are always looking for contributions from teachers. Check them out at empathylab.uk/.

Teaching Tolerance, a project of the Southern Poverty Law Center, shares a variety of lessons and exercises designed to build empathy, on topics such as discovering your identity, organizing against bullying, and putting yourself in someone else's shoes (tolerance.org/lesson/developing-empathy).

Above all, the words of Chris Riddell, Children's Laureate of the UK, resonate with us: "Reading allows us to see and understand the world through the eyes of others. A good book is an empathy engine" (2015). Share that quote with your kids! They need to hear it.

4. Get to know your kids ASAP.

Too often, striving readers arrive in the classroom at the beginning of the year already depleted of confidence. Many of them seem to quickly disappear and develop strategies that ensure they remain hidden. Or, conversely, their behavior causes the kind of attention that doesn't serve them well.

So, our first order of business is to get to know them—to find a way into their hearts and minds—early in the year. The best way to do that is by familiarizing ourselves with their interests and desires. We start by sharing what interests us and what we desire—and model how reading helps to shape our identity. We also provide strivers with multiple entries into information, beyond reading, so they don't get further behind. As such, the actions on the following pages encourage you to provide access to videos, images, artifacts, and the like, as well as to books. The actions that follow include a number of practical suggestions for learning as much as you can about your striving readers, as quickly as possible—to discover their interests, their passions, their questions, and their concerns, and to match them with books, ideas, websites, photos, videos, and stories that matter to them. No time to waste!

The actions on the following pages encourage you to provide access to videos, images, artifacts, and the like, as well as to books.

Meet With Former Teachers

At the start of the year, make time to learn as much as you can about the new strivers in your room. Talk with the previous year's classroom teachers, reading specialists, special ed teachers, administrators, and/or any other adults who worked with them. Find out if there has been any adult who had a particularly strong relationship with each of your striving readers and seek him or her out. If a child has moved frequently, do whatever you can to talk to others who can shed light on previous living situations. Too often, when a child is placed in special ed or pulled out for Title 1 or even RTI Tiers 2–3, he or she becomes a specialist's responsibility, not the classroom teacher's. As such, we often refer to children as "Mrs. Harvey's kids" or "Mrs. Ward's kids." We need to think of all kids, particularly those for whom we have concerns, as everyone's kids. Two heads are better than one, three are exponentially better than two, and so forth. Ongoing communication is key. All of our kids are everyone's kids.

Create Interest Inventories

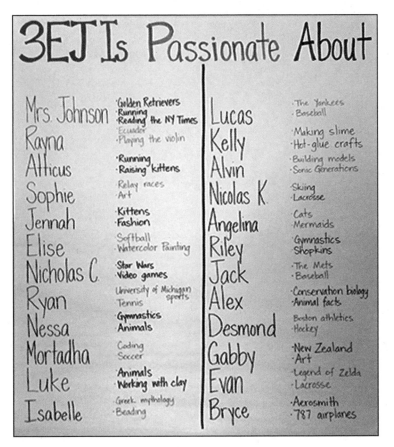

Find out kids' interests on Day 1. Start by sharing your own interests, jotting down at least three of them and telling the story behind one of them. Let kids know that you have a life outside of school, and that you know they do, too. Open up the conversation to any questions they have about your interests.

Create a whole-class interest inventory chart by listing all of the kids' names, as well as yours. Write your interests after your name. Then have the kids jot or draw at least three interests of theirs, talk with a partner about them, and post them on the chart. Bring in texts that relate to your interests and share how much you enjoy reading them and learning more about your interests.

Share Interest Photos and Videos

Bring in a photograph or video of yourself doing something you are interested in or something you care about. If you like to hike, share a photo of you trekking up a mountain. If you are a dog lover, share a photo of your favorite breed. Ask kids to bring in or email you a photo of something they're interested in and/or care about. You can also send them online to find a photo and print it out. During the first week of school, encourage students to share the photos and the stories behind them. Post the photos in the room. If students have a video of themselves doing something they love, share it with the class. This is particularly powerful for strivers. Pay close attention to their photos and stories so that you can begin to find books, articles, websites, podcasts, and so forth that reflect those interests and that they may want to read, watch, and listen to.

Spotlight Important Books

On the first day of school, teacher and writer extraordinaire Cris Tovani brings in a book that has been important to her and has made a difference in her life. Have a go yourself. Share a book with the class on Day 1 that has had a significant impact on you and explain why. Ask kids to bring in a book that has meant a lot to them. It's possible that some kids, particularly striving readers, may not have one that comes to mind or may not have access to one that does come to mind. If that's the case, get the title or a description of the book, and see if you can find it, or at least go online and print the cover. If a student can't come up with a book, make sure you have books and other resources available that focus on a particular interest he or she revealed when you created the interest inventory chart or they shared photos. And don't despair: If kids don't have an important book yet, there will be plenty of them in their future!

Create Your Textual Lineage

Alfred Tatum is the author of many books and the Dean of the College of Education and director of the University of Illinois Chicago Reading Clinic. His work focuses on the literacy development of African American males and the role of text as it relates to their literacy development. He writes and speaks frequently about the notion of textual lineage—in his words, "Our textual lineage includes things we have read that have been significant in shaping our identities." Scholastic's Global Literacy Campaign describes textual lineage as "a reading and writing autobiography which shows that who you are is in part developed through the stories and information you've experienced" (2014). We share our own textual lineage and model how we created it so that striving readers can see the power that reading has had in shaping our identity, in developing us as readers, and in living our lives. (See the Practice entitled "Textual Lineage" on page 256.)

Create Identity Webs

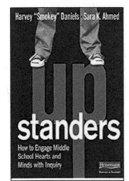

In their terrific book *Upstanders: How to Engage Middle School Hearts and Minds with Inquiry* (2014), Sara Ahmed and Harvey "Smokey" Daniels suggest creating identity webs on the first day or two of school as a way of sharing who we are, helping kids know us as people early in the year, and getting them to think about their own identities. The earlier our strivers get to know us, the more comfortable they will feel working with us. That's true of all kids, but particularly of strivers.

Place a photo of yourself doing something you enjoy, at the center of a piece of chart paper. Talk about what matters to you, people you love, things you like to do outside of school, books that have been important to you, preferences you have, and so forth, making notes as you go on lines emanating out from the photo. Add to the web over a few days' time during the first week of school so kids get a strong sense of who you are. Then have kids create their own identity webs. It's okay if they come up with only one or two things at first because the webs are ongoing. Encourage kids to add to them as they think of and discover things that matter to them.

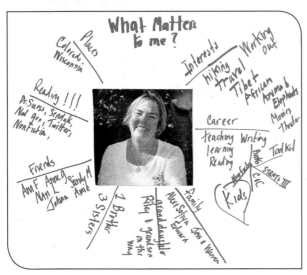

Steph's identity web

Create Heart Maps

In her book *Heart Maps: Helping Students Create and Craft Authentic Writing* (2016), Georgia Heard suggests a wonderful activity, heart maps, for encouraging kids to write about what is important to them: memories, topics, issues, and so forth. The teacher models her own heart map and then the kids have a go. Heart maps help us get to know kids early in the year. They are beneficial to strivers because they provide a visual way into writing about something that matters and inform bookmatching.

Choose Walk-Up Songs

Anyone who has been to an MLB baseball game knows what a walk-up song is. When a batter comes up to the plate or a pitcher takes the mound, a song they chose reverberates throughout the ballpark. Some of the more famous walk-up songs include Alex Rodriguez's "Already Home" and Ryan Spilborghs's "Livin' on a Prayer." When Charlie Blackmon of the Colorado Rockies steps to the plate, the whole park explodes with "I Don't Want to Lose Your Love Tonight."

Steph has kids choose their own walk-up songs, another way to help them explore and represent their identities. A Coloradan for many years, she starts by playing her own song, "Rocky Mountain High," which is also her ringtone! She talks about why she chose the song, how much she loves the state and the mountains, and how lucky she is to live there. Then kids think about possibilities. They can simply choose a favorite song, or they can choose a song that they identify with somehow. They can even write one. Some teachers Steph knows create a chart for all to see with the kids' photos and their walk-up songs as captions. And they play the songs throughout the year, particularly to introduce kids when they're giving presentations.

Have Kids Teach YOU Something

Donald Graves was known to say, "Teachers are the chief learners in the classroom." We agree. The most effective teachers are consummate learners. Seventh-grade ELA teacher Amy Estersohn invites her kids to "teach her something." For example, for fun, they taught Amy to "dab," the popular dance move where you drop your head into the crook of your elbow and raise the opposite arm skyward. Kids know a lot about many topics: contemporary music, social media, and so many more. Inviting them to teach you something sends a powerful message that everyone's a teacher and a learner.

Share Areas of Specialty (AOS)

A fun, powerful way to show early in the year that we are all learners is through Areas of Specialty (AOS), which is inspired by an idea of Donald Graves from many years ago: Areas of Expertise (AOE). AOS is similar, but we refer to ourselves and the kids as specialists rather than experts. (See the Practice called Areas of Specialty: AOS on page 258.)

Bring in Personal Collections

Just as we share our textual lineage with students, we can share our personal lineage with artifacts that matter to us. If you are a collector of anything, you have a leg up. Annie has an amazing Carlton Fisk baseball card collection. Once Steph became a grandmother, she started collecting stuffed animals from every state and country she visits to share with her precious granddaughter Riley. Artifacts like those represent memories and show that we really care about and value them. Richard, a striving fifth-grade reader, was over the moon when his teacher encouraged him to bring in his Star Wars action figure collection, share it with the class, and explain why it mattered to him. Sharing a collection is an accessible entry point for striving readers and lets us in on what really matters to them. Furthermore, reading and researching more about their collection can be naturally motivating and engaging.

Select Whole-Class Read-Alouds to Build Community

One of our most delightful and significant back-to-school rituals involves choosing and sharing read-alouds that foster community among new classmates. We love hearing stories from teachers of how they spend the summer rereading favorite books and discovering new ones—particularly now that social media connects them in one grand conversation. *Nerdy Book Club* bloggers recently polled readers, eliciting a stream of fabulous book suggestions and rationales for them: nerdybookclub.wordpress.com/2015/08/09/poll-first-read-aloud-of-the-year/.

Similarly, "Book Whisperer" Donalyn Miller posted "Books That Build Community," in which she provides suggestions in categories: Communities of Readers and Writers, Communities Who Value All Members, Communities Who Have Fun, and Communities Who Care About the World. (blogs.edweek.org/teachers/book_whisperer/2012/08/books_that_build_community.html. Pay particular attention to those books that you believe will resonate with your striving readers.)

In addition, once you have engaged in some of the interest-building actions described earlier—inventories, collections, important books, and so forth—you will have more information about themes and content that might appeal to specific kids so you and they can search for books that capture them. We can easily visualize a striving reader light up when a book he or she is interested in gets the green light for read-aloud!

5. Create conditions for interaction and boundless reading.

Many of us recall classrooms of our childhoods as magical places in which we made friends, learned about the world, and forged our young identities. Annie can readily conjure a memory of her fifth-grade classroom in Lincoln, Massachusetts—her desk by the window overlooking the kickball court and the large round skylights that caught raindrops, fall leaves, and snowflakes. But it's the Necco-wafer purple rug in the meeting area that lingers in Annie's mind most—the rug upon which Miss Charney would gather the class several times a day and turn it into a magic carpet.

A teacher encourages turn-and-talk during her read-alouds.

Miss Charney read aloud every day after recess, and at one point she read *Mrs. Frisby and the Rats of NIMH* by Robert C. O'Brien. Miss Charney's voice cast a spell, transporting Annie and her classmates into the world of the book. Their hearts ached for the widowed Mrs. Frisby as she tried to protect her family from the farmer's plow. Decades later, this read-aloud remains one of the most potent literary experiences Annie has ever had.

In October 1975, Miss Charney gave the class a bad case of Red Sox fever. Poring over articles, scores, and statistics in the *Boston Globe* became a daily ritual, as the team advanced toward the World Series. Annie learned to savor an event twice—first through lived experience and then through the lens of a favorite critic or reporter.

Miss Charney made extraordinary things happen in an ordinary classroom. She truly knew and valued each of her students, she built community, she cultivated curiosity and a zest for learning, and she shared unforgettable books. She gave her students voice and choice in the classroom to create a personalized learning environment. And she did it all with standard classroom furniture and simple daily rituals.

Fifth-grade co-teachers Lauren Scharfstein and Elena Canneto build community by inviting each child to contribute a photo of his or her family to the class gallery.

In this section, we share ideas for setting up and maintaining your classroom for interaction, collaboration, and, of course, boundless reading. Whether you have a tiny space in a century-old building or a spacious room in a modern building, it likely contains an assortment of desks, tables, chairs, and shelves. In other words, a classroom is a classroom. The magic starts with how you arrange the furniture, stock the shelves, and interact with and communicate to the kids in the space.

Create a Fluid, Navigable, and Flexible Classroom Layout

When researchers Richard Allington and Peter Johnston camped out in exemplary fourth-grade classrooms, they found that the teachers were "more often working alongside students, individually and in small groups, than working from the front of the room . . . . A great deal of instruction was not done by the teacher but by the students, who had learned to consult one another and to make their thinking available to one another. Collaborative learning was common" (2000).

In setting up your classroom, consider the ways you and your students will work. Sometimes, you'll want to gather the class in an intimate space for whole-group meetings and mini-lessons. Sometimes, you'll want students to collaborate in small groups and partnerships. Sometimes, you'll want to confer with individual students. And across the day, you'll want children to read and work independently in comfortable spaces. For those reasons, you'll need to facilitate movement, which means minimizing clutter and moving away from the "all-desks-in-a-row" arrangement of traditional classrooms.

Design a Comfortable Meeting Space for Whole-Group Gathering and Instruction

Questions to consider:

- Will all students be able to see the whiteboard, screen, and/or chart or easel?
- Will all students be able to hear you and one another?
- Will your whole class fit comfortably in the meeting area?
- Is there room for you to move around among students when they are bunched on the floor?
- Is there room for them to take notes and turn and talk to a partner?

Suggestions:

- If you don't have carpet, head to the carpet stores. Retailers will often donate discontinued samples and carpet squares.
- Find bargains on colorful bathmats and carpet runners at websites such as overstock.com.
- If you have a large class and/or older students, use carpet squares to expand a traditional 8' x 11' rug.
- Use benches, milk crates with cushions, and/or love seats to frame the meeting area and provide additional seating. Of course, you'll need to create a system to cycle kids through these popular seats!

Perhaps the best way to find out the conditions under which a child will thrive as a reader is to simply ask him or her.

In this integrated, co-taught classroom, flexible seating and multiple meeting areas with timely book displays promote conversation and collaboration.

Establish Spaces for Small-Group Instruction, Collaboration, and Independent Reading

Questions to consider:

- Will your classroom layout enable students to work frequently and fluidly in groups and pairs?

- Are there niches for kids who work more effectively in quieter, more private spaces?

- Are there spaces that will foster informal, peer-led small-group discussions and small-group work?

- How will you create a space for small-group instruction that enables you to work with students in a group and, at the same time, keep an eye on the kids working independently outside the group?

Suggestions:

- Keep in mind, learning is a social act. Interaction is key. Conversation is a natural means of enhancing comprehension across the day. It just makes sense to have kids in clusters for the majority of the day—even during independent work time—rather than isolated in rows.

- Group four to six kids at tables if you have them, or cluster students' desks to accommodate four to six kids.

- For management and community-building purposes, engage kids in naming the tables or clusters. For example, in one Mamaroneck classroom, tables are named after "famous" local landmarks: Rita's Ice Cream Parlor, Walter's Hot Dog Stand, Hommocks Skating Rink, and Harbor Island Beach.

Teachers and students constructed this unique reading/ writing nook.

Personalize Learning Spaces

Perhaps the best way to find out the conditions under which a child will thrive as a reader is to simply ask him or her. You'll likely be surprised by the amount of information you get—and your gesture will send a powerful message of caring and concern. Annie's district features an integrated co-teaching approach to special ed, where the general educator and the special educator are paired in the classroom with both gen-ed kids and children with special needs in class. In their co-taught fourth-grade class, Melanie Arminio and Mary Alice Pietrapolo got a wide range of responses when they asked students, "What does your classroom need to be like in order for you to be successful?" While one child preferred a "dark and cool/cold" environment, another liked "lots of excitement and fun twists." Just as *The Odd Couple*'s Felix Ungar and Oscar Madison had to learn to get along in a city apartment, kids have to get along in a classroom. They need to know and respect one another's preferences, make their own needs clear, and sometimes negotiate with others to make sure those needs are met.

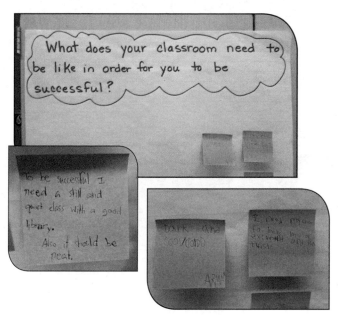

Suggestions:

- Have the kids themselves establish comfortable reading spots throughout the room.
- Have kids share photos and sketches of their favorite places to read outside of school and post them in the room.
- Remember, halls and walls teach! Hang work throughout the classroom. If the work is not complete, or not written in dictionary spelling, display it with either a "draft" stamp or a sticky note with "_____'s work in progress" written on it.

- Feature fresh and interactive bulletin boards on classroom walls and school halls. Place sticky notes and pencils near them so kids can respond to one another's work.

There are many ways to create conditions that promote self-efficacy and engaged learning, and so many amazing teachers who do it. You will see many more captivating classrooms woven throughout this book. But for a start, we suggest you take a look at *Reading with Meaning, Second Edition* (2012) and *Teaching with Intention* (2008), both by Debbie Miller, who, as a teacher, created one of the most inviting classroom communities Steph ever set foot in. The magic starts with how you arrange the furniture, stock the shelves, and interact with the kids in the space.

Nancie Atwell, teacher/author extraordinaire and the 2015 Global Teacher Prize winner, has created an entire school where every classroom reverberates with a culture of joyful reading and learning. Pick up a copy of *The Reading Zone, Second Edition* (2016) from Nancie and her daughter, Anne Atwell Merkel, on creating a classroom that fosters self-efficacy, deep reading, and a collaborative community.

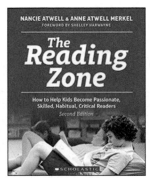

From Striving to Thriving © 2017 by Stephanie Harvey & Annie Ward, Scholastic Inc.

TABLE THE LABELS

Use these questions to drive responsive, learner-focused teaching based on what kids *can* do.

Self-Questions

- Do I believe that an expert, caring teacher is superior to programmatic instruction?
- Do I believe that striving readers can become avid, proficient readers?
- What are some ways I can build confidence in my striving readers?
- Do I share my area of specialty with my kids and encourage them to share theirs?
- Do I share with my kids times I have made mistakes or experienced frustration?
- Do I share stories that show how effort and hard work eventually lead to success?
- Have I designed and created comfortable learning spaces in my classroom? Spaces that make reading more desirable?

Kidwatching Questions

- Does the student believe that he can become a good reader?
- Does the student believe that reading will help her grow more knowledgeable?
- Does the student become frustrated when he loses meaning while reading?
- Is the student willing to try again?
- Does the student easily find reading materials she is interested in?
- What does the student know and care about?
- Are there spots in the room where the student knows he can work most easily and productively?

Conferring Questions

- Do you want to try that again? What will you try differently in the next attempt?
- Did you learn anything you would like to explore further?
- What do you care about most in life?
- What topics do you like to read about most?
- Do you need a more comfortable space to do this work?
- What can I do to help you out?

"Teaching will be learning how to ask the right questions. I was taught to memorize facts. Why remember them? Now you just need to learn how to search for information and sort through the burgeoning data available on computers . . . . Instantaneous access really changes your life. What never changes is the need for curiosity. What you really need to do is teach people to be curious."

—Eric Schmidt, CEO of Google

CHAPTER 2

Cultivate Curiosity

We agree with Eric Schmidt's claim (at left) to a point. Curiosity matters, big time! But do we really have to *teach* kids to be curious? We don't think so. Human beings are brimming with curiosity from birth. You see it in every baby, toddler, kindergartner, or quirky kid you encounter. Questions cascade right out of them. What we really have to do is fan that curiosity flame so it blazes rather than smolders.

A couple of years ago, Steph accepted the joy of babysitting her grand-daughter Riley every Monday. What a special privilege! She quickly discovered how different caring for Ri was from caring for her own two children some 30-plus years earlier. No doubt her energy had diminished and she collapsed for a much needed nap when Ri went home for the evening, but what she had every Monday that she didn't have when her kids were young was *the precious gift of time.* When Riley's mom dropped her off, Steph did nothing but interact with Riley, no doing dishes, no washing clothes, no cramming kids into car seats to get them off to day care as she headed to her classroom. It is simply Riley and Steph all day, every Monday.

See the following Practices and Lessons for this chapter:

PRACTICES

LESSON

These sheets are also available at scholastic.com/ThriveResources.

After a month or two of getting used to the joys and challenges of having a baby back in her life, Steph couldn't resist turning at least some of the day into a project. No surprise, right, being a lifelong teacher and learner? So Steph, a very amateur (which can't be emphasized strongly enough) photographer, decided to take pictures of Ri throughout the day as she engaged in acts of curiosity. With the best of intentions, Steph began chronicling Riley's curiosity episodes through photography. But within two weeks it was clear that if she continued down that road, Riley would never get fed, changed, put down for a nap, or cared for at all, because all Ri was doing all day long was peeking around corners to see what was there, quizzically scrutinizing latches on cupboards, pointing with eyes furrowed at the photos that filled the house, fiddling with water gushing out of the faucet, manipulating knobs and switches, and—thank goodness—peering at images in books. In short, she was curious every waking minute!

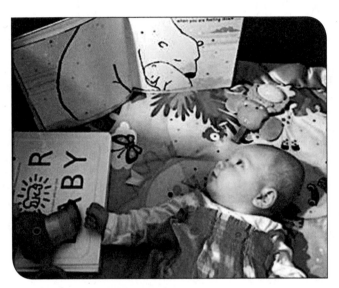

Riley engaged in a curiosity episode.

Curiosity Drives Learning

Recent research has revealed a great deal about young children and their innate appetite for questioning and wondering. Researchers have found that at home three-year-olds ask parents about 26 questions per hour and engage in "curiosity sequences" as early as two-and-a-half years of age where their questions are linked inquiries involving follow-up questions and comments (Engel, 2011). Amazing! In fact, most young kids ask so many questions they might drive us crazy if they weren't so enduringly charming. *Why is the ocean blue? Why are the zebras and tigers the only ones with stripes? Where did the cowboys go?* Science questions, history questions, and cultural questions tumble out of kids who can't yet reach the countertops.

We've all noticed that five-year-olds burst in on the first day of school brimming with questions, but those questions diminish as the year goes on. The number of curiosity episodes at school fall to about one an hour in kindergarten and even fewer than that by fifth grade. Researchers conclude that many children spend hours a day in school without asking a single question (Engel, 2011; Chouinard, 2007).

This we know: The more we learn, the more we wonder. So, ideally, kids should be asking many more questions, rather than fewer, as they grow older. Barbara Logan, a principal investigator at the Efficacy Institute, asked the question, "How do children go from wanting to know everything under the sun to having so few questions?" (Logan, 2010). She concluded, "It's very simple, they learn it." In other words, conventional schooling drums the curiosity right out of kids. In school, we focus so intently on answers that little room remains for kids' questions. But kids will never learn much if they aren't asking questions. And striving readers are likely to learn even less. Questioning is the strategy that propels learners forward. We need to convince striving readers that we truly value their questions and that asking questions makes them more knowledgeable. If they trust that asking questions is a true asset to growing more knowledgeable and learning, they will almost certainly ask more. So we share our own questions, watch our kids closely, and listen to them. By listening and observing, we come to know them better and know what they need, and we are better positioned to help them. Barbara Logan (2010) suggests that good teachers let kids know that their questions matter and teach them to ask questions and search for answers.

When strivers accept that we believe in them and they know that we value their questions, they are far more likely to ask them. Once they start, torrents of questions often flood from them. Often naturally inquisitive, they gaze awestruck at photos of volcanoes and wonder aloud about them. They obsess over tantalizing illustrations of colorful dinosaurs, no longer merely green as most of us learned early on, but now even represented with black, orange, and yellow stripes.

We need to cultivate that innate curiosity and capture our striving readers with compelling ideas, artifacts, issues, and generally irresistible content. Many of their reading difficulties stem from their lack of interest in reading, as much as anything else. Having been relegated to phonetically decodable pabulum that spurs curiosity in few, striving readers typically find reading both nonsensical and BOOOORING. So, immersing strivers in glorious photos, captivating ideas, and rich content drives their curiosity. It is that "puzzle drive," as Nobel Laureate Richard Feynman called it, that can steer striving readers to investigate, learn, and yes, read more to satisfy that sense of wonder. Stephen Krashen notes that self-selected reading in pursuit of questions of personal interest to the reader drives intellectual growth and achievement (2016). So, how do we tap into that innate curiosity and foster a spirit of wonder so kids investigate their questions through reading?

THREE TO KNOW
RESEARCHERS ON CURIOSITY

1. Research by Daisy Yuhas at the University of California shows that when people's curiosity is evoked, not only do they remember information about the topic at hand, they also remember incidental and unrelated information that surrounds the topic (2014).

2. Susan Engel studied the manifestation of curiosity both at school and at home among young children and found that children as young as three years old ask about 26 questions an hour at home. In school, however, the questioning rate dropped significantly with kindergartners asking only about one question an hour and fifth graders fewer than that.

3. Barbara Logan, principal investigator at the Efficacy Institute, asked why children's curiosity declined so precipitously in schools. She could only conclude that their natural curiosity was somehow discouraged at school. Discourse enhances curiosity. In schools with limited discourse, we see an inquiry-reducing effect. Kids learn that their questions and comments lack merit, so they stop asking any. She notes, "Effective educators help students release their questions, teaching them that learning is about asking good questions and discovering the answers."

---

1. Model your own curiosity every day. Make what you wonder visible.

Passion and wonder are contagious. One morning, Steph watched Michele Timble, a fourth-grade teacher in the Chicago Public Schools, welcome her class with, "The birds are back." Half of the heads turned instantly.

"What birds—what are you talking about?" Kyle asked. With all kids now in front of her on the rug, faster than usual, Michele explained, "Remember I told you that every spring these birds build a nest in the eaves outside my bedroom? Well, birds are building a nest there again. But I have all of these questions. *Why do these birds come back each year? Are they the same birds? Do birds really like this location for a nest? Do they know that other birds have been there?* I don't know the answers to these questions, but I can't stop wondering about them, and tonight when I go home, I am going to try to find out. First, I think I'll call my neighbor who is an avid bird watcher and see what she thinks. I bet she has some books she might lend me. I'll also check online to see what I can find."

The next day Michele reported back to the kids on what she found out. "I couldn't find out about these birds exactly, but I did learn that birds like to come back to familiar places to raise their families."

"I heard about a church in California where birds come back every year," Callie interjected.

"Exactly, Callie. That is a place called San Juan Capistrano," Michele responded. And so it went—a short conversation that demonstrated that above all Michele is curious and doesn't just forget about her questions, but takes time to do some research to address them.

We need to show kids that as adults we spend much of our lives asking questions and searching for information (often in text!) to answer them. Each day, we are flooded with one question after another—*How do I find a cereal that is healthy and that Riley will eat? This traffic is insane, should I get off the highway, or will the alternative be worse? Whom should I vote for in the local school board election?* On and on. As a matter of fact, the older we get, the more questions we have. We're not sure our kids recognize this. Many kids, particularly our striving readers, seem to think that adults have all of the answers. And striving readers often believe that asking questions reveals some sort of personal deficit.

So, sharing our curiosity, modeling our questions every day, and showing that thoughtful grown adults have questions and care about finding the answers is essential to nurturing our kids' curiosity and to encouraging participation from everyone. Curiosity is contagious. We can share our questions about daily life, curricular topics of interest, significant issues, and so forth. A day should not go by that we don't let kids know that we are always wondering about something.

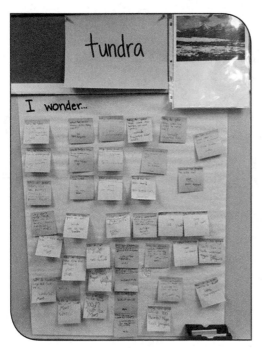

This chart with sticky notes positioned at the bottom invites wondering.

A Life of Wonder

We need to live a curious life, and when we say curious, we're not talking about curious as in "odd." Although we teachers might be considered a bit odd since we are the only folks we know who choose to spend our lives in the company of those much younger than ourselves. And how lucky we are for it! Living a life full of wonder is central to fostering curiosity. How do we nurture passion and curiosity in our classrooms? How do we engage and encourage contributions from our striving readers in the marvelous mix of social activity and inquiry? We make our curiosity visible by:

- asking questions daily and showing we care about reading and research to find answers.
- modeling our thinking and questions so kids see that adults are continually asking questions.
- drawing from a spectrum of resources to search for answers, including talking to others, going online, reading books, doing research, etc.
- remaining alert to new information and revising our thinking in light of new evidence, demonstrating that reading and learning really do change thinking.
- collaborating with others to explore and inform our curiosities.

2. Honor the questioning and the learning more than the knowing.

Too often, we celebrate what kids know more than what they learn. Schools should be incubators for curiosity and havens for learning. We need to convince striving readers that schooling is mainly about learning, not about knowing everything already. We can celebrate learning and model the process with language such as:

I wondered about this and then I found out _____.

I used to think _____, but now I think _____.

Before I read this, I thought _____, but now I learned _____.

Wow, I never knew that before.

I'm changing my thinking in light of new evidence.

It is so great to learn something new even though I used to think the opposite.

Annotate Wonderings on Thinksheets and Sticky Notes

As kids read and research, they can organize their thinking and wondering in

a variety of ways. Annotation is a powerful way to hold onto thinking. Kids can annotate by jotting directly on the page, by writing or drawing on sticky notes, and by leaving tracks of their thoughts, questions, and reactions on graphic organizers. In the *Comprehension Toolkit* series (2016), Steph and Anne Goudvis explain the notion of Thinksheets, a form of graphic organizer and an alternative to fill-in-the-blank worksheets, which require little in the way of thinking. When strivers use Thinksheets, it gives them a place to "work out their thinking." We let them know that writing down or sketching their thinking is like going to the "reading gym." When we designate space on Thinksheets for kid's questions, we send the message that their curiosity truly matters. Some of our favorite Thinksheets include:

- Two-column sheets headed with "I Learned" and "I Wonder," which conveys that whenever we learn something new, it is likely we will have some questions about it.

- Three-column sheets headed with "I Learned," "I Wonder," and "WOW!" on which they jot or draw their new learning, their questions, and their reactions. These sheets are particularly effective with younger children.

- Three-column forms headed with "Facts," "Questions," and "Responses" (FQR), on which kids record text information in the first column, any questions they have about that information in the second column, and their reactions in the third column (Harvey, 1998).

- As teachers, we take care to assure that filling in graphic organizers such as these does not become perfunctory, as in, "Make sure to fill out your FQR chart before lunchtime." These graphic organizers are tools to scaffold learning and understanding while reading and to invite readers to express their thoughts and questions voluntarily.

Create a Trusting Culture Where Kids Feel Safe to Ask Loads of Questions

Curiosity thrives when kids believe that their questions matter. Striving readers tend to refrain from asking questions out of fear of appearing inept. Therefore,

From Striving to Thriving © 2017 by Stephanie Harvey & Annie Ward, Scholastic Inc.

Facts	Questions	Responses
There used to be millions of Elphents in kenya now there is half a million. 100 Afrcan Elphents are killed Every day. US is the 2nd largest market	What is happning in that picture? Where do they relocate them	they are tacking the Elphent to a saffer place. to a Very safe park Type place that is so sad Name Kate Date 5/19/17

we need to create a culture of acceptance where there is truly no such thing as a stupid question, and kids trust that we believe that.

In his book *The Curious Classroom* (2017), Smokey Daniels suggests kids track their curiosity on a two-column form that allows for two types of questions: Self-Questions (in the first column) and World Questions (in the second column). Self-questions are questions that matter a lot to us personally, and world questions are questions that are broader and more far reaching. We model coming up with and organizing both types of questions in our own notebooks and then have kids do it in theirs. We make sure to include different types of questions, some more serious and some a little silly, so that kids see the full range of authentic wonderings that we have. These questions, both self and world, fuel further research.

Self-Questions	World Questions
How can I get Riley to try new, healthy foods?	What will happen in France under the new president?
Why does my car make such a strange noise when I turn the key?	Does diet cola really cause dementia?
What book do I want to read next?	When will climate change cause East Coast seas to rise enough to spill onto people's property?
Why do I bruise so easily?	When and how will cancer be cured?

An example of a chart we might model and share.

As strivers create their own question lists and routinely share them with classmates, they see that wondering is contagious. They begin to believe that their thinking really does matter and their questions are important. This focus on curiosity builds students' growth mindsets and, in the process, their confidence as readers and learners.

3. Build in lots of time for kids to explore, investigate, and research questions that interest them.

American kids spend on average approximately 1,000 hours a year in elementary school (2014). Doesn't it seem reasonable that a certain amount of that time be reserved for exploring topics of interest that they choose, asking questions, and doing some research to address them? One of the best ways to encourage our striving readers to read more is to make sure they are reading and researching topics they care about. Google famously offers an option called Google 20% Time where Google employees are encouraged to spend 20 percent of their time working on projects they choose, projects that are not part of the strategic business plan. Gmail, one of their most successful products, emerged from Google 20% Time.

Build in lots of time for kids to explore, investigate, and research.

We can set aside time on a regular basis, as Google does, for kids to freely explore their own curiosities, whether they are related to the curriculum or not. We believe that striving readers need this time of individual exploration and choice reading even more than most learners. Sadly and ironically, it is the strivers who are often pulled away from this engaging free exploration and left stuck somewhere filling in bubbles and blanks on a worksheet or screen, which not only has no basis in research but also effectively kills reading motivation. Dr. Mary Howard suggests that "our goal is to create a culture of curiosity—not just something we do by the clock, but the air we breathe" (2017).

Structures, rituals, and routines for building in time to wonder and investigate include:

- **Capturing Wonder.** We hold onto our questions and make wonder visible in our classrooms. Wonder Walls, Wonder Books, and Wonder Boxes represent a few ways we do that. See more about these in practices on page 262.

- **"Wonder-ful" Images.** We build in time every day for kids to view, think, and wonder about images. We simply project an intriguing image on the class screen, and ask kids to turn and talk about what they are wondering about. Visual literacy, "reading, viewing, and thinking about images," is increasingly important for all kids. Much of the information this generation obtains will be visual and auditory in nature. Graphics of all sorts scaffold striving readers since images offer a more accessible entry point into information than text on its own. We can't exclude kids from information simply because they are below benchmark in reading, so offering an array of visual entry points allows striving readers to continue to wonder and learn regardless of their reading level.

After watching a video on African animals, Ellie draws the answer to her question, "Why do cheetas have spots?"

- **Videos.** Videos, too, offer a strong entry point for all kids, but are of particular support to striving readers. We teach kids to interact with videos as they view them. We often stop the video and have kids jot or draw their questions and turn and talk, offering yet another entry point for striving readers to express their thoughts, questions, and opinions. Wonderopolis (wonderopolis.com) is a terrific website that hosts a question a day and shares a video that addresses it. Kids can submit questions to Wonderopolis in hopes that theirs will be selected and shared with kids all over the world.

- **Genius Hour.** Genius Hour is an in-school structure that allows students to explore their own passions and address any questions they have about any topic they are interested in. As with Google 20% Time, kids are encouraged to work on a project of interest for 20 percent of the week or even just for an hour each week. Teachers provide a set amount of time every day or every week for students to investigate their questions and research their passion projects. It may happen the last hour of the day every day or perhaps just for an hour or two on Friday. Genius Hour brings joy to learning because it is a whole lot of fun. Randy Pausch famously said, "If you think you can't learn and have fun at the same time, then I don't think you have a good understanding of either." Fun matters. The most direct route to learning is engagement and the most direct route to engagement is fun, particularly for striving readers! Check out www.geniushour.com or #geniushour on Twitter for more information.

- **Open Inquiries.** Inquiry-based learning is about living in a way that kids' questions matter. Open inquiries give us an opportunity to do that. 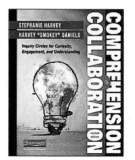 We encourage kids to work together in small inquiry circles to ask questions and investigate topics of interest. While we may not be able to meet the science and social studies content standards with open inquiries, we can teach into the reading, writing, and research ELA standards. Open inquiries allow striving readers to research anything they are interested in, which leads to more fully engaged reading. For more on open inquiries and the role of curiosity in teaching and learning, see Steph and Smokey Daniels's *Comprehension and Collaboration: Inquiry Circles for Curiosity, Engagement, and Understanding* (2015).

- **Capstone Projects.** One specific and extended form of open inquiry is the Capstone Project, in which kids research individual questions of passionate interest and share their learning with others through TED-style talks, expos, web pages, and more. Capstone Projects flourish in concert with the other strategies described in this chapter; if kids spend months poring over compelling images, reading about innovators, and filling wonder walls … then when the time comes for Capstone Projects they will be brimming with ideas and researchable questions! In Annie's district, the inquiry process is woven into the curriculum and culminates in Capstone Projects at grades 5 to 8.

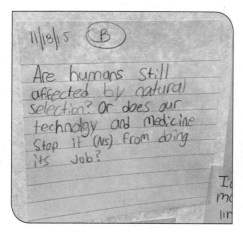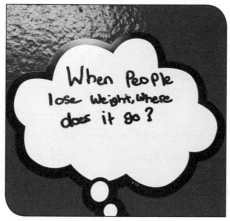

Questions on a Wonder Board drive research for Capstone Projects

Since kids' interests run the gamut, it's an all-hands-on-deck situation with librarians, art and music teachers, physical educators, psychologists, custodians, and community members collaborating as inquiry guides. Kids tap specialists through email and Skype, nearly all of whom are thrilled to be contacted by children and respond in depth and detail. Delightfully, the kids' questions lead adults to learn alongside them, and schools buzz with genuine fascination as learning grows. As the inquiry process unfolds, kids' initial questions evolve and their follow-up questions become deeper and more pointed. Poignantly, one fifth grader's question about the allure of Facebook eventually focused on the impact of social media on the attention parents pay to their children.

- **Real-Time Information Apps.** The tech opportunities from apps such as Google Docs, Drawing Pad, Edmodo, and Padlet are endless for inspiring curiosity, asking questions, and doing research. As we read a text aloud, kids with devices can jot their questions on a Google Doc, which can be displayed in real time on the class screen. Everyone can see all the questions of all the kids. Kids will pick up on other kids' questions and add to their own, quite helpful for those striving learners who have trouble coming up with something they are curious about. We recommend apps like Drawing Pad, which allow kids to draw rather than write their thinking, giving striving readers a boost. We can create surveys with Google Docs. Kids might work together to come up with a whole-class question such as, "What is the best class pet for us?" Individuals can make suggestions based on information they research. The data can be gathered on the Google form, which is projected for all kids to view and see quickly which pet is in the lead. Technology like this helps all our kids to consider responses in real time.

- **Curiosity Quotes.** Many people throughout history have extolled the virtues of asking questions and having a curious mind. Einstein famously said, "I have no special talents, I am only passionately curious." Sir Ken Robinson states, "Curiosity is the engine that drives creativity." And E. B. White speaks directly to teachers with his words, "Always be on the lookout for the presence of wonder."

These are but a few of the powerful thoughts that permeate the minds of creative, passionate, curious individuals. We can begin the year by posting some of our favorite curiosity quotes around the room and filling kids in on the lives and contributions of the people who said these words, reading picture books about them and sharing how they innovated through their sense of wonder and their willingness to keep on trying again and again. Kids can join in and collect, collaborate, and share quotes they encounter, jotting them in their Wonder Books. They can create artistic representations of these quotes until we have flooded the room with the dynamism of curiosity. It is particularly powerful for striving readers to hear the quotes and learn about famous, successful people who truly believed that curiosity was a key to their success and love of life.

"Always be on the lookout for the presence of wonder."

—E. B. WHITE

When these structures, rituals, and routines are implemented in the classroom, kids learn that their thinking and questions matter. Striving readers learn that after years of being made to feel less than others, they, too, can participate fully and contribute mightily to the curious classroom. Eleanor Roosevelt said, "At a child's birth, if a mother could ask a fairy godmother to endow it with the most useful gift, that gift should be curiosity." We wholeheartedly concur! Curiosity matters.

CURIOSITY

Use these questions to drive responsive, learner-focused teaching that cultivates curiosity.

Self-Questions

- Am I modeling my own curiosity every day and keeping my own Wonder Book?
- Have I built in plenty of time for kids to ask, answer, and research questions?
- Is there a structured time each day or week to do this?
- Have I offered viewing and listening entry points, as well as text-based ones?
- Have I noticed more trust and comfort regarding kids' sharing questions?

Kidwatching Questions

- Is the student asking questions more frequently?
- Is the student jotting or sketching questions when reading, listening, or viewing?
- Is the student using a wide range of resources to answer questions?
- Have I seen evidence that the student is revising thinking in light of new evidence?
- Is the student motivated to do further research to address a question?

Conferring Questions

- What are you wondering?
- What are you interested in learning more about?
- Did you learn anything from asking your question?
- Do you need help addressing/answering your question?
- Is there any place you changed your mind? Where and why?
- Does it help to jot your thoughts and questions in your Wonder Book? If so, why? If not, why not?
- Do you think asking questions can help you? If so, why? If not, why not?
- Are you comfortable asking a question in front of the class? If so, why? If not, why not?

"There's no such thing as a kid who hates reading. There are just kids who love reading, and kids who are reading the wrong books. We need to help them find the right books."

—James Patterson

CHAPTER 3

Ensure Access to and Choice of Books

Jen Saul, a reading teacher in Mamaroneck, conferred with Michelle, a fifth grader, about her book choice for the weekend. "The best books are the ones the teachers read aloud," Michelle lamented, "and I can't find anything as good." Jen recognized the poignancy: Michelle had an appetite for story and a desire to read; she knew that books can immerse readers in what Mihaly Csikszentmihalyi describes as "flow experiences" (2008). But she also knew that the texts she perused in the classroom library had not yet stirred these potent responses.

Annie has since referred to this as a "Miss Clavel moment"—the instant when she, like Madeline's teacher in Ludwig Bemelman's classic, knew that "Something (was) not right." Although the collections in Mamaroneck classroom libraries appeared vast, was it possible that they constituted book deserts for striving

See the following Practices and Lessons for this chapter:

These sheets are also available at scholastic.com/ThriveResources.

readers like Michelle? In a quest to promote reading volume, Annie and her colleagues had been studying the matches between readers and books, finding that, when asked about the books they were reading, thriving readers typically clutched and buzzed about books they treasured while striving readers all too often pointed with understandable indifference to worn, leveled books in their desks or book baggies.

To investigate this issue, Annie cleared the way for Mamaroneck reading teacher Maggie Hoddinott to act as a literacy ambassador and conduct a room-by-room inventory of the district's more than 125 elementary classroom libraries. See the next few pages for the findings, most notably the stark mismatches of books to children, which deprived many striving readers of all-important access. These sobering data led Annie and her colleagues to put in place systemic processes to ensure teachers have time and resources to curate their collections.

Although the collections in Mamaroneck classroom libraries appeared vast, was it possible that they constituted book deserts for striving readers like Michelle?

Daily access to irresistible books is essential to all readers' development. Stocking classrooms with compelling books is our joyful responsibility to all students, but it is an urgent, life-saving imperative for striving readers like Michelle who may have limited access to books and time to read outside of school. The best way to provide that access is to build and maintain robust classroom libraries, which Steph has likened to "the beating hearts of the school."

But a classroom library is far more than a large collection of books! Without careful and continuous upkeep, a classroom library can devolve into a sprawling collection of unenticing texts. In this chapter, we focus on specific types of books known to hook striving readers and provide sure-fire success. We offer strategies to curate classroom libraries and make kids aware of their evolving contents, and we emphasize the importance of providing striving readers with continuous access to books when school is not in session.

THE "LEAKY FAUCET" CASE STUDY

Entwistle, Alexander, and Olson (1997) have likened access to books to a "faucet" that flows freely when kids are in schools with well-stocked classroom and school libraries, and when their teachers send home books every night, every weekend, and over every vacation, including summer. Concerned that classroom libraries in Mamaroneck did not contain enough books for striving readers, Annie commissioned a systematic inventory of each one.

Site: Mamaroneck, New York, Elementary Schools

Guiding Question: Are the collections of books in our classroom libraries sufficient, varied, and appealing enough to feed the range of readers in each room?

Procedure: Reading teacher Maggie Hoddinott visited more than 125 elementary classrooms in fall of 2015, and:

- conducted "bin-level" inventory of each library.
- conferred with teachers and students about the library.
- observed students shopping for books.
- took photographs.
- in each classroom, matched levels of books in the library with reading levels of kids in the class.
- identified trends and made recommendations.

Key Findings:

- No systemic processes in place to support teachers in knowing the latest and greatest children's books
- Inconsistent and variable allocations, procedures, and timelines for teachers to order books
- With unreliable supply chains, teachers hoard books and avoid sending them home.
- Grade-level changes and new class sections wreak havoc on libraries.
- K–2 students run out of new books to read at each level before they are ready to move on.
- Children reading below benchmark feel self-conscious reading books that are visibly different from their peers'.
- Seeking out appealing age-appropriate books for striving readers is time-consuming.

Conclusion: Striving readers do not have reliable daily access to the high number of compelling, appropriate books they need to thrive. Read on for details.

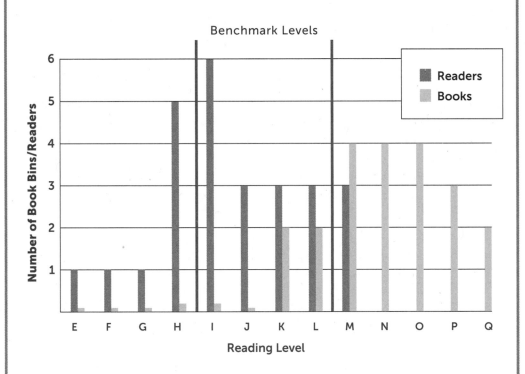

READERS AND BOOKS IN A SECOND-GRADE CLASSROOM

Benchmark Levels

Legend: ■ Readers ■ Books

y-axis: Number of Book Bins/Readers

x-axis: Reading Level — E F G H I J K L M N O P Q

This graph depicts the mismatch of readers and books in a second-grade classroom. Bins of books at each level are plotted in yellow. The actual September reading levels of students in this class are depicted in green. District independent reading-level benchmarks are depicted in red; readers are expected to progress from Level I in September to Level L in June. As you can see, the collection of books is skewed very high; the majority of bins contain books at levels that second graders are not expected to reach by June. This teacher was moved from fifth grade to second grade, and took his books with him anticipating a sparse collection in his new classroom. The eight striving readers in this class who entered at levels E–H found themselves in a veritable book desert.

READERS AND BOOKS IN A FIFTH-GRADE CLASSROOM

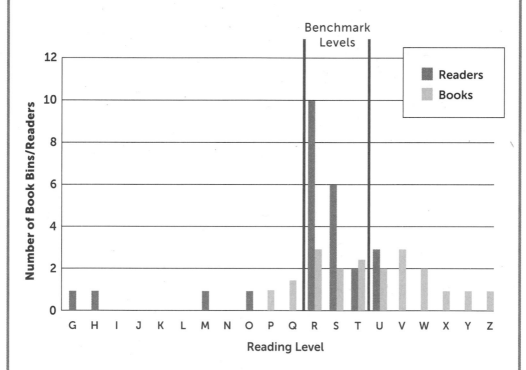

Here is another example of the mismatch of books to readers. By fifth grade, the gaps between striving readers and their classmates are vast; four students entering the year at levels G, H, M, and O find themselves in a book desert. Approximately half the books in this sparse collection are at levels beyond the June benchmark.

It's natural to question how these stark and dire patterns went undetected, particularly in a well-resourced district. The photographs on the next page depict the fifth-grade classroom library graphed. It appears to be robust and varied, doesn't it?

Classroom library depicted in graph

The Leaky Faucet case study reveals the necessity of examining classroom libraries with both wide-angle and zoom lenses. The bulk of the collection should align with the expected trajectory of readers across the grade level. And the collection must be extended and customized to match the needs and interests of the individual readers in the class, particularly those not yet thriving.

THREE TO KNOW

RESEARCHERS ON ACCESS AND CHOICE

1. The 2005 National Assessment of Educational Progress Report (NAEP) demonstrated that students in classrooms with well-designed classroom libraries:

    - interact more with books.

    - spend more time reading.

    - demonstrate more positive attitudes toward reading.

    - exhibit higher levels of reading achievement.

2. John Guthrie and Nicole Humanek (2004) found that assuring students access to an array of interesting texts produced reading achievement gains roughly four times as large as the small effect of systematic phonics instruction, as reported by the National Reading Panel in 2000.

3. In their 10-year-long study of access to books, *Giving Children a Fighting Chance*, Susan Neuman and Donna Celano identified a pattern they called "the more the more, the less the less" (2012). They found that children who had steady access to books read more and followed a dramatic upward growth spiral. Devastatingly, they found that students without reliable access to books read far less and followed a downward spiral of avoidance and disengagement.

RESOURCES FOR CULTIVATING YOUR CLASSROOM LIBRARY

For general guidance on classroom library development, consult these helpful resources:

- "Curating a Classroom Library," a chapter from Donalyn Miller's *Reading in the Wild* (2013): scribd.com/doc/179730832/Reading-in-the-Wild-Curating-a-Classroom-Library

- "The Importance of the Classroom Library" (2001), a concise, research-filled paper by Susan Neuman, suitable to share with families and administrators: teacher.scholastic.com/products/paperbacks/downloads/library.pdf

1. Build a library for the readers you expect; customize it for the readers you meet.

This action is a two-part imperative: first, that you work to build a comprehensive collection over time suited to the typical range of readers at your grade level; and second, that each year you bring in texts that match the interests and capabilities of the actual kids in your class, particularly striving readers and those without ample books at home. The *2017 Scholastic Teacher & Principal School Report* reveals that about half of educators surveyed (46 percent) say their students do not have adequate access to books at home—with 69 percent of educators in high-poverty schools saying the same—and 96 percent of educators believe that "providing year-round access to books at home is important to enhancing student achievement."

With the long-term goal of building comprehensive collections in mind and having diagnosed a systemic need to overhaul classroom libraries, Annie and her colleague Maggie Hoddinott developed a blueprint, shown on the following page, to illustrate the wide range of texts necessary to satisfy all readers. The blueprint includes a variety of genres as well as genre-spanning text formats and topics with high kid appeal and low effort-to-reward ratios.

Here we highlight book formats that have appealingly low effort-to-reward experiences and features of certain genres that beckon striving readers into high-success reading experiences.

CLASSROOM LIBRARY

Build the collection for the readers you expect; customize it for the readers you meet.

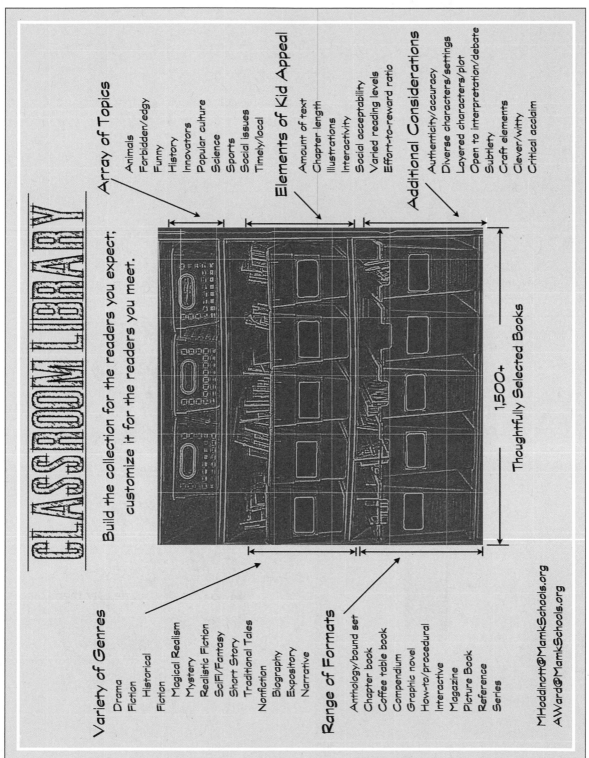

1,500+
Thoughtfully Selected Books

Array of Topics
Animals
Forbidden/edgy
Funny
History
Innovators
Popular culture
Science
Sports
Social issues
Timely/local

Elements of Kid Appeal
Amount of text
Chapter length
Illustrations
Interactivity
Social acceptability
Varied reading levels
Effort-to-reward ratio

Additional Considerations
Authenticity/accuracy
Diverse characters/settings
Layered characters/plot
Open to interpretation/debate
Subtlety
Craft elements
Clever/witty
Critical acclaim

Variety of Genres
Drama
Fiction
    Historical
    Fiction
    Magical Realism
    Mystery
    Realistic Fiction
    SciFi/Fantasy
    Short Story
    Traditional Tales
Nonfiction
    Biography
    Expository
    Narrative

Range of Formats
Anthology/bound set
Chapter book
Coffee table book
Compendium
Graphic novel
How-to/procedural
Interactive
Magazine
Picture Book
Reference
Series

MHaddinott@MamkSchools.org
AWard@MamkSchools.org

Classroom Library Blueprint

BOOK FORMATS WITH APPEALINGLY LOW EFFORT-TO-REWARD RATIOS

In evaluating books for inclusion in your classroom library, consider the "effort-to-reward" ratio each offers. Starting a new book is like pedaling a bicycle from a dead stop. There is a lot of comprehension work to do at the outset. Whereas thriving readers will readily expend effort and tolerate initial disorientation, confident that meaning will emerge, striving readers benefit from immediate gratification as they make their way into an unfamiliar text. We therefore suggest that you weigh the amount of "effort" to be invested (text length and complexity, comprehension challenges) against the "rewards" provided (intriguing characters, compelling illustrations, tantalizing details, gripping plotlines).

For example, middle school reading teacher Nancy Capparelli introduced Annie to the Surviving Southside series, questioning whether it was appropriate for eighth graders. Perusing a few books, it was immediately evident why Nancy's students flocked to the bin and blazed through the series. Each Surviving Southside novel grabs prospective readers with a dramatic title and cover photo of teen character(s) fraught with conflict. The first chapter invariably begins with a scant half-page of text that lays out a provocative scenario. The low "effort-to-reward" ratio of Surviving Southside books makes them irresistible.

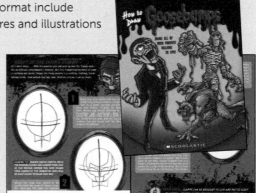

- **Compendium:** These collections of bite-sized, fascinating facts lure even the most reluctant of readers. Open to any page and find compelling tidbits! *The Guinness Book of World Records* is a classic example; Mamaroneck readers are devouring Anna Claybourne's *100 Most* series, which has the added appeal of describing extreme circumstances. Compendia empower striving readers as mavens—possessors of bizarre information that others want to hear.

- **How-To/Procedural:** Books in this popular format include cookbooks and crafts books. Clear text features and illustrations support all readers; they occur naturally and are not viewed as childish. Readers make choices about which recipes and projects to consider. Best of all, these books promote hands-on action and application (making or doing something) rather than the verbal responses so often expected of readers. Procedural books also provide readers with authentic and practical reasons to reread, which builds comprehension and fluency.

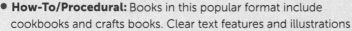

- **Anthology and Bound Set:** These short books gathered in single volumes look as hefty as full-length chapter books, making them socially acceptable. Striving readers experience success and a sense of accomplishment as they finish each book within the set and are motivated to keep reading. Particularly desirable are anthologies of books about familiar and popular characters, which reward readers' copious background knowledge. *Ponyville Reading Adventures*, for example, holds six *My Little Pony* books in a substantial volume.

- **Infographics:** Infographics are pictorial representations of information or data. The inimitable Steve Jenkins has created *Animals by the Numbers: A Book of Animal Infographics*, which includes a fascinating pie chart depicting the prevalence of different species. (1,000,000 million types of insects versus only 5,500 species of mammals!)

- **Joke Books:** Often dismissed as low-brow entertainment, joke books spark spirited conversation about vocabulary, puns, and idioms as readers want to understand the punch lines. "Why wouldn't the shrimp share his Halloween candy? Because he was a little shellfish." Joke books promote rereading and fluency as kids work on their delivery.

- **Interactive Books:** Choose Your Own Adventure books are classic examples; contemporary additions to this highly engaging, agency-building format include the Can You Survive series, which has history, survival, and Doomsday branches. Teachers have reported that kids often reread these gripping books, making different choices and discovering the outcomes until they have exhausted all possibilities.

- **Free Verse Novels:** Hesse's *Out of the Dust* and Creech's *Love That Dog* introduced many of today's teachers to this spare, impactful format when they were young. Free verse poems (i.e., unrhymed and without metrical patterns) pack individual punches and combine to form powerful narrative arcs. Ample white space enables readers to mull each page. Alexander's *The Crossover* and *Booked*, Pinkney's *The Red Pencil*, Woodson's *Brown Girl Dreaming*, and Burg's *Unbound* are powerful and critically acclaimed recent examples.

ANATOMY OF A BOOK WITH
LOW EFFORT-TO-REWARD RATIO

Short chapters spur continued reading.

Small amount of text on the page rewards the reader with a quick page turn.

Illustration provides an accessible entry point and offers an immediate reward.

Page-ending cliffhanger urges the reader to read on.

CHAPTER 1 JUNK MAIL

Alexander Bopp was almost home when he heard the screaming. It was coming from his house.
He ran to his yard. His dad was on the front porch, twisting and shouting.
"Dad?!" he yelled.

Briefly recapping previous books in the series cues readers to access background knowledge and scaffolds understanding for those reading nonsequentially.

Alexander had seen lots of weird things since moving to Stermont. Weird things like *monsters.* He'd battled balloon goons, shadow smashers, tunnel fish, and other creepy creatures.

Alexander looked from the porch to the trees to the driveway. No monsters.
Oh, wait — Dad's not under attack, he thought.
He's dancing!
"Good news, Al!" his dad said. "It's finally here!"

Alexander's dad boogied into the house. Alexander followed, dropping his backpack by the door. "What's here, Dad?"
His dad spun around, holding a padded envelope. "The Reflecto-900 is here!" he said. He ripped open the envelope and pulled out a golden wand. "It's the perfect dental tool!"

REFLECTO-900
Built-in light
Fog-proof mirror
Solid gold!

Diagrams add visual interest and additional opportunities to engage with print.

Thought bubbles reinforce visualizing.

Rewarding illustrations are frequently interspersed among small chunks of text.

Must-Have Genres for Striving Readers

Access and choice can't happen without offering students a full range of genres and formats.

Nonfiction. Nonfiction matters—preeminently! Steph literally "wrote the book" on it. In *Nonfiction Matters* (1998), she asserts, "Passion is at the heart of inquiry. Interest and curiosity breed engagement . . . . Nonfiction reading, research, and writing stoke the inquiry engine as it chugs towards solutions to big questions." With fascinating, real-world topics, jaw-dropping illustrations, and a wide array of interesting text features, nonfiction is a highly accessible and appealing genre for all readers, but it is particularly engaging and rewarding to striving readers for the following reasons:

- **Nonfiction shows us that the world is endlessly fascinating!**
  Who can resist learning about the planet's slimiest yet endearing deep-sea creature in Keating's *Pink Is for Blobfish: Discovering the World's Perfectly Pink Animals*? What terrifying circumstances in 1907 prompted a young cook named Mary Mallon to lunge at visitors with a sharp fork? The opening paragraphs of Gail Jarrow's *Fatal Fever: Tracking Down Typhoid Mary* are a riveting introduction to the plight of Mary and her unfortunate victims. Outstanding nonfiction books enable readers to deepen existing interests and explore compelling new realms.

- **Nonfiction is highly navigable and provides multiple entry points.** Whereas fiction is linear and demands to be read from beginning through middle to end, nonfiction puts the reader in the driver's seat and offers choices. The index and the table of contents empower the reader to find relevant and interesting sections efficiently. The layout and features on individual pages provide options as well. For example, in *Goal!*, Taylor and Vilela's colorful celebration of soccer around the globe, each page contains a box with information about the game in a

particular country. Readers choose whether to pause and attend to these boxes as they go or to read the narrative first.

- **Nonfiction brims with text features that support comprehension.** In just 32 vibrant pages, *Oklahoma's Devastating May 2013 Tornado* by Mariam Aronin provides readers with arresting photographs taken before, during, and after the storm; clear captions; informative headings; bolded important words and an accompanying glossary; inset quotations; maps; a time line; profiles of people who showed courage and compassion; a bibliography; and additional recommended books and websites. See Chapter 6, "Teach Thinking-Intensive Reading," for strategies to build striving readers' skills in using text features to navigate nonfiction.

- **Nonfiction helps kids relate the new to the known.** *National Geographic Kids Ultimate Bodypedia* uses a flabbergasting array of comparisons to illustrate the complex workings of human and animal bodies. In the section on the circulatory system, a "bet you didn't know" graphic states that a blue whale weighs up to 200 tons—as much as 40 elephants. The blue whale's heart is the size and weight of the Mini Cooper car pictured alongside it!

- **Nonfiction builds social energy.** It's inevitable that a reader poring

over a compelling nonfiction book is soon swarmed by peers eager for a look themselves. Information about topics of interest—timely, important, and, yes, bizarre— is currency in the classroom. Readers can't wait to share their newfound knowledge and revel together in it. Second graders relish books from the *Weird but True!* series and trade tantalizing tidbits.

For all of these reasons, nonfiction is welcoming and inclusive. It ignites curiosity, sparks conversation, and impels kids to read more. One of the most important things we can do for striving readers is to flood our classrooms with irresistible nonfiction books on every topic under the sun.

Series Books. Citing the overwhelming correlation between series reading as a child and avid lifetime reading, Kylene Beers recently (2016) asked her Facebook friends, "Which series rocked your reading boat?" Hundreds of comments, likes, and shares ensued in which Kylene's followers reminisced about the impact Nancy Drew, Encyclopedia Brown, Little House on the Prairie, Baby-Sitters Club, Harry Potter, and others had on their reading trajectories. Series books are to the striving reader what spinach is to Popeye: a super food! It is imperative that we stock our shelves with these potent books and keep our collections current and complete.

Series books are to the striving reader what spinach is to Popeye: a super food!

- **Series books are page-turners—and turning pages means volume!** We quote Michael Lewis at the beginning of our volume chapter because it's no accident that this highly acclaimed author of bestsellers such as *The Blind Side, Moneyball*, and *The Big Short* whiled away countless hours of his youth in the Hardy Boys mysteries! Plot twists and cliffhanging chapters propel readers forward and leave them hungry for the next installment.

- **Series books are predictable and highly comprehensible.** Whether it's a first grader opening his next Biscuit book or an adult reaching for her umpteenth Michael Connelly mystery, the series reader is drawn by the promise of familiar pleasures. Predictable structures and recognizable characters and settings make series books particularly accessible to striving readers.

- **Series books invite readers to join the "literacy club."** Frank Smith uses this metaphor to describe the social nature of literacy learning. Enthralled series readers swap books with friends, gossip about characters as if they are real, and commiserate together during the long wait for new releases. Fifth-grader Yandel recently told Annie proudly that he was "on the Post-it" for *Firelight*, the seventh book in Kazu Kibuishi's graphic novel Amulet series. Annie assumed Yandel meant that he was using sticky notes to track his thinking, but Yandel clarified. "I'm on the waiting list. I get it after Sophie and Jose." Yandel had joined the literacy club. The Big Nate series had catapulted him forward and now he was among his peers, itching for his turn with the popular Amulet book. Given the powerful social currency that series books carry, we offer a few caveats pertaining to striving readers.

- **Be aware that specific series are commonly associated with specific grade levels because the majority of readers are ready for them at that time.** For example, many third graders fly through the Magic Tree House series, trading books with one another and eagerly awaiting new releases. Reading popular series at the typical grade levels puts proficient readers in the social mainstream and fuels their reading volume. Striving readers often attempt to catch the wave by selecting these books, which do not yield the high-success reading experiences so necessary for growth. Or, when counseled to select more accessible books, they endure the stigma of reading something visibly different from what their friends are reading.

- **Don't expect striving readers to read things their friends finished months or years ago.** The social energy generated by popular series books is a double-edged sword. A well-intended but insensitive comment like, "Oh, I loved the Magic Tree House books when I read them in third grade" to a fifth grader reading those books is damaging. Even when these comments aren't made (and in our experience they frequently are!), striving readers find the tame and simplistic characters, conflicts, and plot lines of series at their level to be boring.

- **Seek out high-interest, mature-looking but accessible series for striving readers in the upper grades.** They're hard to find, but they're out there! When Mamaroneck's literacy ambassador Maggie Hoddinott discovered Scholastic's Branches division, she knew that series like Eerie Elementary would be perfect for intermediate students reading substantially below benchmark. The spooky cover illustrations and mysterious plot lines appeal to older readers while providing much-needed volume.

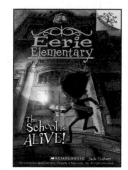

- **Consider reserving certain high-interest, accessible series specifically for striving readers at each grade level.** After diagnosing the problem that striving readers have few new and appealing series to discover, Maggie recommended that certain ones be held in reserve specifically for this niche in the upper grades. This way, when readers are introduced to them, there is novelty rather than yet another reminder of the gulf between them and other readers in the class.

Graphic Novels. Until recently, graphic novels have been the Rodney Dangerfields of literature because they "don't get no respect." This misunderstood format deserves recognition, rebranding, and a prominent place in classroom libraries! Graphic novels grow out of the comic book tradition (which provided volume for Michael Lewis and so many of us) and contain many of the same characteristics: an appealing blend of text and sequential art, eventful stories told through progressions of frames, and exposition and dialogue provided in captions and speech balloons. But whereas comic books typically comprise short episodes, most graphic novels are full-length texts with sophisticated subjects and themes. The combination of accessibility and literary richness makes graphic novels a uniquely satisfying format for striving readers!

- **Graphic novels are explosively popular with people of all ages.** We need to catch the wave, because enthrallment leads to volume; love leads to habit (as Dav Pilkey advises in his illustrated story at the beginning of this book). From primary-grade readers hooked on *Babymouse* to adults like Annie who appreciate the wry wisdom of Roz Chast's *Can't We Talk about Something More Pleasant?*, people gravitate naturally to this compelling format.

- **Graphic novels contain sophisticated themes and complex story lines.** In *Drowned City: Hurricane Katrina & New Orleans*, Don Brown chronicles the storm's devastation with haunting watercolor images. *Hidden: A Child's Story of the Holocaust* uses flashbacks to tell the story of a young Parisian girl's rescue by neighbors from the Nazis after her parents are sent to concentration camps.

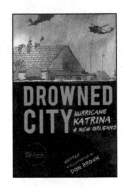

- **Graphic novels make complex content accessible and concrete.** Although the text is relatively spare, vocabulary in graphic novels is often sophisticated. Illustrations provide natural scaffolding, enabling striving readers to infer meaning and keep reading. Notice, for example, that this image from *The Keeper's Treasure*, part of the Explorer: The Mystery Boxes anthology, readily conveys the meaning of "bog," a word unfamiliar to many middle-grade readers. Sophisticated literary elements such as flashback and metaphor are likewise conveyed pictorially. In Judd Winnick's *HiLo*, for example, the title character's backstory is depicted in a different color and figure size. Image size in graphic novels enables readers to determine their importance; bigger frames signify more important information.

- **Graphic novels are gateways to other reading experiences.** In recent years, graphic novel adaptations of everything from classics to contemporary series have sprung up. For example, Gareth Hinds has made complex works like *The Odyssey, Beowulf,* and Shakespearian plays accessible while preserving their timeless richness. Raina Telgemeier has adapted Ann M. Martin's wildly popular Baby-Sitters Club series, enabling readers to distinguish the four main characters more readily. In addition to providing pleasurable, high-success reading experiences in their own right, graphic novel adaptations often serve as springboards for readers to tackle the originals.

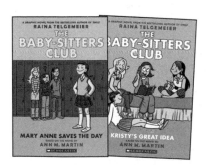

For example, reading researcher Stephen Krashen documented the dramatic reading growth of Ramon, an emerging bilingual student from Mexico, who progressed from manga graphic novels to read and reread Venditti's graphic novel adaptations of Rick Riordan's Lightning Thief series. Ramon moved on to Riordan's original novels—reaching grade-level expectations in the process. (Read more about Ramon's reading arc in Chapter 5, "Book-Match Relentlessly.")

- **Graphic novels are now receiving the critical recognition and acclaim they deserve.** *March: Book 3*, the final installment of John Lewis, Andrew Aydin, and Nate Powell's memoir of Lewis's role in the Civil Rights Movement, won the 2016 National Book Award, Prinz Award, Sibert Medal, and a host of other high honors. *El Deafo*, CeCe Bell's humorous and poignant memoir of growing up with a hearing disability, earned a Newbery Honor in 2015.

In Annie's district, infusions of graphic novels into classroom libraries resulted in viral popularity that posed some interesting problems. Not only did kids' demand for the books exceed the available supply, a number of parents—and even teachers—questioned whether the format was appropriately academic for mass consumption in school. This skepticism led to a healthy and illuminating exploration of graphic novels in professional development sessions and parent workshops. Resources such as Teri Lesesne's guide (randomhousekids.com/media/activities/GraphicNovels_EducatorGd_15_WEB.pdf) have helped adults develop visual literacy and appreciation of graphic novels.

Short Texts, Text Sets, Images, and Objects. At the height of the Rainbow Loom craze in which tweens spent hours weaving rubber band bracelets, Annie conferred with a pair of fifth graders in a special education class who were reading a nonfiction article about thunderstorms. Struck by their wrists full of elaborate bracelets, Annie asked about the designs and patterns.

This unleashed a torrent of information; Isaiah and Steven were working to master a new pattern called the "Mohawk" with loose band loops sticking up from the middle of the bracelet. "Did you know that the man who invented the

Rainbow Loom made it in his basement so he could join his daughters' bracelet making?" Annie asked. "His fingers were too big to manipulate the tiny rubber bands. The real breakthrough happened when his daughters posted how-to videos on YouTube."

The boys were curious to know more, and Annie mentioned a recent article in *The New York Times* about the inventor Cheong Choon Ng, a crash-test engineer for Nissan. Later that day, the boys' teacher, Mary Conroy, emailed Annie asking for the link since the boys were eager to read more. Annie sent the piece, "Rainbow Loom's Success from 2,000 Pounds of Rubber Bands" by Claire Martin (nytimes.com/2013/09/01/business/rainbow-looms-success-from-2000-pounds-of-rubber-bands.html), along with an op-ed piece about Ng and American entrepreneurship written by Bill Keller, "Toy Story" (nytimes.com/2013/11/18/opinion/keller-toy-story.html).

When we think of classroom libraries, we typically think of book bins, but short texts such as articles and interviews are a key genre to include for the following reasons.

- **Short texts are, in a word, short!** Length alone intimidates striving readers. The brevity of articles makes them appealing and non-threatening to striving readers who can read them in a single sitting and have a complete experience. The Rainbow Loom article is two pages long.

- **Short nonfiction has all the supportive features of book-length texts.** The online version of the *NYT* article includes color photographs of Mr. Ng with the loom, one of his daughters with several elaborate creations, and a close-up of the loom itself.

- **Short nonfiction is easy to find and relatively inexpensive to print or copy.** The Internet enables us to respond to students' interests and questions immediately while the curiosity flame is lit. A quick search for "Rainbow Loom" turned up a plethora of articles from vetted sources, photographs, and YouTube videos on all facets of the story. While not every classroom has Internet access, a printer, or e-readers, there is no doubt that the Internet enables us to locate appropriate, compelling texts on any topic, usually for free, and put them in children's hands efficiently.

- **Short texts facilitate differentiation.** The ease with which we can retrieve high-quality material enables us to tailor readings to individual students' interests, reading levels, and appetites. The ability to cut and paste articles into a word-processing program enables us to change font size, insert more white space, and so forth, if needed.

- **Short texts may be bundled into source sets to foster collaborative inquiry and build volume.** One can easily imagine a bin or binder filled with articles, images, and objects connected to children's passions, local happenings, or global current events. As the Flint, Michigan, water crisis unfolded, for example, Mamaroneck teachers compiled articles and infographics in folders in response to children's questions and outrage. Students added resources to the collection as they paid attention at home. A bin grew with nonfiction books on the water cycle and water pollution. Multi-genre source sets like these naturally spark collaborative inquiry. Sometimes sources contain discrepant information; students have authentic reasons to check publication dates and assess the credibility of sources when they care deeply about the content. (See the Source Set lesson on page 284.)

Articles covering the water crisis from Science World *and* Scholastic News

- **Short texts provide interesting and authentic occasions for students to develop reading skills and strategies.** "The content is seductive," Steph regularly reminds teachers. If a lesson objective targets an element of the reading process such as inferring or synthesizing, why not get students to practice it in the most fascinating text possible? For example, Steven and Isaiah grasped the big idea that the Rainbow Loom's success resulted from the daughters' YouTube videos and demonstrations in Learning Express toy stores. "To want to buy the looms, people needed to know how to use them," one of the boys commented, successfully synthesizing.

Poetry. "Poetry is the synthesis of hyacinths and biscuits," wrote Carl Sandburg. This compact, powerful genre has the power to capture striving readers' ears, hearts, and imaginations so long as we choose carefully and tread lightly. If we select vibrant, varied, and startling works—and if we strike an invitational rather than instructional tone—striving readers find delight in poems.

- **Poetry is compact.** Poems are small packages surrounded by white space. What could be less intimidating? In fact, the gorgeous anthology *Firefly July* announces that fact in its subtitle: *A Year of Very Short Poems*. Melissa Sweet's brilliant illustrations are paired with poems selected by Paul Janeczko, such as Raymond Souster's "Spring": "Rain beats down,/Roots stretch up./They'll meet/In a flower."

- **Poetry is visual.** Concrete poetry delights the eye with shapes that convey meaning. Anthologies of child-friendly concrete poems abound; In *Ode to a Commode*, for example, Brian P. Cleary turns words into pictures to create poems such as the swirling "Flush," inspired by the anthology's title.

- **Poetry is playful.** Brimming with clever rhymes, startling word choices, novel comparisons, and rich imagery, well-crafted poems delight the reader and inspire rereading. Doug Florian's rollicking anthology, *Shiver Me Timbers! Pirate Poems and Paintings*, contains a poem called "Pirates Wear Patches" with this satisfying stanza:

> *Pirates have parrots*
> *And eat alligator.*
> *Pirates shoot first*
> *And then ask questions later.*

- **Poetry is soul stirring.** No genre matches the power of poetry to captivate readers with unforgettable lines and images. While the text in poems such as Langston Hughes's "Dreams" is simple, the ideas are complex: "Hold fast to dreams/For when dreams go/Life is a barren field/

Frozen with snow." Don't underestimate striving readers' capacity to read, write, ponder, and savor poems with enduring literary richness.

For some great ideas on how to capture striving readers with poetry, check out the work of poets Sara Holbrook and Michael Salinger. In particular, *Outspoken* (2006), a performance poetry book, and *High Definition* (2010), a poetry/vocabulary book, will fire them up.

Wordless Picture Books. Wordless picture books are eminently inviting and accessible. As Nerdy Book Blogger Kristen Remenar writes, "The most important reason to share wordless books is because they draw us into a world where even those who struggle with letter recognition can successfully read a fantastic story."

- **Wordless picture books encompass complex topics with narrative arcs.** *The Arrival* by Shaun Tan is a tour-de-force depiction of immigration in sepia frames. The lack of words belies its complexity.

- **Wordless picture books foster attention to detail.** Ninth grader Russell couldn't resist *Stick Man's Really Bad Day* on Annie's office shelf. In spite of his self-diagnosed "allergy to books," Russell breezed through Steve Mockus's book about a catastrophe-laden day in the life of the stylized stick man told exclusively through road signs. Initially assuming the book was a spoof, Russell noticed that the endpapers contained photographs of real albeit outlandish road warning signs. He then reread the book more carefully to determine whether Stick Man's "really bad day" was real.

- **Wordless picture books promote partner dialogue.** Given the amount of inferring that goes on in readers' minds between frames, wordless books are provocative fodder for discussion. *Robot Dreams* by Sara Varon depicts the fleeting friendship between a robot and a dog. When one loses a friend, how long should he grieve before moving on? Does it dishonor the friendship to forge new relationships?

Coffee (or Cocoa!) Table Books. These gorgeous tomes can do far more than decorate living rooms. Put them to work in your classroom library captivating young readers! Maggie Koerth-Baker describes the appeal of coffee table books to tween readers: "You're at an age where you still enjoy picture books but are looking for a bigger, deeper view of the world than most picture books provide. Coffee table books bridge that gap, offering grown-up perspectives in kid-friendly packages. Whether the topic is art, architecture, history, culture, or science—coffee table books can be a kid's first step into a subject they'll come to love as an adult." Coffee table books:

- **provide a distinctive and novel reading experience because of their size and heft.** They are meant to be savored in segments rather than read cover to cover. Rather than daunting readers, coffee table books invite perusal.

- **spark curiosity about real-world topics.** The spectacular, full-page images in _Rarely Seen: Photographs of the Extraordinary_, for example, introduce kids to mysterious phenomena that they will want to learn more about.

- **reward prolonged attention and conversation.** Dazzling photographs paired with dense, complex text are a satisfying combination of scaffolding and challenge. Kids love to pore and puzzle over them, making meaning gradually.

A coffee or "cocoa" table is an inviting extension of your classroom library. Borrowing coffee table books from school or community libraries is an affordable way to curate timely collections.

IT TAKES A VILLAGE

We recognize that no school's budget, even a well-resourced school's, is sufficient to purchase the vast and evolving range of titles needed for a truly robust classroom library. It's therefore imperative that teachers partner with school and community librarians to assess kids' interests, book-match relentlessly, and maximize circulation. Fierce and knowledgeable guardians of children's independent reading lives, librarians are invaluable allies. School and public libraries are vaster than classroom libraries, so we must tap them as a steady source of compelling books. Here are some collaboration strategies to consider:

- Invite librarians to your classroom frequently to book-talk new titles.

- Ask them to lend you a temporary "satellite collection" of books for a specific content area or in a specific genre.

- Keep school and community librarians updated on curriculum changes so they can order new titles with those changes in mind. Most librarians welcome these requests enthusiastically.

- Make sure each of your students has a public library card. Perhaps your school or district identifies a grade level at which to register children for cards. In Mamaroneck, for example, second graders register and make field trips to the village libraries as part of a social studies exploration of community resources. If it doesn't, register on your own any of your students who don't have cards.

During a narrative nonfiction unit, fourth-grade teacher Matt Porricelli augments his classroom library collection with books from the Mamaroneck Public Library. Steph reports that in Denver, teachers may check out 100 books for three weeks and renew them without hold requests.

- Invite community librarians to Back-to-School Night to help families get library cards.

- Take advantage of public libraries. Librarians happily gather collections of books to check out for your classroom.

- Take your students on field trips to the public library. Encourage lifelong patronage by teaching them how to reserve books online and retrieve, check out, and renew them.

- Invite librarians to describe appealing library programs and resources (e.g., book clubs, speakers, "maker" spaces) and notify parents of them.

- Head up community "One Reads." For example, the Larchmont Public Library partnered with the school district to read *Boys in the Boat* (adult and YA versions) by Daniel James Brown and invited Olympic rower Esther Lofgren to speak at the library and schools about her journey, from gangly teen to world-class athlete.

IN WITH THE NEW

It's vital to develop a system to add the latest, greatest titles to your classroom library efficiently. It's important to handpick titles. While it's expedient to order pre-bundled collections, we find that they often lack the quality and novelty our readers deserve. Also, to establish the breadth of topics, genres, and formats necessary to hook our strivers, it's crucial that we identify books outside our own reading comfort zones. We rely on the following reliable sources:

- **The Cooperative Children's Book Center:** CCBC librarians post and archive Books of the Week, which inevitably include gems not reviewed elsewhere. The center's compilation of awards and Best-of-the-Year lists is all-inclusive. CCBC's Bibliographies and Booklists on myriad themes and topics not only help teachers choose specific titles, but also remind us of the breadth necessary to reach all readers.

- **The American Library Association:** Our "mother ship" bestows a slew of book, print, and media awards each year. Ordering the top 10 in as many categories as one's budget permits is an efficient way to jumpstart a collection. In Mamaroneck, for example, we seek the Alex Award winners for our high school classroom libraries because ALA has vetted them as adult books widely read and enjoyed by teens.

- **The National Council for Social Studies:** This organization releases Notable Trade Books for Young People each year in thematic strands. Recent selections in Biography include *Miss Moore Thought Otherwise*, Jan Pinborough and Debby Atwell's account of how Anne Carroll Moore ensured that all children were welcomed in libraries!

From Striving to Thriving © 2017 by Stephanie Harvey & Annie Ward, Scholastic Inc.

- **The National Science Teachers Association:** The NSTA also selects Outstanding Trade Books each year. 2015 picks include Katherine Applegate's *Ivan: The True Story of the Shopping Mall Gorilla*, the author's nonfiction follow-up to *The One and Only Ivan*, which includes a tribute from the gorilla's zookeeper and one of Ivan's paintings signed with a thumbprint.

- **The Orbis Pictus Award for Outstanding Nonfiction for Children:** Each year, the National Council of Teachers of English bestows this award, commemorating the 1657 book by Johannes Amos Comenius, *Orbis Pictus* (*The World in Pictures*), which is considered to be the first book actually published for children.

- **Children's Choices and Teachers' Choices:** Each year, in projects co-sponsored by the International Literacy Association and the Children's Book Council, children, teachers, librarians, and reading specialists from regions across the country are invited to voice their opinions about favorite books, resulting in annotated lists of 100 sure-fire hits.

- **Indefatigable bloggers at the Nerdy Book Club:** These writers, led by Donalyn Miller, Colby Sharp, Katherine Sokolowski, Franki Sibberson, and Cindy Minnich, post a steady stream of lively and timely reviews—and they welcome contributions! The Goddess of YA, aka Teri Lesesne, posts "pearls" and book recommendations on her blog and on Twitter @professornana.

OUT WITH THE OLD!

It's not enough to flood our classrooms and libraries with books; administrators need to provide time for teachers and librarians to weed and update. A key component of access is freshness. It's not enough to have shelves full of books; the collection needs to be carefully curated, weeded, and updated regularly in order to ensure it has books to entice every reader in the room. Just as produce managers remove bruised peaches and limp lettuce from the aisles, we need to review our collections regularly, adding recently published gems, replacing worn-out favorites, and eventually removing books that don't circulate. Administrators need to bless the process because most teachers hate to discard books!

Finally, weeded books should be thrown out and not donated to families in need. Such "charitable" efforts are misguided and could be insulting. We must work to ensure that striving readers, particularly those from low-income homes, have access to the freshest, most appealing books from classroom, school, and public libraries, not worn-out cast-offs! See Practice entitled "Weeding Your Classroom Library" on page 268.

2. Display, read aloud, and book-talk a wide range of titles.

Having worked to build a robust and diverse collection, it's vital that we enthusiastically endorse wide and wild reading without judgment. Linda Gambrell has taught us the power of the "teacher blessing of the book" to influence children's motivation to read (1996). We bless books by displaying them prominently, choosing them for whole-class read-alouds, and book-talking them animatedly. Children infer that the books receiving this attention are worthy, as indeed they are. However, children also infer the inverse—that un-blessed books are not worthy. This conclusion marginalizes striving readers! As Teri Lesesne has blogged, "A good educator does not shame books nor limit what students can read" (April 27, 2017 blog post "Standing Room Only"). The following easy-to-implement strategies eradicate book snobbery and include everyone.

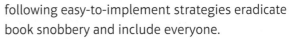

- Use inexpensive wire easels to display the alluring covers of books in your library. Be sure to include cookbooks, graphic novels, picture books, and series books alongside the latest Newbery-winning novels.

- Vary the genre, format, and length of your read-alouds. Why not treat your class to a joke book or a trivia book like *National Geographic Kids Quiz Whiz*? (For more on interactive read-alouds, see Chapter 6, "Teach Thinking-Intensive Reading.")

- Deliver frequent book-talks, and keep a running chart of titles you've endorsed so kids can add to their next-up lists. Make sure to bless books that are at lower reading levels than the mainstream. Include accessible formats like compendia (e.g., *Wacky Facts About Space*) and bizarre or "forbidden" topics (e.g., *Dr. Proctor's Fart Powder*) to sanction these options. See the Practice entitled "Book-Talking" on page 270.

From Striving to Thriving © 2017 by Stephanie Harvey & Annie Ward, Scholastic Inc.

Mamaroneck second-grade teacher Stefan Kuzcinski made a point to read aloud Mo Willems's Elephant and Piggy books when several striving readers gravitated to them. With his blessing, the entire class fell in love with the series, and it sparked sophisticated conversation about the characters and their friendship. Although the books were well below some students' reading levels, Stefan noted that thriving readers used Willems's books as mentor texts for punctuation and that everyone benefited from the joy of sharing these delightful books.

SAMPLE BOOK TALK

I'm excited to share *Ivan, the Remarkable True Story of the Shopping Mall Gorilla* by Katherine Applegate and illustrated by Brian Karas. We haven't been able to stop thinking and talking about Ivan since we finished reading *The One and Only Ivan* aloud last week, so I know you'll be fascinated by this nonfiction account of his life that Applegate wrote following her novel.

Look at how she dedicates the book: "For everyone who loved Ivan." That's certainly us! The book tells the story of Ivan's life, from his birth in Africa to his final, happy years at Zoo Atlanta. When we finished the novel, a lot of us had questions about Ivan's time at the zoo, and this book answers many of them. Look at the emotion in Brian Karas's illustrations alongside Applegate's beautiful language: *"In leafy calm, in gentle arms, a gorilla's life began."*

(Turn to marked page.) This page depicts Ivan and Burma's arrival in the United States: *"The jungle, green with life, was gone. The gorillas had traveled halfway around the world to Tacoma, Washington. A man who owned a shopping mall had ordered and paid for them, like a couple of pizzas, like a pair of shoes."* (Pause for impact.)

Like many nonfiction books, this one has interesting features that help us learn more and keep learning if we want to. There's a photograph of Ivan at the zoo alongside Karas's illustration. There's also an "About Ivan" section in the back in which Applegate describes all her research. For example, she first learned of Ivan from an article in *The New York Times* called "Gorilla Sulks in a Mall as His Future Is Debated." We might want to track down that article. Finally, on the last page, there is a remembrance from Ivan's zookeeper, Jodi, who took loving care of him in the last years of his life. She includes a painting by Ivan in his favorite color, red, signed with his thumbprint.

I'll leave this fascinating book out on the chalk rest alongside the books we found about elephant sanctuaries. Do any of you want to add it to your next-up list?

3. Send books home nightly, on weekends, and over school vacations.

We believe passionately that access to books is a social justice issue. Striving readers require voluminous, pleasurable reading every day to grow. In our experience, the vast majority of striving readers do not experience that nourishing volume due to some combination of inadequate access, choice, and time to read. When the faucet flows freely, the following are in place:

- Abundance of books in the classroom library the child can read and wants to read
- Safe, quiet time and a place to read uninterrupted in school and at home
- Books sent home nightly from school
- Access to knowledgeable librarian(s)
- Continuous school library circulation
- Community library card
- Frequent visits to community library
- Ability to navigate library collections; identify, reserve, and retrieve appealing books
- Connectivity and resources to download books to e-readers

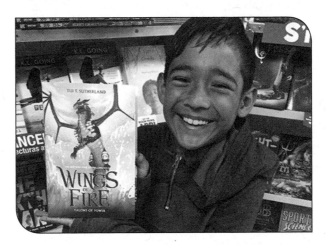

From Striving to Thriving © 2017 by Stephanie Harvey & Annie Ward, Scholastic Inc.

We cannot make assumptions—particularly for children in poverty—that these elements are in place, nor can we judge and blame parents if they are not. Instead, we must champion children's reading lives by ensuring that the first three conditions on this list are met for every child, every day. It's within our power, and it's our responsibility!

With respect to the first condition, we've provided recommendations for robust classroom library contents. And we've cautioned that striving readers may find themselves in de facto book deserts—*even when they are surrounded by books*—if we haven't carefully ensured there are appealing and accessible options for them within our libraries. With respect to the second condition, we emphasize in Chapter 4, "Pump Up the Reading Volume," the need to provide copious amounts of time for kids to read in school during the day and suggest strategies for so doing.

The third condition makes it imperative that we send home appealing and appropriate books every day and not rely on parents to procure books. While we should monitor and guide all students' book choices, it's particularly important that we check to see that striving readers are well matched to the books in their backpacks and equipped to read them.

We need to redouble these efforts before school breaks and summer vacation, cognizant that many of our striving readers, particularly those in poverty, lack access to books at home.

SUMMER SLIDE PREVENTION

The pernicious phenomenon of "summer slide" is well researched: Typically, students from low-income homes lose two months of reading growth during the summer while students from more affluent homes make modest gains. This means that even if poor children grow at the same rates as their advantaged peers during the school year when the faucet is on, the gap widens each year because of summer slide.

But summer slide is preventable! And the solution is simple and heartening: books. Richard Allington and Anne McGill-Franzen found that a book giveaway program in which children received 12 to 15 self-selected books over three consecutive summers resulted in gains equal to summer school for children in poverty—with double the impact of summer school for children in greatest poverty (2013). This powerful intervention costs less than $100 per child whereas often ineffective summer school programs run into the thousands. In Mamaroneck, Annie and her colleagues have replicated Allington and McGill-Franzen's summer slide prevention initiative with remarkable success, allowing children from low-income homes to select and keep 15 high-interest books from June book fairs and tracking the impact on their reading trajectories.

Ideally, committed schools and districts could identify funding sources for book giveaway programs as Mamaroneck has. But if not, it's still vital to send kids home with backpacks full of summer reading material. Allington urges us to clear the library shelves by letting kids select piles of appealing books before they leave for vacation. Because librarians typically inventory, weed out, and organize their collections at year's end, it's important for administrators to provide extra clerical support and/or volunteer assistance to handle the summer circulation. In Mamaroneck, we support and publicize days across the summer when school libraries will be open for book exchanges, read-alouds, and ice cream.

ACCESS AND CHOICE

Use these questions to drive responsive, learner-focused teaching that ensures children's access to and choice of books.

Self-Questions

- Am I sending every child home with books every night, taking particular care to ensure strivers are well matched?
- Am I preventing "slide" by sending stacks of books home before long weekends, school breaks, and summer vacation?
- Have I taken kids on field trips to the library so they learn how to navigate the collection, use the electronic catalog, reserve and/or locate books, and check out and renew them?
- Have I modeled the ways in which I learn about great new books and develop my next-up list (e.g., trusted friends, reviews, bookstore and library browsing, social media, awards lists)?
- Do I book-talk and read aloud books of all genres, formats, and levels nonjudgmentally?

Kidwatching Questions

- Does the student always have books and other reading materials?
- Does the student use his classroom/school/public library privileges to the fullest? If not, have I intervened to ensure unfettered access?
- Does the student have an electronic device onto which I can download e-books?
- Does the student ask whether specific books are available? Does she mention authors and titles she's heard of?

Conferring Questions

- When you think about the best book(s) you've read recently, how or where did you find it/them?
- Do you have books at home? If so, what kinds? Do you visit the public library? Do you have a library card?
- Do you have a quiet time and place to read at home? Are there ways to minimize distractions?
- (If the student cares for a younger sibling) Shall we choose some books for you to read to [sibling's name] at home?
- Do you have a copy of your next-up book? Let's find one.
- What are your plans for the school break? Let's make sure you have a stack of terrific books to read!

"As a kid I lived on a steady diet of the Hardy Boys and Archie comic books, without the slightest sense there was anything better I might be doing with my time."

—Michael Lewis

CHAPTER 4

Pump Up the Reading Volume

Annie and her daughter Mimi commuted to school together for 17 years, a ritual that Annie sorely misses. During Mimi's junior year of high school, she got her learner's permit and needed to log hours of driving. Annie took the wheel in the mornings when time was tight, and Mimi drove home. At one point, Mimi suggested (much to Annie's delight) that they read aloud Jane Austen's *Pride and Prejudice* to one another during the commute.

Several chapters in, during a description of Elizabeth and Darcy's first verbal sparring match, Mimi paused in a thicket of unfamiliar terms, realizing that she no longer understood what was going on. "Oh well. The point is that sparks are flying between them," Mimi said. "We'll see if that landowning thing is important later." Annie noted how readily Mimi, an experienced reader, stopped reading, determined importance, and moved on, aware that she needed to monitor whether the passage she'd skipped would eventually interfere with meaning.

See the following Practices and Lessons for this chapter:

PRACTICE

LESSON

These sheets are also available at scholastic.com/ThriveResources.

That same day, on the commute home, Mimi exclaimed, "What do I do? What do I do?" Annie looked up from the book to see a string of brake lights looming ahead. A huge tree limb had fallen, blocking several lanes of traffic. "You could start by slowing down," Annie said wryly, noting that Mimi's foot hadn't come off the accelerator. "You'll need to get into the other lane. Watch the cop; he'll signal you when to merge."

Throughout the spring, Mimi encountered other navigational challenges and gained experience behind the wheel. She learned how to parallel park and how to make her way around a rotary. She learned that you can't always trust a blinker because sometimes drivers leave them on, with no intention of turning. With each experience, her competence and confidence grew. She passed her driver's test on the first attempt and made a triumphant solo trip to CVS.

From Striving to Thriving © 2017 by Stephanie Harvey & Annie Ward, Scholastic Inc.

FOUR DECADES OF DICK ALLINGTON'S "GREATEST QUIPS" ON VOLUME

- "Few can learn to do anything well without the opportunity to engage in whatever is being learned . . . . To become a proficient reader one needs the opportunity to read" (1977).

- "Based on this massive sample, this finding suggests the stunning conclusion that engaged reading can overcome traditional barriers to reading achievement, including gender, parental education, and income . . . ." (2009).

- "Sadly, struggling readers typically encounter a steady diet of too-challenging texts throughout the school day as they make their way through classes that present grade-level material hour after hour. In essence, traditional instructional practices widen the gap between readers" (2012).

- "Struggling readers just participate in too little high-success reading activity every day. This is one reason so few struggling readers ever become achieving readers" (2013).

- "We fill struggling readers' days with tasks that require little reading. If we want to foster reading development, then we must design lessons that provide the opportunities for struggling readers to actually read" (2013).

Reading Makes Readers

Mimi's progression as a driver helped Annie recognize the analogy: Readers gain skill from experience, and there's no substitute for it. Experienced readers have read countless texts and, as a result, they have acquired strong navigational skills. They have learned how texts work. They take their experience with them from text to text, and their inner voice tells them, "Oh, I've seen this before." They know that italics often signify a character's thoughts; they recognize flashbacks when they encounter them. In expository nonfiction, they know they have choices: They can read linearly from cover to cover or they can use the table of contents to navigate to topics of particular interest.

- Toddlers who pore over Richard Scarry's busy illustrations are thrilled to discover funny vignettes such as Mr. Fixit's flawed "repairs." They learn that pictures often contain important details not mentioned in the text. This knowledge serves readers later, when they know to use illustrations, charts, and other graphic features in textbooks and nonfiction to make meaning.

- Emergent readers who encounter Junie B. Jones meet a classically unreliable, albeit lovable narrator and learn to take her "stretchers" with a grain of salt. A decade or two later, those readers will know to question the credibility of Nick Carraway, the unreliable narrator of F. Scott Fitzgerald's *The Great Gatsby*, when they encounter him.

- Middle grade readers whose hearts have been expanded by R. J. Palacio's *Wonder* learn to assemble a whole truth from multiple perspectives as Augie's narrative baton is passed to Via, Summer, Jack, Justin, and Miranda. If they read William Faulkner's challenging novel *As I Lay Dying*, these readers will be equipped to piece together the whole from each part a character narrates.

Like drivers, readers acquire confidence by logging miles in books; they recognize challenges they have seen and navigated before. They make judgments about when to slow down, stop, veer around, or keep going.

From Striving to Thriving © 2017 by Stephanie Harvey & Annie Ward, Scholastic Inc.

THREE TO KNOW

RESEARCHERS ON READING VOLUME

1. Arguably the most ardent advocate of reading volume is Richard Allington, researcher at the University of Tennessee and past President of the International Literacy Association. Dick has been writing and speaking about reading volume for over four decades. In a 1977 article, "If They Don't Read Much, How They Ever Gonna Get Good?" Allington asserts, "The best way to develop reading ability is to provide abundant opportunities for experiencing reading." In his most recent book, *What Really Matters for Middle School Readers*, he argues yet again that expanding the amount of high-success reading that students do should be our highest priority (Allington, 2015, 2012, 2009, 1977).

2. Stephen Krashen, Professor Emeritus at the University of Southern California, is a linguist and educational researcher known for his work on language acquisition and development. Krashen advocates zealously for "free voluntary reading" (FVR), which he defines as "reading because you want to . . . no book reports, no questions at the end of the chapter, and no looking up every vocabulary word . . . the kind of reading most of us do obsessively all the time." In a meta-analysis of over 50 studies, Krashen found that reading volume was the single greatest factor in reading achievement—greater than socioeconomic status. He calls "light reading," such as comic books, teen romance books, and magazines, "a great conduit to heavier reading" because it motivates students to read and make them feel linguistically competent. Krashen rails against traditional reading incentives and rewards, which are shown to be ultimately harmful (2004, 2011).

3. In "one of the most extensive studies of independent reading yet conducted," Anderson, Wilson, and Fielding (1988) traced reading growth to independent reading and reading volume. They found that the amount of time students spent in independent reading outside of school was the best predictor of reading achievement. The chart to the right captures the results of the study. Note the number of words students consume during independent reading—and the enormous differences in reading volume between higher- and lower-achieving students across a year.

Variation in Amount of Independent Reading		
Percentile on standardized test	Minutes of reading per day	Words read per year
95	67	4,733,000
90	33	2,357,000
80	25	1,697,000
70	17	1,156,000
60	13	722,000
50	9	601,000
40	6	421,000
30	4	261,000
20	2	134,000
10	1	51,000
2	0	8,000

1. Trust the book, trust the reader.

The overwhelming benefits of voluminous engaged reading compel us to give all kids a whopping daily dose and make it a foremost intervention for striving readers.

A compelling book has important work to do in the heart and mind of the reader. Although we fervently believe in—and devote our longest chapter to—explicit and energetic reading instruction, the overwhelming benefits of voluminous engaged reading compel us to give all kids a whopping daily dose and make it a foremost intervention for striving readers.

Those benefits range from the acquisition of reading skills to the development of readers' humanity.

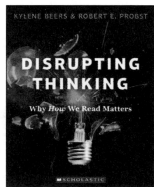

Children not only become better readers through voluminous, engaged reading, they also become more informed, principled, empathetic people. In *Disrupting Thinking: Why How We Read Matters*, Kylene Beers and Robert E. Probst (2017) provide the following summary of the benefits of voluminous reading:

9 REASONS TO READ MORE

Builds Knowledge

Cunningham & Stanovich, 1991 • Cunningham & Stanovich, 2003 • Pressley, 2000

Improves Achievement

Allen, Snow, & McNamara, 2015 • Anderson, Fielding, & Wilson, 1988 • Allington, 2012 • Blachowicz & Ogle, 2001 • National Assessment of Educational Progress Report, 2015 • Worthy & Roser, 2010

Increases Motivation

Atwell, 1987 • Feitelson & Goldstein, 1986 • Guthrie, Klauda, & Ho, 2013 • Ivey & Broaddus, 2001 • Lapp & Fisher, 2009 • Lesesne, 2003 • National Endowment for the Arts, 2007

Increases Vocabulary

Krashen, 1989 • Nagy, Anderson, & Herman, 1987 • Nation & Cody, 2013 • Read & Hodges, 1982

Improves Writing

Bazerman, 1980 • Goodman & Goodman, 1983 • Langer & Flihan, 2000 • Raphael, Kirschner, & Englert, 1988

Builds Background Knowledge

Anderson, 1984 • Anderson, 1985 • McVee, Dunsmore, & Gavelek, 2005 • Ozuru, Dempsey, & McNamara, 2009 • Smagorinsky, 2001

Improves Understanding of Text Structures

Armbruster, 2004 • Fletcher, 2006 • Kendeou & van den Broek, 2007 • Meyer & Rice, 1984 • Snyder, 2010

Develops Empathy

Allington, 2013 • Bal & Veltkamp, 2013 • Johnson, 2012 • Koopman & Hakemulder, 2015 • McLean, Breen, & Fournier, 2010

Develops Personal Identity

Abodeeb-Gentile & Zawilinsky, 2013 • Begum, 2014 • Fives, Russell, et al., 2014 • Hall, 2012 • Harste, 2009 • Jesweak, 2015 • Tatum, 2009

A CASE FOR VOLUMINOUS, ENGAGED READING: YANDEL

Anne Marie and Yandel

Yandel entered fourth grade lacking confidence. An emerging bilingual, he kept to himself, preferring video games to classmates' company. When he did interact with peers, conflicts often resulted, which required adult mediation. The oldest of three children, Yandel had caretaking responsibilities for his two younger siblings while his parents worked. Acutely aware of his reading deficits, he finished very few books.

When the district provided funding for classroom libraries, Yandel's teachers flooded the room with graphic novels, including the Big Nate and Amulet series. Yandel gravitated to Big Nate and fell for it hard. Special education teacher Anne Marie Finlan described what happened: "The next few weeks, the only books in Yandel's hands were Big Nate, and the other students even began to notice. It was obvious that independent reading was his favorite. He was the first to take his book out and the last to put it away. Every time he came back from the library he had a Big Nate book. After reading the entire series once, he began reading it again. His reading log from February to April consisted of every Big Nate book that was available."

Not only did Yandel progress through five independent reading levels in six months, his confidence and social skills grew as he read voluminously. "He was transforming before our eyes," Anne Marie wrote. He participated throughout the day actively, and he developed conflict-resolution skills, which drew the assistant principal's attention on the playground. Anne Marie procured a Big Nate poster for Yandel, which he proudly hung in the living room of his family's apartment. His mother commented that he seemed much happier at home and would read avidly, even when his brother was acting up.

By June, Yandel reached the year-end reading benchmark for fourth grade. He had moved on to Amulet, jockeying with his friends for copies of the "gone-viral" series, while still rereading beloved Big Nate books. District funding enabled Yandel to select 15 high-interest books from a summer slide prevention book fair; he took this stack to sleep-away camp and read during "flashlight time" every night.

Before school reopened in September, Annie and Anne Marie visited Yandel and his family at home to talk with him about his summer reading experiences. When Annie asked Yandel how teachers could help children read voluminously, Yandel had this to say: "Teachers should ask kids what they're really interested in and try to find the books that have those things in them. If a kid likes comedy and action, you can try to help them find a book that's comedy and action. And then they would read it and like it and continue on. And I think that would help teachers help students become better readers so they can read and learn at the same time."

2. Build in time for students to read independently.

Given the indisputable link between reading volume and achievement, all children should have substantial time to read independently every day in school. Why is it, then, that daily independent reading is not practiced in many classrooms? *The Scholastic Kids and Family Reading Report* (2017) contains the following statistics:

- One-third of children ages 6–17 (33 percent) say their class has a designated time during the school day to read a book of choice independently, but only 17 percent do this every or almost every school day.

- Half of children ages 6–17 who read independently as a class or school (52 percent) say it's one of their favorite parts of the day or wish it would happen more often.

- School plays a bigger role in reading books for fun among children in lower-income homes. Sixty-one percent of children ages 6–17 from the lowest-income homes say they read for fun mostly in school or equally at school and at home, while 32 percent of kids ages 6–17 from the highest-income homes say the same.

READ FOR YOUR LIFE!
Voluminous, Engaged Reading Lengthens and Enriches Lives

- In 2016, researchers at the Yale University School of Public Health found that, of 3,635 participants, those who read books for a half-hour a day had an average "survival advantage" of two years over those who didn't read books—even those who read newspapers and magazines—presumably because of the extended cognitive and emotional engagement that comes from reading books.

- The British Cohort Study, sponsored by the British Institute of Education (1970), follows over 17,000 people who were born in England, Scotland, and Wales within the same week, April 5–11, in 1970. Among the many findings of this vast ongoing study is that children's pleasure reading from the ages of 10 to 16 has been linked more to their cognitive development and academic success than their parents' levels of education.

In other words, in-school reading is highly pleasurable and inextricably linked to reading development, and yet it happens daily in fewer than one-fifth of the classrooms surveyed. Something is wrong with this picture!

READING ON SCHOOL TIME

Why We Don't Do Enough of It	Why We Should Double Down on It
Perception that if reading is "fun," it must not be rigorous.	High volume of high-success reading is the number-one factor correlated with reading development (Krashen, 2011; Allington, 2009). Many recent studies have demonstrated the positive cognitive benefits of engaged reading (Berns, Blaine, Prietula, & Pye, 2013).
Higher standards call for students to be reading challenging texts and moving up the "staircase of complexity."	High volume of high-success reading at the base of the staircase leads readers to take step after step into more complex books over time (Allington, 2009), whereas putting hard books into striving readers' hands is a recipe for disaster.
Assumption that teachers should be teaching during class, not just letting kids read.	Teachers have vital teaching opportunities before, during, and after independent reading: selecting books for their classroom libraries, matching kids with books one by one, and monitoring the matches relentlessly, just to name a few. Reading conferences, which often happen during independent reading time, are valuable formative assessments that provide data to inform whole-class, small group, and one-to-one instruction.

An unhurried daily block of independent reading should be the centerpiece of our reading curriculum. Time to read in school gives kids a leg up on their reading. When kids get "into" their books in school, they are far more likely to continue reading at home.

While reviewing middle schoolers' quarterly reflections on independent reading, Annie was struck by an additional benefit: It provides a peaceful, quiet interval in students' otherwise noisy and fast-paced day. Students frequently described reading time as a period of calm. One even called it (with a nod to Jon Stewart) a "moment of Zen."

Research bears this out: A 2009 study at the University of Sussex found that reading reduces stress more effectively and quickly than listening to music or taking a walk. Six minutes of engaged reading was found to reduce subjects' stress levels by 68 percent. Mamaroneck administrators display appealing books in their offices, in part so that children who end up there for whatever reasons can calm themselves by reading.

In-class reading time provides us with invaluable opportunities to confer with students about what they are reading and to verify that each one is well-matched to a book. An intimate face-to-face conversation is a highly effective way to measure a child's engagement. It enables us to diagnose a mismatch or a comprehension challenge. See the Practice entitled "Conferring for Engagement: Reader to Reader, Heart to Heart" on page 276. For example, when Annie pulled alongside fifth grader Elijah, he appeared to be engrossed in *Semper Fido*, the first book in C. Alexander London's Dog Tags series about soldiers and dogs. Elijah told Annie, "There's a part in Chapter 21 where I almost cried. Would you like to see it?" *Would I ever*, Annie thought! Elijah flipped back page by page; as he neared the pivotal passage, Annie noticed his breathing quicken and his chest heave with anticipation. He pointed at the page, inviting Annie to read it. It was immediately apparent why this moment had arrested Elijah: The protagonist, a Marine, was faced with the decision to shoot his beloved stray companion to prevent the dog's barking from giving away the platoon's position to a sniper. When Annie felt her own chest tighten and her voice begin to crack, Elijah reassured her, "Don't worry; Gus didn't have to shoot Loki."

After bonding with Annie over this intense passage, Elijah said, "Would you like to see something else?" *Would I ever*, Annie thought again. Elijah reached under his shirt and pulled out a pair of dog tags on a chain that had been packaged with the book. "I don't take it off," he said. Annie remembered hearing Mem Fox once say, "Children's hearts need to ache with caring over what they read." Elijah was clearly deriving all the benefits that engaged reading provided, and Annie's only remaining objective in the conference was to ensure that he had access to other books in the series.

PREDICTABLE STRUCTURES FOR INDEPENDENT READING

There are many ways to schedule independent reading during the school day, but only one rule of thumb: It's your responsibility to guard this sacred time against intrusions. Reading should be seen by all as the main event and not as "filler" when other assignments have been completed.

- **Beginning-of-day independent reading.** Steph has long advocated that we begin each day with a half hour of independent reading, when students are fresh and focused. Kicking off the day with independent reading signals its importance and ensures that it won't take a back seat as other demands of the day kick in—and it doesn't require school-wide support and buy-in.

- **Reading workshop.** This instructional model calls for a brief (10-minute) mini-lesson followed by an extensive block of time (45+ minutes) for independent reading. While students are reading, the teacher confers with them individually or convenes small groups, based on students' needs or interests. The workshop typically ends with a brief (5-minute) cross-pollinating share session.

- **Daily, school-wide reading break.** Schools with teachers and administrators who understand the importance of independent reading carve out a sacred time each day during which the entire school reads. This is a wonderfully visible endorsement of independent reading. Whereas in the past teachers were encouraged to read alongside their students during independent reading, we encourage you to confer and book-match, while making your own, authentic reading life visible to students. For example, middle school teacher Stacy Peebles keeps a running roster on her whiteboard of what she is reading.

Let's make every classroom a reading oasis.

3. Remove barriers to volume.

Just as doctors vow to "do no harm" when they take the Hippocratic Oath, we educators must vow to do no harm to striving readers and provide them with the reading volume they need and deserve. Although this may sound like a no-brainer, we find that if we're not careful, certain pervasive, daily structures erode the amount of time striving readers spend reading in school and at home! We must rethink and revise any structure that does that. Be on the lookout for the following potential barriers to volume.

Curriculum Calendars

Let's begin with the "elephant in the classroom": the curriculum itself! This sounds like heresy, but hear us out! Many curriculum calendars contain genre-specific units of study (e.g., mystery, historical fiction). Unless we take extreme care to procure a wide range of appealing books within these genres, striving readers will likely encounter books they cannot or do not want to read for the duration of the unit. Not only does a lack of suitable reading material prevent striving readers from accessing the curriculum, it also stalls their reading lives—just what they don't need.

Annie recently conferred with Charlotte, a third grader engrossed in *Little Robot*, Ben Hatke's graphic novel featuring a resourceful heroine. Charlotte's book box also contained a Nate the Great book, which was prohibitively challenging for her. When Annie saw that every child's book box contained a Nate the Great book along with other, self-selected texts, she knew what was up: Although the teacher had ensured that every child had chosen a just-right book for independent reading, she was dutifully devoting class time to the whole-group study of mystery, as required by the district. She was using Nate the Great as a shared text because it matched the expected reading level for third graders and, frankly, because there were enough copies in the bookroom.

Annie knew that Charlotte and several of her classmates were reading many levels below the expected reading level for third graders. The best fuel for Charlotte's reading growth at that moment would be a ladder of texts, built on *Little Robot*. (See the discussion of reading ladders in Chapter 5, "Book-Match Relentlessly.") There is a high cost anytime a striving reader like Charlotte spends time in books that are too challenging: the loss of the gains she would have made if she had been spending time in high-success texts.

We must "crack open" curriculum units so that their objectives may be met using a broader array of book genres, formats, and levels. For example, Mamaroneck literacy coach Laurie Pastore suggests reframing a historical fiction unit as a study of the impact of setting (place and time) on character development. In addition to historical fiction, students could read graphic novels, contemporary realistic fiction, fantasy, and other genres to meet unit objectives. Another approach is to frame units around themes, concepts, or essential questions rather than genres.

Revising curriculum this way likely requires a systemic commitment. If we truly have striving readers' best interests in mind, however, we must advocate for changes and resources, especially when the curriculum limits volume. (See Chapter 8, "Advocate Tirelessly.") In the meantime, a classroom-level solution is to advance a unit with short texts and whole-class read-alouds, while enabling children to self-select books in all genres for continuous, voluminous, and high-success independent reading.

THE REALITY OF READING TIME

According to the *2017 Scholastic Teacher & Principal School Report*, the overwhelming majority of educators agree that students should have time during the school day to read independently a book of their choice, but only 36 percent of pre-K–12 teachers set aside time every day for such reading. Teachers cite "the demands of the curriculum" as the primary barrier.

"Canned" Reading Responses

When what we read stirs our hearts and minds, our impulse is to think deeply, talk with others, or pick up another book—and not to make a character puppet or to map a book setting. Mike Schmoker coined the phrase "Crayola Curriculum" to describe the excessive coloring, cutting, and pasting that often occur during time allocated for reading (2001). We must slay these inauthentic, time-sucking, volume-robbing monsters!

Having kids log their reading is a good idea as long as the method is efficient and enables readers to track and reflect on their progress. Beyond logging their reading, we encourage students to respond authentically by doing the following:

- **Talking with others.** In a 2012 study, Gay Ivey and Peter Johnston found that middle schoolers who had read gripping YA books were compelled to discuss them with classmates who had read them, whether or not they were friends. Reading and talking about reading breaks down social boundaries! And spontaneous, student-initiated talk increases comprehension more than teacher prompts.

- **Taking action.** During the run-up to the 2016 presidential election, Steph's friend and co-author, Anne Goudvis, worked with Karen Halverson, a fifth-grade teacher at the Boulder Community School of Integrated Studies, on a voice and voting inquiry project.

  The project sprung from the outrage of Karen's students when they read that fewer than half of college-aged students had voted in the previous election. They went to C.U. Boulder with painted signs to get out the vote by marching and forming a tunnel for college students to pass through. To their delight, NPR picked up and broadcast their story: http://www.npr.org/sections/ed/2016/11/07/500997105/these-fifth-graders-think-its-really-really-important-that-you-vote.

- **Linger in the world of the book.** Having finished David Guterson's evocative novel *Snow Falling on Cedars*, a ninth grader commented that he was "still in his book hangover" and wasn't yet ready to leave the setting and characters for another book. To promote volume while respecting the reader's urge to linger, his teacher helped him find related short texts.

> "I do not think (great) readers would tell us about making shoebox dioramas of beloved novels or writing new endings to published stories. They wouldn't talk about sending make-believe letters from one character to another, or about cutting books into sentence strips and reassembling them. Instead, I think that great readers would tell us about weaving reading together with the people and passions of their lives. They would tell us that reading, like writing, is a big thing we do with our whole lives."
>
> —*Lucy Calkins*

- **Inquire into the book and read around it.** Fifth grader Nina wasn't ready to move on when her teacher finished reading aloud *The One and Only Ivan* because she was so moved by it. Annie sympathized because the novel had moved her deeply, too. She shared with Nina the results of her own inquiry into the real "shopping mall gorilla": the *New York Times* article that had inspired Katherine Applegate; Ivan's obituary from NPR; a nonfiction book on elephant sanctuaries called *Just for Elephants*; and a YouTube video of an elephant reunion at the sanctuary that may have inspired the character of Stella.

- **Selecting a next-up book and moving on.** The ultimate volume-builder is simply to pick up another book, whether it relates to the previous one or not! In *Book Love*, Penny Kittle likens real readers' paths to roller coaster rides—not linear and ever-ascending but rather filled with twists and turns (2012). After finishing something long and hefty, many readers indulge in something quick and light—and vice versa. Or they choose something else long and hefty. There is no "right" next-up book.

Homework

Whether to assign homework to children at various grade levels—and, if you do, how much—is controversial, but one thing is clear: The more we clutter children's backpacks with busywork, the less we support their independent reading at home. We send a mixed message when we call for 30 minutes of independent reading each night, but send home a sheaf of worksheets to be completed, too. Busy parents acknowledge, "What's in the folder is what gets done," which means that worksheets all too often trump independent reading. We need to make reading the main event, rather than something kids turn to only at bedtime when they are tired.

In *No More Mindless Homework*, part of the Not This, But That series, Kathy Collins asserts, "It's important that reading at home gives children a chance not only to practice reading, but also to grow a self-directed reading life, positive attitudes toward reading, and highly functional reading habits."

Test Prep

There is no widespread practice more detrimental to reading growth than excessive amounts of test preparation. Yes, we all wince when we think of our striving readers facing long, complex passages and convoluted questions on standardized assessments. And at the same time, we want all our students—striving readers included—to be as prepared as possible to tackle them. However, there is scant evidence that test prep actually improves test performance (Allington & Gabriel, 2016). There is overwhelming evidence, however, that engagement in high-success reading advances kids' confidence and competence as readers, better equipping them for life (and, incidentally, the tests).

Dick Allington concurs. In summarizing the results of "exemplary teacher research" in six states, he writes, "I must also note that we observed almost no test prep in (exemplary teachers') classrooms. None of the teachers relied on the increasingly popular commercial test preparation materials. Instead, these teachers believed that good instruction would lead to enhanced test performance. The data bore out their beliefs. It was in the less effective teachers' classrooms that we found test-preparation activity. It seems that less effective teachers truly don't know what to do and, as a result, drift toward the use of packaged test preparation activities in the hope that they will make up for less effective teaching throughout the year" (2002).

Voluminous Reading Changes Lives

Voluminous, engaged reading fosters literacy and changes lives. And the proof is in the Harry Potter series—the bestselling book series of all time. Millions of kids from around the world have become thriving readers by feverishly following Harry, Hermione, and Ron across thousands of pages.

Those readers have also become more empathetic human beings. In 2015, researchers in Italy, led by psychologist Loris Vezzali, met weekly with groups of fifth graders to read and discuss passages from Harry Potter books. At the outset of the study, all children were surveyed about their attitudes toward immigrants and refugees. Children in the "treatment" groups read passages in which Harry reacted strongly to the persecution of out-groups such as "mudbloods," muggle-born wizards like Hermione. Meanwhile, children in control groups read passages unrelated to prejudice, such as a description of Harry's first wand purchase. When surveyed again, the children in the treatment groups demonstrated significantly warmer feelings toward students from other countries than did children in the control groups. "Unfortunately, the news we read on a daily basis tells us we have so much work to do (around tolerance)," Vezzali says. "But based on our work, fantasy books such as Harry Potter may be of great help to educators and parents in teaching tolerance."

While vacationing in Scotland, Annie dined at The Elephant House, the Edinburgh pub in which J. K. Rowling penned installments in the series while her baby daughter napped. In the loo, from floor-to-ceiling, graffiti honors Rowling and her unforgettable books. Comments range from bawdy ("I'd get sleazy for Ron Weasley") to poignant. One fan wrote, "Thank you, J. K., for having made my childhood extraordinary." Sarah King from Florida thanks Rowling for "life lessons" delivered by wise, beloved Dumbledore: "It is our choices, Harry, that show us what we truly are, far more than our abilities." The expansiveness of readers' gratitude to Rowling is significant. Readers author their lives through their choices of books, and those choices expand readers' abilities while opening their hearts.

Tributes to J. K. Rowling in the loo of The Elephant House, Edinburgh

VOLUME

Use these questions to drive responsive, learner-focused teaching of voluminous, high-success reading.

Self-Questions

- Have I modeled my own volume-building habits (e.g., having nonfiction downloaded on my phone, keeping books in my car)?
- Have I modeled my own reading plans for weekends and vacations?
- Am I certain kids are well matched with the books in their hands?
- Do I confer regularly with kids about their reading and reading materials to ascertain their level of engagement?
- Have I modeled how I get myself ready to read (e.g., by finding a block of distraction-free time, particularly for a new book)?
- Have I modeled my own process of getting into books, particularly challenging ones?

Kidwatching Questions

- Does the student activate knowledge about the book and/or author? Does she read the flap? Peruse the contents?
- Watch the student in the early stages of reading. Does he get into the book readily and progress at a reasonable pace?
- Does the student maximize downtime and build volume by seizing opportunities to read?
- Does the student abandon books? If so, is there a pattern?
- Does the student initiate conversations with peers about what she is reading?
- Does the student express curiosity and search for additional information about what he has read (e.g., about the real Ivan the gorilla)?

Conferring Questions

- (At the outset) Are you getting into the book? Is it easy to get into? If so, why? If not, why not?
- (Mid-book) How is it going? What is the book making you think about?
- I've noticed that during the week you don't seem to read as much at home as on weekends. Let's talk about that.
- What does this book make you curious about? What would you like to know more about?
- Do you think this author has written anything else? Let's check . . .

Part II: Teach

"Let us remember: One book, one pen, and one teacher can change the world."

—Malala Yousafzai

▶ scholastic.com/ThriveResources

"For students of every ability and background, it's the simple, miraculous act of reading a good book that begins to turn them into readers. . . . The job of adults who care about reading is to move heaven and earth to put that book into a child's hands."

—Nancie Atwell & Anne Atwell Merkel

CHAPTER 5

Book-Match Relentlessly

"**W**ould you like to hear a joke?" Jamir whispered to Annie when she visited his third-grade class during independent reading time. "What do you get if you cross a chicken with a cow?" "Hmmm…," Annie responded, eyeing the unopened Goosebumps book in his hand and pondering possible plays on mooing and milking. "You get a *roost* beef," Jamir answered gleefully. The teacher, Andrea Ochiogrosso, noted that Jamir told jokes to break the ice with peers and adults. "I'm good at jumping in," he had assured her. Andrea also noted that Jamir was new to the class, having recently entered a local shelter with his mother. He had gravitated to Goosebumps because it looked like what his new classmates were reading, but the series was a challenge for him.

Annie and Andrea discussed Jamir's reading selection, and decided that a joke book might be a better choice, but there were no such books in the classroom library. The school library, however,

See the following Practices and Lessons for this chapter:

PRACTICE
Going the Extra Mile to Put the Right Book in a Striving Reader's Hands 280

LESSON
Making a Reading Plan 282

These sheets are also available at scholastic.com/ThriveResources.

had a sizeable collection. The next day, with the help of the librarian, Pam Tanenbaum, Jamir chose *Just Joking: 300 Hilarious Jokes About Everything, Including Tongue Twisters, Riddles, and More!* Andrea saw that Jamir's sense of humor and desire to expand his repertoire kept his nose in the book. He wasn't shy about asking for the meanings of puns or the pronunciation of certain words if it helped with his delivery. Jamir pored over the book and memorized favorite bits by reading them again and again. In addition to clever jokes, *Just Joking* contains intriguing animal facts and features. His interest sparked, Jamir soon began to choose nonfiction books about animals from the classroom library.

Assuming you have fabulous books in your school and classroom libraries, it's likely that many of your students will choose appealing titles and topics to read on their own, with some guidance and support. It probably comes as no surprise, however, that striving readers often have trouble finding just-right books, and when they do, staying in them. In fact, this is a key factor that distinguishes striving from thriving readers. Stalls, interruptions, and gaps in kids' reading lives mean they are not getting the volume of high-success reading they need! Book-matching is vital in putting striving readers on a reading path. It's labor intensive, but it's a labor of love. As Nancie Atwell and Anne Merkel put it, it's heroic, heaven-and-earth-moving work in certain cases, but well worth it!

RESEARCHERS ON RELENTLESS BOOK-MATCHING

1. Can a single positive experience ignite a child's reading life? Research suggests "yes! "Vinnie Henkin and Stephen Krashen document "The Naruto Breakthrough," the story of Ramon, a teenager and his "home run book experience." Ramon immigrated to Arizona and entered ninth grade, speaking very little English and having completed only sixth grade in Mexico. Ramon discovered Naruto, a Japanese manga series about a teenage ninja, based on a Spanish-language television series he had watched in Mexico. Hooked by the first Naruto book, Ramon sought library passes to check out others. After Ramon exhausted his school's supply, he found more Naruto books in the public library. Ramon's academic performance improved dramatically and measurably, and he joined the soccer team. His reading branched out, too—from graphic novel adaptations of Rick Riordan's *The Lighting Thief* and *The Red Pyramid* to his original novels. Ramon's goal was to obtain all As in his mainstream 11-grade classes. Henkin and Krashen note, "The importance of the home run book phenomenon is that a reading habit will result in improvement in all aspects of literacy and greater school success" (2015).

2. No one believes more passionately in every child's right to a wide and wild reading life than Donalyn Miller, the self-proclaimed "Book Whisperer." Although Donalyn claims, "I am not a reading researcher" (2009), we beg to differ. She has assembled a powerful body of action research over the decades that explains the glorious reading arcs of thousands of students and galvanizes teachers worldwide. Donalyn's blog (bookwhisperer.com/) is a trove of thoughtful reflections on teaching and invaluable professional resources, including her must-read post, "I've Got Research. Yes I Do. I've Got Research. How About You?" (2015). Share this pithy essay with anyone who doubts the power of self-selected independent reading!

3. The incomparable Teri Lesesne has an ever-evolving, encyclopedic knowledge of children's literature and a flair for book-talking, which make her a spectacularly effective book-matcher. In *Making the Match*, Teri talks about the power of "the right book for the right reader at the right time," pairing practical chapters with delightful essays by prominent children's authors. In *Reading Ladders*, Teri lays out concrete strategies to meet readers where they are and put them on progressions, or "ladders," of compelling books for high-success reading. Teri blogs and tweets as "Professor Nana," and her "pearls" are not to be missed: professornana.livejournal.com.

1. Tap the power of watershed books.

In 1947, critic and writer Clifton Fadiman said of his earliest indelible reading experience, "One's first book, kiss, home run, is always the best," giving rise to the term "home run book" that Henkin and Krashen would use decades later (2015). As baseball fans, we love the metaphor and love even more recalling our own home run books. For Steph, it was Carol Ryrie Brink's rollicking novel *The Pink Motel*; for Annie, it was the Discovery Book biography *Florence Nightingale: War Nurse*. Not surprisingly, we've both tracked down copies of these long-out-of-print favorites that so enthralled us and put us on reading paths.

Earlier, we described how the first book in the Naruto series was a home run book for young Ramon. But given the torrent of engaged reading it launched, we think of it more as a "watershed" book. There was no turning back for Ramon— no subsequent dry spell or slump, but rather a continuous stream of engaged reading that transformed him. Watershed reading experiences are the catalysts that transform many readers from striving to thriving. Witnessing these transformations regularly inspires us to book-match steadily and faithfully.

From Striving to Thriving © 2017 by Stephanie Harvey & Annie Ward, Scholastic Inc.

And watershed reading experiences needn't be restricted to school. Annie's daughter Mimi was a competent but unenthusiastic reader in third grade. Annie recalls having to set the timer on the microwave to enforce the nightly 20 minutes of reading. When the timer would ding, Mimi would slam the book shut immediately. Annie recalls brokering a deal: "Mimi, you don't have to finish the chapter . . . or even the page. . . . But you do have to finish the paragraph!" Mimi's lack of engagement was evident and chagrining.

The Right Book at the Right Time

Once, returning home at the end of a long day, Annie and Mimi found a mysterious, brown-paper-wrapped package crammed in their mailbox. It was addressed to Mimi with a tantalizing return address: "The Reading Fairy." Although Annie recognized the handwriting, she could honestly say she knew nothing about the package's origins. Mimi clutched it in the elevator up to the apartment and disappeared into her room. Annie peered surreptitiously as Mimi unwrapped *Into the Wild*, the first book in Erin Hunter's Warriors fantasy series about cat clans, and began to read.

Mimi's bookshelf

Into the Wild was a watershed book for Mimi. She devoured it and sped through the other books in the series as quickly as Annie could supply them. Eventually, Mimi read them all; for the first time, she experienced the agonizing pleasure of awaiting the publication of a favorite author's next book. That summer, while on vacation in Maine, Mimi pleaded for a long drive to Portland to procure the just-released next Warriors book. She braved carsickness and read ravenously on the ride back . . . only to discover a misprint in her copy that omitted a huge chunk of the book! It was a few long days before a new copy could be located, during which time Mimi wrote an indignant letter to the bookstore.

The "Reading Fairy" turned out to be Mimi's stepfather, Bill, who was an elementary principal at the time. He had received the Warriors book as a sample and thought Mimi might like it. He wrapped it in a grocery bag and sent it through the mail in the hopes that mysterious delivery might pique her interest. It did that—and so much more. The book changed her trajectory as a reader and a student. Now a college senior, Mimi keeps her beloved Warriors collection intact on her shelf at home.

For striving readers, the path to high volume often begins with a single watershed book. It's our mission to serve as "Book Whisperers," Donalyn Miller's apt term for those who know kids well, help them get their hands on that compelling initial read, and keep the right books coming. Change the book, change the reader!

2. Make and monitor individualized matches.

Book-talks and next-up lists, which are described in Chapter 4, are effective whole-group strategies to help most thriving readers find appealing reading material. The following individualized book-matching strategies, though more labor intensive, are effective because they zoom in on each child's particular needs and desires:

- Procure copies of next-up books
- Offer preview stacks
- Provide book introductions to usher readers in
- Increase volume with reading ladders
- Create custom books

Procure Copies of Next-Up Books

When you ask a Barnes & Noble associate about a particular book, he or she doesn't merely direct you to the appropriate aisle. The mega-retailer trains its employees to escort you to the appropriate shelf, locate the book, and put it directly into your hands because this dramatically increases the likelihood that you'll buy it. In a similar vein, if a striving reader lets us know his "next-up book," it behooves us to find a copy and hand it to him, rather than trust that he will be able to procure a copy himself.

For example, after stirring interest among seventh graders in Gordon Korman's action-packed series debut novel *Masterminds*, English teacher Amy Estersohn reached out to Annie to see whether she could obtain copies for kids who might not otherwise have access. The idea snowballed when Amy realized that the second Masterminds book, *Criminal Destiny*, would be published right before February vacation. Amy bet she could boost volume dramatically by sending interested readers off with copies of both books if Annie could supply them.

It was an experiment worth pursuing. Literacy ambassador Maggie Hoddinott secured 10 copies of each book in time for vacation. From there, Amy enthusiastically tracked the impact of this $200 intervention and emailed a report to Annie and Maggie after the break. In it, she wrote:

---

1. The students who gravitate towards the Masterminds series tend to be the students who are the hardest to match with a book.

2. Five readers came in during office hours to discuss the second book in the series, *Criminal Destiny*, with me.

3. A reader told me, "I actually read *Masterminds* for an hour and a half over spring break." I have been working with this reader all year to choose a "just-right" and enjoyable book in order to increase his reading volume. Yesterday, after he finished *Masterminds*, he tried a new book in a different series. After about 10 pages into this book, he recognized that he wasn't enjoying it as much as he had enjoyed *Masterminds* and decided to pick up *Criminal Destiny* because he "wanted to know what would happen next."

4. Students are much more eager to pick up other books by the author now that they have the Mastermind series as a reference point. Gordon Korman is a great author to love because he's so prolific and so consistently appealing to kids! He has a new book coming out in a few weeks.

Using Nancie Atwell's term for productive reading enthrallment, Amy reported that, because of the Masterminds series, seven difficult-to-please readers had entered the "reading zone." Clearly, we need to pay close attention to striving readers' next-up lists and go out of our way to find copies of books on them.

Of course it's not always possible or even necessary to purchase multiple copies, particularly if we hype books that have been out for a while. Librarians remind us that whereas brand-new releases are in high demand and short supply, older titles can accumulate quickly through inter-library loan once their initial wave of popularity has ebbed. And since any title is new to readers who don't know about it, we suggest identifying books of any age that deserve to be viral, and make them so through spirited book-talks and read-alouds. Take note of the striving readers you hook and get copies for them right away!

Offer Preview Stacks

Donalyn Miller coined the phrase "preview stacks" and pioneered the use of them to assess kids' reading preferences and match them with books (2009). This simple strategy is a game changer for striving readers! When presented with a stack of books, kids who might have appeared "passive" or "turned off to reading" readily offer opinions, as well as easy-to-read body language, that help us understand them as readers and make progressively more targeted book recommendations. The idea is to gather alluring titles that students can easily read and will want to read because they reflect their interests. Offering kids an array of concrete choices and gauging their reactions like this is far more illuminating than probing them with out-of-thin-air, abstract questions such as, "What kinds of things do you like to read?" or, worse, "What was the last book you read and really loved?"

The idea is to gather alluring titles that students can easily read and will want to read because they reflect their interests.

In the preview stacks you assemble, make sure there's variety in terms of length, genre, format, illustrations, and text features. Briefly and nonchalantly introduce the books one at a time, making it clear that you are genuinely trying to help the reader make a just-right personal book match. There is no need for her to be polite or feign interest; it helps you to know exactly what appeals and what doesn't.

When a student discards a book right away, ask why. When she keeps a book in the "maybe" pile, ask why as well. Recording these data will help you refine your recommendations. Like any good salesperson, you want to make thoughtful suggestions while respecting the shopper's tastes and opinions. Practice 1 on page 280 provides guidelines for creating and using preview stacks. Here are two variations of Donalyn's technique.

Getting-to-Know-You Preview Stacks. Literacy ambassador Maggie Hoddinott recommends the "Getting-to-Know-You Preview Stack" (illustrated on the next page) conference as a diagnostic assessment at the beginning of the year, alongside other universal screening measures. She has two main goals:

1. to inform herself about the child's reading stance, preferences, and aversions.

2. to get the child up and running as a reader by matching him or her with one or more appealing books.

As you let the child peruse each book and point out its features, make note of her physical reactions (e.g., reaching for the book eagerly versus pushing it away) and her comments. Also, listen for and make note of evidence of prior reading experiences; openness to new authors, genres, and formats; and topic preferences stemming from personal interests. For example, when Maggie presented fourth grader Leyna with a popular how-to book on hairstyling called _Fabulous Hair_, Leyna shrugged and commented that she "didn't really like reading about hair." Fair enough! Maggie then asked whether Leyna would be interested in how-to books on other topics. Leyna replied enthusiastically, "Yes, like how to ride a skateboard!" giving Maggie an important lead.

Jump-Start Preview Stacks. As the year progresses and you come to know readers' proclivities, use jump-start preview stacks to guide them back onto reading paths if they stall.

For example, Annie's colleague Waldina referred Jack, a ninth grader, to her. Jack had read two books from the classroom library—_The Zodiac Killer_, Brenda Haugen's biography, and _My Friend Dahmer_, Derf Backderf's graphic novel about his high school friend, Jeffrey Dahmer—but he had nothing on his next-up list. After confirming that Jack was still interested in true crime, Annie assembled a stack of books from the high school library, which, because of the science department's forensics elective, has a surprisingly robust collection of books about serial killers.

Get-to-Know-You Preview Stack

Grade 3

- Compendium
- Series
- Shorter Texts
- Graphic Texts
- Popular Characters
- Procedural
- Expository

Books in stack:
- TOTALLY WACKY FACTS ABOUT LAND ANIMALS
- the CRITTER club — Amy and the Missing Puppy
- GALAXY ZACK — HELLO, NEBULON!
- March of the Mini Beasts
- SUPER-PETS SHOWDOWN
- X-MEN · DAYS OF FUTURE PAST
- BALLET CAT — The Totally Secret Secret
- BIRD & SQUIRREL ON ICE
- Unicorn on a Roll
- SUPERHEROES AND CHARACTERS FROM CARTOONS, TV SHOWS, & MOVIES
- New Junior Cook Book
- FIRST BIG BOOK OF THE OCEAN

A Mix of Kid-Appeal Elements

Different Amounts of Text per Page

Various Navigational Choices

A Range of Topics

Animals

Popular Characters

Hobbies

A Variety of Reading Experiences

Cover to Cover

Dip In and Out

Read the Illustration and the Text

She began with *The Jeffrey Dahmer Story*, thinking that Jack might be interested in learning more about Dahmer and his eventual fate in prison, since that isn't addressed in the graphic novel. He ruled it out immediately: "Too long." Annie assumed he would also reject the full-length book on the *Zodiac Killer* and moved on to *The Crime Archives*, which contains artifacts from crime scenes and documents from case files. Jack thought it looked "confusing," which Annie interpreted to mean "too much effort." Finally, Annie showed Jack *The World's 20 Worst Crimes: True Stories of 20 Killers and Their 1000 Victims* by Kate Kray, which contains 20 short chapters, each on a notorious killer. Match made.

Annie gleaned from this conference that, although Jack was still interested in serial killers, he was not inclined to tackle another full-length text. What appealed to him about Kray's book was that he could read it in short bursts and learn a little about a lot of crimes; it had a lower effort-to-reward ratio.

This example raises the issue of whether books about edgy, controversial topics belong in classroom and school libraries. These decisions are best made locally, with teachers, librarians, and administrators poised to weigh in and accept or reject such topics after careful consideration. For example, *My Friend Dahmer* was an ALA Alex Award winner and was named one of the top five nonfiction books of 2012 by *Time* magazine, major reasons why it was part of Mamaroneck High School's collection. (Incidentally, at the time of this writing, Jack is a high school senior taking AP Government, a course that requires copious amounts of reading.)

Provide Book Introductions to Usher Readers In

With a thriving reader, our book-matching responsibilities are usually finished when the right book is in his or her hands. A striving reader, on the other hand, usually benefits from additional "escorting." If the book doesn't provide a clear, inviting pathway, it may help to spend a few minutes orienting the reader by providing background information, reading aloud the first few pages, drawing attention to important text features, and/or demonstrating ways to navigate the book.

For example, Annie helped Emily, a seventh grader, choose *Miss Spitfire*, Sarah Miller's fictionalized biography of Annie Sullivan. Emily was intrigued by the Braille subtitle on the cover. She knew that Helen Keller was deaf and blind, had learned sign language, and had gone to college. Thinking that Emily might not know what "spitfire" meant, Annie told Emily a bit about Annie Sullivan's fiery personality and her visual impairment. She offered to read a few pages aloud over cocoa, knowing that the opening diverges from a more traditional narrative:

"Ticket, please."

"I wipe my eyes and thrust the wretched thing at him. I've already had to change trains six times since Boston. On top of that, I have to take this train north to Knoxville to catch yet another train south to Alabama."

Whereas an experienced reader would readily infer that a train conductor is asking Annie Sullivan for a ticket—and perhaps even that she is traveling from Boston to the Kellers' home in Alabama to assume the position as governess—to Emily this opening was a confusing jumble of ideas. She was interested in the book and motivated to read it, but she needed help getting started.

Even when a striving reader is off and running, it's important to monitor the match carefully. Like a delicate flame, the striving reader needs attention, but not so much that it smothers him or her. When eighth grader Molly reported "being obsessed with" *The Giver*, Annie helped her find the second book in Lois Lowry's quartet, *Gathering Blue*. Annie watched from across the room as Molly dove into it.

After a few minutes, Annie noticed Molly flipping back through the pages. Then Molly's eyes rose from the book and stared out the window. Annie was concerned that Molly didn't seem to be getting into the book. So, she ventured over and asked, "So what do you think so far?" Molly responded, "It's kind of confusing. There's someone named Kira but not Jonas."

Annie sat down and perused the book jacket and opening pages with Molly. "Oh, wait a second. This seems to be a companion novel to *The Giver*, not a sequel. I'm thinking that it takes place maybe in the same time period, in a world with some of the same characteristics, but we're meeting new characters." Molly seemed relieved to have Annie validate her confusion. Nonetheless, it was clear that she would need additional support to get into the novel. If Molly could make her way successfully into *Gathering Blue*, she had *Messenger* and *Son* to look forward to. Annie read aloud the opening pages to Molly in a comfortable corner of the room. "I'm curious now myself," Annie said. "I've always thought these books were a series, but now I'm wondering if and how the characters and storylines intersect." Annie was genuinely confused and let Molly know. Striving readers need to know that experienced adults need to ask questions to clarify meaning.

From Striving to Thriving © 2017 by Stephanie Harvey & Annie Ward, Scholastic Inc.

As we've stated, getting into a new book can be like trying to bicycle uphill from a dead stop. There is often a lot of heavy-duty comprehension work to do. Who are these characters? Where is this taking place? What's going on here? Thriving readers have the confidence and experience to know that this initial effort is par for the course. They develop theories and read on to confirm or refute them. They flip back and reread when things aren't making sense. After a few pages, they get the literary wheels turning and off they go. Striving readers, however, often need to be shown that this is what it's like at the outset and that pleasures await if they pedal hard. By the end of the period, Molly was far enough into *Gathering Blue* to begin rooting for Kira.

Increase Volume With Reading Ladders

Success is a powerful motivator! So once a striving reader has his or her nose in a good book, don't wait to think about the next one. Teri Lesesne coined the term "reading ladders" for the vital, volume-building progressions readers make from book to book, with our support. In her book by the same name, she writes, "Many of us are searching continually for that just-right book for each and every one of our students. It is my hope to help you find those books. More importantly, I hope to help you guide students to the next great book and the one after that. That is the purpose of reading ladders. Because it is not sufficient to find just one book for each reader" (2010).

As we seek to move striving readers up their personal reading ladders, we must remember to keep pleasure and success at the forefront of our minds; there must be a favorable effort-to-reward ratio in each of the successive texts we recommend. In other words, there mustn't be too much space between the "rungs" or it will feel like too daunting a climb.

When making recommendations, it's important to introduce only a few new elements in order to foster manageable increments of growth. For example, Annie, a passionate dog lover, has assembled the "Dogs of War" ladders (shown on the next page) to extend students' natural curiosity about dogs. She often starts by coaxing striving readers of all ages to read in one sitting Major Brian Dennis's gripping nonfiction picture book, *Nubs: The True Story of a Mutt, a*

Marine, and a Miracle. The book tells the story of a Marine in Afghanistan and Nubs, a stray dog, and the lengths they go to in order to stay together and make it back to the United States. This book has been a "watershed" book for numerous strivers, drawing in self-avowed nonreaders and compelling them to wonder and read more.

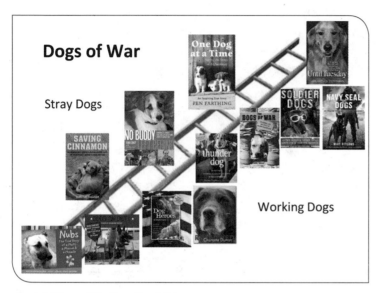

Annie's "Dogs of War" reading ladder

One pathway up the ladder moves students from *Nubs*, the story of a stray dog, to progressively more complex books about working dogs. Dorothy Hinshaw Patent's book *Dogs on Duty* looks similar to *Nubs*, making it a good second-rung book. It, too, has full-color photographs and interesting sidebars. The contribution of Cairo, a Belgian Malinois, to the raid on Osama Bin Laden's compound always heightens students' interest in military service dogs, making this rung of the ladder very appealing.

Next, Annie introduces a coffee table book called *Dog Heroes of 9/11.* Although this book is significantly longer and more complex than *Nubs* and *Dogs on Duty*, it, too, is loaded with photographs and interesting, easy-to-digest sections: two-page profiles of dogs and handlers from around the country who went to Ground Zero in New York for search-and-recovery missions. Readers can navigate the text on their own terms and enjoy poring over it together.

Some students wanted to learn more about the stray dogs of Afghanistan and Iraq after reading *Nubs*, giving rise to the other branch of this reading ladder. Annie did some research and discovered that a number of organizations have sprung up dedicated to rescuing dogs from those countries, and many books have been published chronicling rescues. *Saving Cinnamon* is one of them. It follows Navy Reservist Mark Feffer and the stray that he befriends in Afghanistan. Its arc is similar to *Nubs*'s but more complex: A dog handler inexplicably loses Cinnamon during her rescue. (Don't worry. As one of the kids commented, "If they wrote a whole book about it, there's probably a happy ending.")

Carefully curated reading ladders are a phenomenal way to promote voluminous reading. As kids acquire background knowledge on each rung, their confidence and appetite grow. One carefully selected book gives them a strong foothold to the next. Annie likens it to the relief one feels at a cocktail party upon seeing a familiar face across the room—the known makes the unknown less challenging. When designing ladders, err on the side of making the growth increments very gradual rather than too precipitous; the goal is to extend volume above all else!

Create Custom Books

Toni Morrison says, "If there's a book you want to read but it hasn't been written yet, then you must write it." Taking our cue from her, we suggest that if you haven't been able to ignite a child's reading life with published material, then you must write the incendiary book yourself or help him or her write it!

First-grader Khalil was sporting a meticulous Mohawk, a neon-trimmed Old Navy tracksuit, and a pair of carefully unlaced Timberland boots when Annie met him in principal Katie Andersen's office. Katie and assistant principal, Emily Macias, had invited Khalil in to read with them to celebrate the progress he was making in Reading Recovery. He dutifully pulled *Baby Chimp* from his book baggie and read it fluently, but with little enthusiasm. After Khalil left, the group lamented, "If only there were a book about fashion and style just right for him!" Later that morning, Annie spent a few minutes searching, cutting, and pasting nuggets from the Internet to create in PowerPoint *Khalil's Boot Book*, and emailed it to Katie and Emily to print out. Each page featured a photograph of a type of boot with a caption (e.g., "Ugg boots"). The last page featured a photo of his beloved Timberlands, with the caption "Khalil's boots." Pleased as he was with his custom book, Khalil pointed out some gaps in the types of boots featured, which provided an opportunity for additional, collaborative page-making and labeling.

When dual language teacher Kate Wessman consulted Annie about Mattias, a third grader who rejected most books, Annie drew on the Reading Recovery strategy of beginning with what the learner knows and "roaming around the known" together: She suggested empowering Mattias to make his own book about his idol, Argentinian footballer Leo Messi.

Kate and Mattias working together

Kate invited Matti to select images of Messi from the web and to dictate what he wanted to say about each image, while she transcribed his words on PowerPoint slides. As the custom book took shape, Matti's interest and investment grew; he expanded his table of contents and took an increasingly active role in composition. Matti wrote the final book in Spanish, citing sources, and Kate bound and laminated copies for him, the classroom library, and Annie. Matti's mother Giamileth wrote to Kate, "I love hearing this story and knowing that Matti is very enthusiastic about reading. Of course, we will read the book at home—it is a great way for him to practice."

When Annie gave Matti a copy of Sean Taylor and Caio Vilela's nonfiction book *Goal!*, Matti appreciated the photographs and information about young footballers in countries across the globe, but he was disappointed to find no page for Venezuela, his home country, nor one for the USA. With Kate's guidance, Matti made his own supplemental pages (including action shots of him trapping and kicking a soccer ball) and emailed them to Annie. Kate printed out the pages for Matti to insert into the book.

Not only do student-generated books satisfy kids' cravings for niche topics, they also build fluency, confidence, and agency through the reciprocal processes of writing and reading. Furthermore, they build relationships: Children flourish when they feel known and valued under what psychologist Shefali Tsarbary refers to as an adult's "appreciative gaze."

From Striving to Thriving © 2017 by Stephanie Harvey & Annie Ward, Scholastic Inc.

3. Set kids up to read outside of school.

All the techniques we've mentioned thus far are designed to light the reading flame at school. But significant amounts of reading outside of school are vital if striving readers are to thrive. The following strategies are designed to promote reading at home:

- Have kids make reading plans.
- Send them home with books.
- Communicate with families about kids' reading.

Have Kids Make Reading Plans

Thriving readers plan their reading lives like mini-vacations. They anticipate when there will be opportunities to read for long blocks of time, and they track down titles on their next-up lists in preparation. Before school vacations and long weekends are excellent times to model this kind of planning and engage kids.

A couple of years ago, given the way the calendar fell, Annie's district had two full weeks of vacation at the end of December and the beginning of January! This provided an excellent opportunity to channel kids' mounting excitement about the break into concrete reading plans. The lesson on page 282 describes how Annie modeled her own plan for students and guided them to create their own day-by-day reading schedules.

Devoting class time to book selection, acquisition, and schedule making is far from frivolous. The social buzz around reading is highly motivating, and the "bird-in-the-hand" value of striving readers leaving school with appealing books in their backpacks is enormous!

Send Kids Home With Books

We must not assume that striving readers have abundant access to appealing books outside of school. Therefore, we cannot emphasize enough the importance of sending kids home with books. While doing this doesn't guarantee that kids will read those books, it increases the likelihood dramatically.

Some teachers express reluctance to send books home because they fear the books will be damaged or lost. While we understand those concerns, we give you the rationale for doing it:

- Volume is vital to striving readers' growth.

- Access to books is social justice in action.

- Not all families are able to borrow books from community libraries due to work schedules, transportation limitations, childcare, and other legitimate challenges.

Even when books are damaged or lost, the money spent on replacements pales in comparison to money spent on reading interventions.

- Communicating with families about the importance of books generally results in the return of books.

- Even when books are damaged or lost, the money spent on replacements pales in comparison to money spent on reading interventions for children who have not read voluminously!

It is penny-wise, pound-foolish, and utterly unjust to let fear of damaged or lost books impede circulation! See Chapter 8, "Advocate Tirelessly," for ideas for securing funds for book acquisition and replenishment.

Kids' backpacks are filled with books to take home every day.

Communicate With Families About Kids' Reading

The following steps help families understand the power of reading at home and equip them to support their kids' reading lives.

- At the beginning of the year, send home an upbeat letter explaining the benefits of voluminous, engaged reading. Explain that children will read in school every day and take books home almost every night. Urge parents to prioritize reading at home by providing time for books and a quiet space to enjoy them. Encourage them to contact you with any caveats about their child's book selections so you can use that information to help them make selections at school.

- At back-to-school night, show parents the classroom library. Highlight the books you've read aloud, and book-talk some terrific new titles. Choose a book to read out loud and show how you think aloud about the text and how you engage kids in conversation. Encourage your administrator to invite community librarians to back-to-school night to explain and assist with the library card acquisition process.

- Encourage parents to create what Donalyn Miller calls "reading moments" (2009) by putting reading material in places where kids have down time, such as the kitchen table, the car, and—yes—the bathroom!

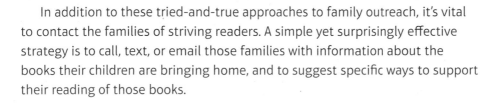

- Host a family reading group. Choose compelling titles that adults and children would enjoy and borrow multiple copies from the school and community libraries. To broaden participation, select short texts such as feature articles and short stories, which can be translated from English into other languages, sent electronically, and read more quickly than full-length texts.

In addition to these tried-and-true approaches to family outreach, it's vital to contact the families of striving readers. A simple yet surprisingly effective strategy is to call, text, or email those families with information about the books their children are bringing home, and to suggest specific ways to support their reading of those books.

From Striving to Thriving © 2017 by Stephanie Harvey & Annie Ward, Scholastic Inc.

For example, Mamaroneck teacher Alison Ivler sent the following note to the mother and grandmother of her student Matthew, equipping them to support his reading over the Thanksgiving break:

From: "Ivler, Alison" 📎

Date: November 17 at 8:22:27 AM EST

To: "Matthew's Mom Desiree, " "Matthew's Grandma Mrs. O."

Cc: "Ivler, Alison"

Subject: Matthew's reading :)

Good morning Mrs. G. and Mrs. O.:

I just wanted to fill you in on some of the reading that Matthew is doing. With the help of Ms. Hoddinott, the district literacy ambassador, we have found some books he seems excited about. As you know, Star Wars and superheroes are areas of interest for him. Matthew is currently reading the following three books:

- *Mighty Marvel Chapter Book: Astonishing Adventures*
- *Laff-O-Tronic Monster Jokes*
- *Star Wars Crafts* .

Matthew and I made a plan together regarding his reading of these books. We talked about the possibility of him picking one craft from the Star Wars book and making it over the Thanksgiving break. He thought it might be something fun to do with Grandma. I would love for you to ask him about his reading. I have been seeing a happier Matthew at school and want to continue to build excitement around reading.

Thanks for all your support. Let me know how these conversations go.

Warm regards,

Alison

 Mighty_Marvel.jpg

 Laff-O-Tronic.jpg

 Star_Wars_Crafts .jpg

Communicate frequently, directly, and productively with the families of striving readers:

1. Find out who takes care of the child in the late afternoons and evenings (e.g., Mom, Dad, grandparent, older sibling, babysitter, neighbor) and what their preferred modes of communication are (e.g., text, email, phone call, personal meeting).

2. Introduce yourself and explain you'd like to partner with them to help the child grow as a reader. Provide several ways and ideal times for them to contact you.

3. Let them know in writing the specific books the child is bringing home, including images of the covers, as Alison did in her message.

4. Use your knowledge of the child's home life and family structure to make specific suggestions:

   » If you know quarters are cramped and/or noisy, provide caregivers with ideas or tools for minimizing distractions while reading. (*"I'm sending home some disposable ear plugs or headphones for Nikolas to wear so that he can focus on his* I Survived *book. He's about to start an exciting chapter."*)

   » If there are younger siblings at home, send home books for your student to share with them. (*"Jack mentioned that he plays with Carmen while you give your other son a bath. He's bringing home some board books to read to Carmen that he thinks she'll enjoy."*)

   » Keep parents abreast of the child's reading plans and timelines. (*"Sofia thinks she can finish* Lumberjanes *this weekend after her aunt's birthday picnic. It would be great if you could encourage her to do so and remind her to bring the book back on Monday so I can give her the sequel."*)

   » Share and build on success. (*"Luisa discovered Christine O'Connell George's* Little Dog Poems, *which she's loving because the illustrations remind her of your dog, Chloe. Ask her to read some of her favorites to you and Chloe tonight!"*)

» Take advantage of the family's talents and reading opportunities. (*"Malcolm mentioned that his grandfather is good at magic and card tricks. He checked out two magic books from our school library, and he'd like to practice to surprise his grandpa. I've put a deck of cards in a baggie in case you don't already have a deck at home."*)

Too often, only negative communication is shared with the parents of striving readers—a litany of their child's achievement deficits. Imagine instead the impact of receiving a timely, encouraging message with concrete suggestions and resources!

David and Jason's mother fuels their voracious reading habits with weekly trips to the library.

BOOK-MATCHING

Use these questions to drive responsive, learner-focused teaching based on relentless book-matching.

Self-Questions

- Am I showing how to preview a book to assess its appeal and level of challenge (effort-to-reward ratio)?

- Have I modeled my own process for getting into new books? Have I demonstrated the "heavy lifting" (questioning, rereading) that's often required at the outset?

- Am I modeling my process for prioritizing next-up reads? Do I think aloud about what I'm going to read next and why?

Kidwatching Questions

- How does the student shop for books in the classroom library? Does she choose deliberately or somewhat aimlessly?

- Does the student display the physical signs of enthrallment (eyes tracking, pages turning, facial expressions)? Does he or she spontaneously express delight, amazement, disgust, etc., while reading?

- Does the student abandon books, and under what circumstances?

- Does the student choose next-up book(s) while still reading the current book?

- Does the student seek and follow recommendations from peers, teachers, librarians, and reviews? Does he or she make recommendations? Is she open to suggestion?

Conferring Questions

- Let's look at the books in your book baggie/box. Why did you choose these specific books?

- You're starting [book title]. What makes this book easy or challenging to get into?

- What do you think the reading experience is going to be like? How do you know?

- What are you thinking about as you read?

- Show me how you've been moving through the book. What choices have you made about how to read it?

- With whom do you like to talk about books?

- Who else do you think would like this book? Go ahead and tell him or her about it.

PART II • TEACH

"Every effort must be made in childhood to teach the young to use their own minds. For one thing is certain, if they don't use their own minds someone will do it for them."

—Eleanor Roosevelt

CHAPTER 6

Teach Thinking-Intensive Reading

Leave it to Eleanor Roosevelt to underscore the purpose of education. She made the statement (see to the left) in 1939, a horrific time in history as Hitler marched across Europe. But the truth is, she could have made it 20 years ago, 50 years from now, or this very minute. For us teachers, nothing is more important than encouraging children to use their own minds, to have the confidence and agency to believe in themselves, and to make the best possible choices. Reading is a direct route to those destinations, which is why it is so critical that all students, particularly our strivers, see reading as a meaningful act that will make a real difference in their lives.

The point of this chapter is to share a variety of strategies that we teach to the whole group and in small groups—comprehension, fluency, and meaning making in general—that give striving

See the following Practices and Lessons for this chapter:

These sheets are also available at scholastic.com/ThriveResources.

readers the edge they need to turn their struggle around. We want all of our kids to become confident, thinking-intensive readers who build knowledge as they go. They need to know that whenever they are reading, listening, viewing, speaking, writing, drawing, making, researching, and so forth, they need to be thinking as well. So, we spend a good deal of time teaching them to think about their thinking and to think strategically. All of the instruction recommended in this chapter, both whole class and small group, has kids interacting with the teacher, the text, and, most importantly, with one another. We immerse them in rich talk about text, information, and experiences so they can continue to build knowledge in a variety of ways. In order for striving readers to make gains, they need to be engaged during instruction. Growth and achievement are directly linked to engagement, and engagement flourishes when kids are interacting and having fun.

It is so critical that all students, particularly our strivers, see reading as a meaningful act that will make a real difference in their lives.

We are particularly elated when a striving reader like Anthony, the fourth grader we met in Chapter 1, realizes that reading is truly about thinking. To help striving readers get that message, we offer interactive, whole-group, community-building instruction to all readers, and, for those who need it, additional support in temporary and flexible needs-based small groups. Above all, we want our striving readers to recognize the power of their own thinking. When striving readers come to understand that reading is thinking and that strategies are tools to aid understanding, confidence grows, reading flourishes, and possibilities open.

THREE TO KNOW
RESEARCH ON THINKING-INTENSIVE READING INSTRUCTION

1. In the late 1980s, researchers led by P. David Pearson identified and systematically investigated the thinking strategies that proficient readers use to comprehend text in an effort to determine what might be missing for striving readers. Building on that work, researchers then explored ways to teach those strategies to children. Pearson, Dole, Duffy, and Roehler (1992) summarized the strategies that active, thoughtful readers use to make meaning, including monitoring and repairing comprehension, asking questions, connecting what they know to new information, drawing inferences, distinguishing important ideas from less important ones, and synthesizing information within and across texts. See pages 170–176 for details on teaching comprehension strategies.

2. In the early 1980s, P. David Pearson and Meg Gallagher (1983) developed a framework for instruction known as the Gradual Release of Responsibility. Gradual release includes five stages—modeling, guided practice, collaborative practice, independent practice, and sharing the learning. The point of gradual release is to move kids toward independence so they can read on their own and apply what they have learned. Adaptations have emerged (Duke & Pearson, 2002; Harvey & Goudvis, 2016), but they remain grounded in and true to the original work of Gallagher and Pearson. See pages 176–179 for details on using this framework with kids.

3. Interactive read-aloud is a powerful instructional strategy where the teacher reads aloud to children, stopping briefly to share their thinking and asking students to turn and talk and jot about their thoughts, questions, and ideas from the text. According to Irene Fountas and Gay Su Pinnell, through interactive reading aloud, students build more intricate networks of meaning than they could build by reading on their own. They also build comprehension and story knowledge (Fountas & Pinnell, 2006). See pages 180–183 for details on interactive read-aloud.

1. Teach comprehension strategies explicitly.

Too often, kids who have difficulty with reading receive repetitive phonics instruction, isolated from meaningful text; indeed, researchers such as Krashen (2004), Goodman et al. (2016), and Smith (2012) argue that sound-letter relationships are most easily acquired embedded inside cohesive, meaningful text. Repetitive phonics instruction, devoid of meaning, is especially confusing for striving readers and too often results in them becoming disengaged readers who don't understand what reading is or why anyone should want to do it. Furthermore, according to Krashen, it "has no significant effect on tests of reading comprehension given after grade 1. The best predictor of performance on reading comprehension tests is how much the children have read. What really does work in raising reading achievement is access to lots of good books" (2017).

To help strivers overcome this confusion, we focus on meaning by putting comprehension front and center. When striving readers come to understand that reading is above all about meaning making—telling a story or sharing information—rather than calling out individual letters, sounds, and words one by one, their perception of reading changes. They begin to see the value in it. Reading suddenly has a purpose—to question, to learn, and to understand. They actually want to do it! Isn't that refreshing?

In the 1990s, P. David Pearson and his colleagues posited that if they could isolate what proficient readers do automatically to make sense of text, they could teach less experienced, less developed readers to employ those same strategies deliberately when needed. Their research revealed the following six comprehension strategies that proficient readers use (1992).

Monitor Comprehension

Reading is thinking! When thriving readers monitor for meaning, they keep track of their thinking as they read, listen, or view. They notice when the text makes sense and when it doesn't. They listen to their inner voice and silently "converse" with the text. They are aware of their thinking and take steps to maintain and extend their understanding. They might ask a question, make a connection, or draw an inference as they read. Striving readers, on the other hand, often simply run their eyes across the page without thinking about what it says. Many have learned over the years that reading is about calling the words, rather than thinking about them. They haven't yet learned that they need to listen to their inner voice as they read.

Monitoring comprehension is an over-arching umbrella for meaning making. We teach "fix-up strategies," such as rereading, reading on, and stopping to refocus thinking, so readers can get back on track when meaning is lost. We teach readers to listen to their inner voice to make meaning, but we also teach them to notice when they stray from meaning. These strategies are particularly helpful to striving readers so they have tools to use when they space out while reading or when the reading gets tough. See the Lessons entitled "Monitoring Comprehension: Following the Inner Conversation" on page 288 and "Using Fix-Up Strategies" on page 290.

Connect New Information to the Known

Whether we are inferring, synthesizing, or determining importance as we read, listen, or view, our background knowledge is foundational. We simply can't comprehend what we read without thinking about what we know. Nothing colors our learning and understanding more than our previous experiences and prior knowledge. Using previous experiences and prior knowledge to learn and understand new information is crucial, especially when it comes to striving readers who would be lost without the ability to do that. Activating their schema allows them to climb the rungs of text complexity. But we need to make sure that their prior knowledge is not laced with misconceptions. To construct meaning, they must not only think about what they already know, but also revise their thinking in light of new evidence.

Ask Questions

Questioning is the strategy that propels readers forward. When readers have questions, they read on to find answers, discover new information, and delve in more deeply. But not just any questions—thoughtful questions. If we hope to develop critical thinkers, we need to teach kids to ask rich questions about what they read, listen to, and view. We teach striving readers to ask questions for many reasons: to find out what is to come, to clarify confusion, and to do further research. Finally, we do whatever we can to help them understand that asking questions is a hallmark of thoughtful, smart readers. This is crucial because striving readers often believe that asking questions might "expose them," when, in fact, it is paramount to moving them—and all readers—forward.

Infer and Visualize Meaning

When we infer, we consider what we know—our background knowledge— and merge it with clues or evidence in the text to come up with ideas that are not explicitly stated. Inferring allows readers to figure out the meaning of unfamiliar words, draw conclusions, make predictions, construct interpretations, surface themes, and create mental images. It is likely the most helpful strategy for striving readers, because they often encounter so many unfamiliar words and ideas as they read. Knowing how to infer the meaning of unfamiliar words and ideas opens up meaning in text. It allows strivers to figure something out by using context clues to help them in the absence of background knowledge.

Visualizing is kind of a first cousin of inferring. It is like inferring except instead of using language to create meaning, readers use mental images. They see, hear, taste, touch, and even smell in their imaginations. However, many striving readers do not seem to visualize effectively, or at least do not think they do. As such, they are often quick to abandon books. They often quit reading before they've even given themselves time to "get into it." So, we teach visualizing lessons to help them more easily create mental images when they read. Visualizing keeps readers engaged and brings joy to reading.

When kids infer and visualize as they read, listen, or view, they respond with a range of emotions: glee, hope, and even dread. Inferring and visualizing engage kids and nudge them to a deeper, more robust reading of the text.

Determine Important Information

Determining important information is a complex, often challenging task. That's why, too often, we reduce the strategy to a "find the main idea" activity. But important information and the main idea are two very different things. What we determine to be important in a text depends on our purpose for reading that text. So, we teach kids to sort and sift details to identify bigger concepts, to separate what is interesting from what is important, and to determine what the author most wants us to get out of the text. These last two points in particular can trip up striving readers, who often think the information they find most interesting is the most important. Consequently, they may miss some of the author's big ideas, so we teach them to distinguish between their thinking and the author's thinking, without sending a message that their thinking doesn't matter. After all, one reason striving readers give up on reading is because they have come to believe that their thinking doesn't matter. See the Lesson entitled "Surfacing the Big Ideas" on page 293.

Synthesize Information

Synthesizing information nudges readers to see the big picture as they read, listen, or view. When synthesizing information or ideas, readers use a variety of strategies—including asking questions, inferring, and determining importance—to construct meaning. It's not enough for them to simply recall or restate the facts. Thriving readers integrate new information with their existing knowledge to come to a more complete understanding of the text. As those readers encounter new information, their thinking evolves. Synthesizing presents a real challenge for striving readers, so it is imperative to break information down into smaller chunks and share how those chunks come together to form a bigger idea.

Although proficient readers tend to employ these research-based comprehension strategies automatically, striving readers do not. They often merely call the words on the page without thinking about their meaning, questioning the text, or connecting to the ideas. So, as we teach striving readers, we share these strategies as tools for understanding, engagement, and building knowledge. We remember that we are not teaching strategies for strategies' sake. We don't teach kids to make connections so they can be the best connectors in the room. We teach them to make connections to better understand what they read. Comprehension is a knowledge-building activity, and a recursive, dynamic one at that. When we think about information and comprehend it, we add to our store of knowledge. Then when we activate that knowledge—that new schema—while reading, listening, or viewing, we comprehend more and continue to build knowledge (Cervetti et al., 2015). Knowledge building is essential if striving readers are to become confident, capable readers and learners.

Charlie synthesizes the big ideas on a three-column thinksheet.

Pacing Strategy Instruction. We teach several lessons on a specific strategy to striving readers so they can wrap their minds around it, understand how it works, and see how it can help them make sense of what they read. But we don't dwell on one strategy for too long, because readers don't simply employ one strategy at a time while reading. They weave strategies together into a tapestry of understanding.

From Striving to Thriving © 2017 by Stephanie Harvey & Annie Ward, Scholastic Inc.

For example, the moment we have a question while reading, an inference generally follows quickly on its heels. Strategic reading truly is a "mosaic of thought" as Keene and Zimmermann shared in their seminal book (2007). So, we give strivers just enough time to practice the strategy so they develop the skill and confidence needed to crack open meaning and move on relatively quickly to another strategy. The ultimate goal is for striving readers to have a small repertoire of strategies at their disposal to construct meaning and build knowledge.

In addition, it is often helpful to demonstrate how to use these strategies outside of text *before* demonstrating how to use them while reading. For example, synthesizing involves taking the parts and putting them together into a whole. So, we might explicitly show kids what synthesizing looks like by baking cookies—demonstrating how all the separate ingredients come together to create a brand-new whole known as a cookie! Or we might play an inferring game by filling a waste paper basket with different types of trash, perhaps an old airline-boarding pass, a Snickers wrapper, and a chewed-up tennis ball. Then we ask the kids what they infer about the family from what they find in the trash: they travel, have a sweet tooth, have a dog, and so forth. These activities make strategies concrete and engage strivers from the get-go. For more on how to make comprehension concrete, check out Tanny McGregor's *Comprehension Connections* (2007).

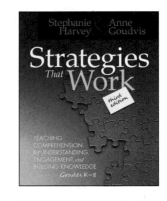

Ultimately, comprehension strategies are the striving reader's super power. They give striving readers a quiver full of strategic arrows to attack words and sentences when they don't understand. In fact, comprehension strategies offer striving readers a robust lifeline. When we teach comprehension strategies to our striving readers, they begin to believe that they are the kinds of kids who can figure things out, who can learn independently and with agency. Check out *Strategies That Work, Third Edition* (2017) and *The Comprehension Toolkit* series (2016) at www.ComprehensionToolkit.com by Stephanie Harvey and Anne Goudvis for a much deeper dive into comprehension strategy instruction.

2. Teach with the Gradual Release of Responsibility framework.

For too long we have been telling kids what to do rather than showing them how to do it. Demonstrating how we learn is far more effective than simply giving directions. But we must be explicit in our demonstrations in order for kids to grasp what we want them to do. That's why we teach using the Gradual Release of Responsibility framework (Pearson & Gallagher, 1983). The phases of GRR include:

- Teacher Modeling
- Guided Practice
- Collaborative Practice
- Independent Practice
- Sharing the Learning

Teacher Modeling

To start, we open up our own cognitive process to show kids how we read. We peel back our layers of thinking for kids to get a good look at how we make meaning when we read. We share both our successes as readers and our love of reading, as well as our challenges along the way. This is particularly important for striving readers to help them see that reading can be not only rich and rewarding, but also tough, even for adult readers. We send a strong message that they are not alone in working through reading obstacles. Specifically, we choose a strategy, describe it, and explain when and how it should be used. Then we model how to use it by thinking aloud, conducting shared readings, and reading aloud interactively. For example, to model the strategy of inferring, we might say, *As I look at this picture, I see a little girl walking on a winding road in the countryside. There are dark clouds in the distance with a strike of lightning on the edge. I'm inferring that a storm is headed her way. And I am a little nervous that she could be in trouble.*

Guided Practice

Much of our teaching occurs during the guided practice phase of the GRR framework. During guided practice, kids try the strategy themselves while we pay close attention to what they are doing. Through shared reading, kids reason through the text, jot down their thinking, and co-construct meaning through discussions with the teacher and one another. It allows us to watch kids carefully as they are gathered up close, so we can scaffold to meet their needs and determine who is ready to work collaboratively and independently and who may need further instruction. It is particularly effective for striving readers because they can participate even though they may not be able to read the text on their own. That said, we take care to avoid "over-instructing" our striving readers. It is tempting to continually build in time to instruct striving readers. But there is a fine line between appropriate scaffolding and over-scaffolding. Whoever does the most work does the most learning, so like any reader, kids need time to practice, once we show them how.

Fourth-grade teacher Kai Johnston conferring with students during reading guided practice.

Collaborative Practice

During collaborative practice, kids apply the strategy in pairs and small groups throughout the room, working and talking together as we move around and conferring with groups, partners, and individuals as needed.

Independent Practice

The ultimate goal of instruction is to move kids toward independence. We want all kids to become confident, capable readers and thinkers who initiate learning. So, we allow plenty of class time for kids to read, write, and practice on their own as we confer, assess, and coach.

Sharing the Learning

As a community, we share informally throughout the entire GRR process. Kids turn and talk briefly during the modeling phase. They read and share their thinking with classmates during guided and collaborative practice. At the

close of the workshop, they come back together as a class to share more formally, teaching one another and responding to one another's ideas.

Although the GRR framework may seem like a linear process, it's not. It's a dynamic, recursive one. We typically model, guide, model again, encourage kids to collaborate and reflect, encourage them to practice independently, model again, and so on.

As with any good instruction, comprehension instruction is paired with continuous assessment. Teachers monitor students' use of comprehension strategies and their success at understanding what they read. The monitoring, in turn, informs the teacher. If the student is still off the comprehension mark, the teacher responds with additional instruction. At the same time, students

should be monitoring their own use of comprehension strategies and become aware of their strengths and challenges as capable, confident readers.

We keep our modeling short and sweet so that kids can dig in quickly, sort of like the "catch and release" method used by savvy fishermen: reel them in, toss them back, then reel them in again.

As Debbie Miller reminds us in her chapter, "Not So Gradual Release," from *Comprehension Going Forward* (Keene et al., 2011), "I now understand the importance of releasing responsibility to children much earlier than before,

Triads share their learning.

inviting them to 'have a go' even on day one of launching a strategy. Why so early? Independence is my goal. When we want children to be active, thoughtful, and independent readers, our teaching and their learning situations must be active and thoughtful. Engaging children in the process and bringing their voices into the mix deepens and increases their capacity for learning, understanding, and remembering and scaffolds them for success during independent practice."

But the GRR framework does not merely provide a structure for strategy lessons. For instance, we also use the framework to help students read increasingly complex texts. If we are teaching a particularly complex strategy, we choose the most accessible, interesting text we can find. Once kids begin to get the hang of the strategy and use it independently, we choose a more complex text, since they are now more skilled at using the strategy flexibly as needed. When we use the framework to teach collaboration strategies early in the year, we rein kids in a bit more than we do later in the year. Over time, when we're confident they can collaborate productively, we loosen the reins.

In these and other ways, the GRR framework permeates our classroom culture. By year's end, if we have been successful, kids are running the show pretty much on their own, with us dipping in and out as needed, but far less frequently than in September.

3. Use interactive read-alouds.

In an interactive read-aloud, we model our own thinking as we read a page or so of the text. Kids are typically bunched up close on the floor without the text, but with clipboards, sticky notes, graphic organizers, and/or notebooks for responding. As we read and share our thinking, kids turn and talk and jot down or draw their thoughts and questions. They are all free to listen, think about, talk about, and process the information and ideas, regardless of their decoding level. As a result, the interactive read-aloud builds community and engagement, as well as comprehension.

Because our mantra is "no pullouts during the reading block," all kids in the class participate in interactive read-alouds, including our striving readers. With the clarion calls around the country for students to read more complex text, we can think of no better way to engage striving readers in complex issues, ideas, and problems than through interactive read-alouds. Students think about, process, jot, and discuss sophisticated ideas in texts that would likely be out of reach if they had to read those texts independently. When teachers with whom we work engage their students in interactive read-alouds, they frequently comment that their striving readers shine, because the technique allows their creative, critical thinking to flourish and go public. Other kids in the class tend to be quite impressed, too, which is profoundly powerful for striving readers who often feel inferior to their more proficient classmates. We hold kids back if we allow them to get information only from texts they are able to decode.

Our mantra is "no pullouts during the reading block."

For example, Steph modeled an interactive read-aloud of Eve Bunting's *Gleam and Glow* to a class of sixth graders, including readers both well above and below benchmark. *Gleam and Glow* is based on the true story of a Bosnian family forced to flee its home in the early 1990s during the war between Bosnia and Serbia, which emerged after the partitioning of the former Yugoslavia. The Serbs, in an effort to promote Serbian nationalism and tragically engage in ethnic cleansing, were driving Bosnians from their homes. The father of the Bosnian family leaves to fight with the resistance. The mother and two children are driven from their home and make a long, arduous journey to a refugee camp outside of the Bosnian border. When they leave their home, they are forced to leave behind their pet goldfish, Gleam and Glow, in a pond in their backyard. As the story progresses, Gleam and Glow come to symbolize the family's hope and resilience. Ultimately, the father is reunited with his family in the refugee camp, and they return home. But when they arrive, their house has been burned to the ground and all that is left is the pond, where the children not only find Gleam and Glow alive, but also hundreds of healthy, active fish.

As Steph read, kids discussed the story and jotted their thinking on sticky notes. Savannah, the most proficient reader in the class, could have easily read the text on her own. Her notes revealed a thoughtful understanding of the story. She infers that home is about family more than material things, but can't fathom, to the very end of the story, why the book is named after the fish.

> *We hold kids back if we allow them to get information only from texts they are able to decode.*

The man is Fair to animals and he onderstands that the Fish need to live to. What is so important about fish that the book would be named after them?

Poor Gleam and Glow! They can't get left behind... Well, at least I hope they find their father...

Finally, something good happens.

Their mother is very courageous. She doesn't give up. Where does the stuff come from? Whats takin care of them? Did they have food before?

It's home, even without the mother things.

They can't die because its the name of the book. IF they died, they wou't. Float to the top. Are they Freshwater? Maybe they're hiding...

I so glad they found their father at the camp. And he can stay too so they are together. They came home! But will their house be there? What about Gleam and Glow? Ohno' How will they live now? At least they are alive together. Gleam + Glow are ok! There are more and more too.

How scary where the storgs?

What ciand of whill?

why did they bren the houses? How could people do such a thing?

there a live!

there gest like humens.

How meny people died?

mom whonts to keep her family safe + to gether.

are the fish still alive?

thats amsing!

warren

Warren, on the other hand, could not have read this text independently, and Steph suspected a processing issue based on his inaccurate spelling and semantics. However, he asked the most important question of all: *How could people do such a thing?* This became an essential question in an upcoming unit on persecution. Moreover, he nailed a profound observation about the fish: *They are alive, and they are just like humans*, two thoughts that inspired a lively class discussion.

Although Warren is a striving reader, he is a highly accomplished thinker. Without the interactive read-aloud, he would not have been able to share his thinking, and, equally importantly, the class would not have had an opportunity to benefit from his deep insights. Interactive read-alouds give everyone a chance to advance his or her thinking—and send a strong message that just because you are not the best reader in the class doesn't mean you can't be a deep thinker.

Print-Reference Read-Alouds

The print-reference read-aloud is an effective strategy for improving readers' awareness of print (Duke, 2017; McLeod, 2013). To build print knowledge, we search for "print-salient text" that highlights print that appears somewhere on the page, not merely along the bottom of it. We seek out books that are filled with extra text like this, books like Cronin's *Duck for President*, where the placards the animals carry include written words urging others to vote, or Patricelli's *Faster Faster*, where the word *splash* appears in large bold font above an illustration of the ocean. We share books with bubbles that contain the character's words or thoughts. We also point out various punctuation marks and share their purposes. This is particularly effective for emergent readers, as well as early striving readers. But we are careful not to overdo print-reference read-alouds because our primary goal is to help kids construct meaning and fall in love with literature.

"Sheer Joy" Read-Alouds

If we only read aloud for the purpose of instruction, we will ruin reading! We need to read aloud every day for the sheer joy of it. We read to our kids to immerse them in words and sounds; to expose them to interesting issues, ideas, and information; to intrigue them and build their curiosity; to entertain them; and, of course, to nurture their souls and help them fall in love with reading. Striving readers, in particular, need "sheer joy" read-alouds every day because, too often, joy is absent from the reading they do.

Every child should hear a proficient reader read aloud every day. Striving readers need this in spades.

4. Build fluency, comprehension, and confidence.

Dick Allington and Rachel Gabriel say that every child should hear a proficient reader read aloud every day (2012). Striving readers need this in spades. They need to hear what natural, fluent reading sounds like. One way to build fluency is to read aloud with expression frequently.

Fluency expert Timothy Rasinski explains that fluency is about automaticity and prosody, "the melodic features of oral language" (2010). Fluency is about reading aloud with expression and it depends on a natural pace, a rhythmic cadence, and, if the content demands it, even a dramatic flair.

However, in recent years, because of a variety of programs such as DIBELS, fluency has erroneously come to be associated with reading speed—how quickly one can read. Fluency is not about reading nonsense words quickly, or, for that matter, about reading real words quickly. Indeed, sometimes in order to understand text, especially complex text, readers may need to slow down their rate so they can process the information.

Fluency is closely tied to comprehension. We can tell that readers are comprehending a text when they read it aloud with expression and their reading "sounds like talking" (Rasinski & Samuels, 2011). Fluent oral readers place emphasis on words and ideas that show they are constructing meaning as they read. The big reward in reading is constructing meaning, and fluency provides a route to get there.

It is for this reason that we need to make sure that strivers are practicing in text they can read. Otherwise they will be hobbled by "word calling"—a failure to realize that the words form a connected, cohesive, meaningful text, resulting in one-word-at-a-time dysfluent reading. Once strivers experience reading in text that they can read with comprehension and fluency, they become more confident. They start to believe that they can read like the other kids, which is a grand-slam home run! What follows are some practices to get them there.

Listening Centers

Tim Rasinski explains that fluency is a skill that can be taught. He suggests that we create listening centers where kids listen to recordings of stories, poems, and informational texts so that they can hear proficient readers reading fluently and construct meaning from what they hear. You can record these readings yourself, or purchase or borrow pre-recorded readings.

Repeated Readings

Repeated readings are helpful in developing fluent readers. As kids read in small groups, we might ask them to reread texts, practice together, and "sound as though they are talking."

Choral Reading and Chanting

We write poems on anchor charts and read them aloud with expression on our own and then read them with the group, as we point to each word. Daily choral reading and chanting like this builds fluency.

Read-Aloud

We teachers need to read fiction, nonfiction, and/or poetry with expression every day. When we do that, we model fluent reading. Kids can hear us emphasize the important parts of texts and use the appropriate tone based on what's going on in the text. For example, we can read funny parts in a humorous tone and scary parts in an eerie tone. For more on helping readers build fluency, check out Tim Rasinski's *The Fluent Reader, Second Edition* (2010).

Fluency Development Lesson (FDL)

Rasinski (2004) suggests a practice for fluency instruction called the Fluency Development Lesson (FDL), which is especially effective with striving readers. See the Practice on page 286.

Echo Reading

A powerful strategy for early readers especially, echo reading develops expressive, fluent oral reading and builds print knowledge. It has also been proven effective in building word knowledge, print knowledge, fluency, and comprehension in striving readers (Duke, 2016).

Some other powerful fluency practices include

1. script reading
2. reader's theater
3. chanting
4. singing song lyrics
5. rap poetry reading
6. hip hop singing and dancing

In an echo reading small-group session, the kids all have the same book at their reading level. We read a page or so of the text in a fluent, expressive way, while running a finger under the words. Then the kids echo the reading by rereading the text the same way: with expression and running a finger under the words. We also echo read using a big book at the student's level. The kids may not use their fingers, but they see the words clearly and echo them after we read them. We can engage in the same process by projecting text on the white board. We might also engage strivers in echo reading in one-on-one conferences. We begin by reading the title and having the child echo it.

Regardless of how you carry out echo reading, it's important to make sure the kids are following the print, and not just remembering what you said and repeating it. Keeping the text short, pointing to the words, and uttering them with expression is key to developing fluency.

These activities engage striving readers from the get-go because they are a lot more fun than filling in bubbles and blanks. And BONUS for us: The research is clear—striving readers will become better readers and meaning makers by hearing experienced readers read, becoming familiar with print, and by reading orally with expression themselves, thereby developing automaticity, prosody, and comprehension.

5. Attend to signposts: text features, graphic features, and signal words and phrases.

Striving readers need support to make sense of text. We can teach them to take advantage of every opportunity that arises that makes text more accessible. Text features, graphic features, and signal words and phrases do just that. Once readers become aware of these entry points and practice using them, their reading really starts to take off. They get so much more information from text when they attend to these signposts. We also teach the purposes of features and signal words and phrases. After all, there's no reason to have kids identify the signposts without knowing their rationale. We model how to discover and use them while reading so kids can discover and use them on their own.

Text Features and Graphic Features

Reading page after page of running print is tough for striving readers. It's one of the reasons that long fiction can be challenging for so many of them and why they often gravitate toward graphic novels, vibrant nonfiction, and poetry with images. The visual nature of graphic features breaks up the text and makes it more appealing and accessible. Text features highlight aspects of text itself. We teach a variety of features so strivers can add more arrows to their meaning-making quiver. We also co-construct anchor charts as kids come across text and graphic features and recognize their purposes. What follows are some common text and graphic features.

Strong visuals support complex descriptions about types of snow from **Weather**.

From Striving to Thriving © 2017 by Stephanie Harvey & Annie Ward, Scholastic Inc.

Text Feature	Purpose		Graphic Feature	Purpose
Title	To convey what the text is about		Photographs	To provide visual images of someone or something
Heads and Subheads	To indicate what a section is about		Illustrations	To show what information in the text looks like
Labels	To name an image or parts of an image		Charts	To present information visually
Captions	To explain a photo or illustration		Graphs	To show relationships
Bold Print	To stress the importance of a word or phrase		Maps	To show where things are located
Italics	To make a word or phrase stand out		Diagrams	To illustrate what something looks like or how it works
Map Key	To provide information to interpret information on a map		Cutaways	To show the inside or inner workings of something
			Close-ups	To see something magnified

Signal Words and Signal Phrases

Signal words and signal phrases are powerful signposts. They cue the reader toward meaning. Paying close attention to them is a potent strategy to enhance comprehension for strivers. When thriving readers see a signal word such as *surprisingly*, they recognize that a surprise is coming. Striving readers tend to run their eyes right over the words without noticing the cue. Have you ever seen a striver come to a phrase like *most importantly* and just keep reading on? We sure have! Striving readers benefit from developing an awareness of signal words and phrases, because by noticing them, they are likely to pay attention to what is coming up. And although it's not a primary motive, teaching kids about signal words not only helps them as readers, but also as test takers.

Fiction and nonfiction are rife with signal words and phrases. So, to prepare for instruction, peruse some articles, pinpoint the signal words and phrases, share a few examples with students, and then encourage them to be on the lookout for noticing and using them as well. Below are lists for your convenience. But the best way for kids to learn about signals is for you to share a few you have noticed and then nudge kids to find some on their own.

Signal Word	Purpose
Surprisingly	Signals the unexpected
Importantly	Signals importance—pay attention
But	Signals change to come
Significantly	Signals importance—pay attention
Likewise	Signals a similarity
Consequently	Signals a result or effect of a cause
Before Next After Then Finally Now	Signals a sequence

Signal Phrase	Purpose
In conclusion In sum	Signals a wrap-up or synthesis of the big idea(s)
There are several reasons There are several factors There are several purposes	Signals an answer to a question or an idea. The most important reason always comes in the first position or last, but never in the middle.
As opposed to On the other hand	Signals a change or contrast
In addition to	Signals more information on the same topic
Because of	Signals a result or cause of something
In other words	Signals a restatement of the message

6. Teach with images, videos, graphics, and artifacts.

Too often, kids in low-achieving schools are given a "uni-source curriculum": one textbook to teach science, one basal reader to teach reading, and so forth. Conversely, kids in high-achieving schools are often given a "multi-source curriculum" (Allington, 2005). A multi-source curriculum should include multimedia, multi-level, multi-cultural, multi-genre, and multi-perspective sources (Harvey & Goudvis, 2016). All kids deserve the latter. In a multi-source curriculum, the teacher uses images, videos, graphics, and artifacts, as well as text. This is good news for striving readers because they have a variety of accessible entry points into ideas and information. In fact, we ignore auditory and visual literacy at our striving readers' peril. Much of the information all readers will encounter in the 21st century will be auditory and visual. So, the multi-source curriculum provides a real break for kids who have a tough time with reading.

Read, Listen, and View Across the Curriculum

We don't save reading for the literacy block. We advocate for classrooms where kids read, write, draw, talk, and think their way through the day, across the curriculum. Immersing striving readers in a variety of content resources and giving them multiple entry points into information allows them to build knowledge even when the text eludes them and written expression is difficult. We can turn science and social studies into the most engaging parts of the day by making the information accessible.

P. David Pearson has a motto that we would like to see posted in every classroom across the planet: "Read it, write it, talk it, do it" (2014). Simple yet profound.

Share images. Throughout this book, we have extolled the value of using images to build knowledge and engage striving readers. Images offer entry points into sophisticated information and ideas that strivers might not be able to access in text. Pearson says, "Today's new knowledge is tomorrow's background knowledge" (2014). So, we want to make sure that our strivers have plenty of opportunities to acquire knowledge through images.

The New York Times features a visual thinking activity every Monday called "What's Going On in This Picture?" The editors post a captionless image and students join a virtual conversation throughout the week. On Thursday, a *Times* editor reveals

David's sketched summary of an interactive read-aloud of Four Feet Two Sandals *shows a deep understanding of the refugee narrative.*

information about the photo, including a caption and a bit of backstory. Another thinking routine we advocate is known as "See Think Wonder" from http://Visiblethinkingpz.org. We share it in more detail in the Close Viewing Practice on page 264. We also encourage kids to demonstrate their understanding through drawing, as David did on his sticky note responses to an interactive read-aloud. Through these image-focused routines, striving readers gain access to information, build confidence, share their thinking, participate in discussions, and have some fun.

Share video clips. Streaming videos abound on the Internet. Web cams in real time show everything from bald eagles hatching to NASA launches. Kids can go to authoritative websites such as the Discovery Channel, the History Channel, and *National Geographic* to find information that relates to a topic of study and then post it to the entire class. YouTube is a virtual new form of schooling; there is almost nothing you can't learn there. When we share videos with kids, we show them how we stop to think, jot, and talk about the content, just as we do in a text-based interactive read-aloud.

Create Text Sets and Source Sets to Build Knowledge

According to Gina Cervetti, knowledge building is the next frontier in literacy teaching and learning (2011). We don't read merely for the sake of it; we read to build our knowledge store. So, when we limit striving readers to only texts they can read, they may miss out on that important act. Text sets and source sets give all kids the chance to build knowledge about a content area, inquiry topic, or just about anything, because of the easy access to materials at every point on the developmental spectrum.

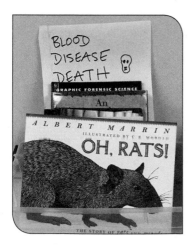

Text Sets. Text sets are collections of texts at a variety of levels, on a common theme or issue, or for a particular content area. They ensure that all readers, including striving readers, have texts at their particular reading levels and, therefore, can participate in the collective knowledge building and discussions that ensue. Teachers can team together to create text sets, often with the help of kids, based on topics they are investigating in science or social studies, authors they are studying in English language arts, or a self-selected topic.

From Striving to Thriving © 2017 by Stephanie Harvey & Annie Ward, Scholastic Inc.

Source Sets. Source sets go beyond text sets. Inspired by "Touch Carts" in museums, where patrons can handle specimens, such as the fossilized dinosaur bones, source sets include not only texts, but also images, videos, artifacts, and just about anything else we can find to engage kids in the content. They replicate how we often gather, research, and gain information outside of school. Teachers and students frequently co-create source sets focused on significant, relevant, and authentic topics and concepts in the curriculum.

Fourth graders explore an Ancient Egypt source set.

The wide range of sources offers a variety of entry points to information and, therefore, helps to differentiate instruction. For instance, a second-grade source set on transportation might include a variety of books and articles at different levels. But it would also be filled with Match Box vehicles of every imaginable type. A source set for a rainforest habitat study could include amazing images, videos, and text, but also realistic rainforest animal figures. A marine biology source set for older kids might include seashells, fish in an aquarium, and so forth. See the Practice entitled "Source Sets" on page 284.

7. Engage kids in temporary, flexible, needs-based small-group instruction and small-group work.

In addition to receiving daily, high-quality whole-class instruction, kids need to spend a large part of the day working in small groups or reading independently in both reading workshop and the content areas. Many before us have written about a form of small-group instruction known as guided reading, where children are grouped according to their reading level, the teacher explicitly teaches a reading skill for about 30 minutes, and, hopefully, children progress

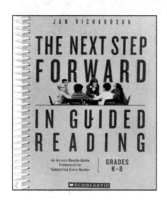

in reading. When children have similar decoding needs, it is expedient and useful to group them for targeted instruction. Striving readers, in particular, benefit from that kind of short-term, small-group instruction. But we believe that instruction should be temporary, needs-based, and flexible. If children remain in the same group for an inordinate amount of time, that is *not* guided reading. These fixed long-term groups more closely resemble ability-group reading, which leads to labeling and more labeling. In other words, it's hazardous to a striving reader's health. Research in support of ability-group reading is sparse to nonexistent. However, needs-based small-group reading is a powerful way to move kids forward. But because kids make gains at different rates, these groups need to remain flexible. (For more on guided reading groups and instruction, see Fountas & Pinnell, 2017, and Richardson, 2016.)

Keep in mind, guided reading groups are not the only kinds of groups that support striving readers. Kids should be working in groups throughout the day, some for the purpose of instruction and others for the purpose of collaborative work and inquiry (Routman, 2014; Harvey & Daniels, 2015). America has a long history of students working in isolation. Desks in rows and no talking were the norm for many years. However, America has changed. If we want our kids to be ready for the 21st-century workplace, they need to spend a good deal of the day working in small groups. In organizations around the country, workers who used to toil alone all day are now working in teams, work groups, and task forces. So, to prepare striving readers for life outside of school, we want to make sure they are collaborating in book clubs, partnerships, and inquiry circles. Next, we describe several small-group configurations that are useful for all kids, but particularly striving readers.

Strategy or Genre Groups

A small-group configuration that is particularly effective for striving readers is based on a common strategy or genre. Small groups such as these are terrific confidence builders for striving readers, because they find themselves reading with classmates at a variety of levels, but who may need help on a specific strategy or genre. Kids have an uncanny way of knowing the most proficient readers in the class, regardless of how closely the teacher keeps that information to her chest. A striver's confidence quotient rises when he or she is called to a group that includes one or more of those proficient readers, considering that the striver may have been relegated to the same group of strivers year after year. Suddenly the stigma begins to evaporate.

Since these groups are based on a strategy or genre need rather than reading level, a common book is generally not provided by the teacher. Each student brings the book he or she is reading independently. As with guided reading groups, the meetings last about 30 minutes. The teacher conducts a very brief mini-lesson on applying the strategy, and then has the kids practice it, as they read their own books.

The teacher moves from one student to another to confer for two or three minutes while the others read. During the final five minutes, the kids share their learning, thinking, and questions in relation to the mini-lesson. These small groups provide targeted, needs-based instruction for sure, but they also give kids more time to read each day. Too often when kids participate in teacher-led small groups, they don't get any time to actually read. We are always on the lookout for squeezing more reading time into the day. With groups like these, strivers not only gain confidence and reading skill, they also get more time to read.

Book Clubs, or Lit Circles

Book clubs, also known as lit circles, are peer-led discussion groups. Modeled on neighborhood book clubs, kids read a common text and discuss it together. We are both big fans of book clubs and are thrilled to see how they have proliferated in schools. In their original form, kids typically read grade-level chapter books or novels. They would choose a book, divide it into chunks, make a plan to meet every week or so to discuss each chunk, and then have a final discussion when they completed the book. However, these book clubs were tough on striving readers, because, for many of them, reading a grade-level novel was not yet in the cards.

But book clubs can look different now. We can use shorter, more accessible texts such as picture books, short stories, nonfiction articles, nonfiction trade books, poems, and plays. This approach opens up book clubs to striving readers unlike ever before. Even if the text is a bit above their level, the short length makes it likely that they can read and discuss it, especially if they are interested in it. We are particularly fond of "picture-book book clubs." Many picture books today offer deep, moving themes in a short, accessible form. Picture-book book clubs organized around a rich theme, such as resilience or hope, offer striving readers an attainable entry

point. The same goes for picture-book book clubs organized around a specific content-area topic, such as Civil Rights or climate change. Picture books on content-area topics abound. When we show all kids how much we value picture books, striving readers begin to see them as more than "baby books."

Book clubs offer so many powerful learning and social benefits. So, we make sure that striving readers have opportunities to read novels in book clubs when they want to and seem ready. We always remember the power of the word *yet*. We would never say, "But Robert can't read that novel." We'd say instead, "Robert can't read that novel *yet*."

Read, Write, and Talk

Read, Write, and Talk (Harvey & Goudvis, 2006) is quite effective with striving readers. In *RWT*, kids choose between three or four nonfiction articles, read

From Striving to Thriving © 2017 by Stephanie Harvey & Annie Ward, Scholastic Inc.

through one, annotate their thinking in the margins, and then discuss it with someone who read the same article. This is a great way to get kids reading about science and social studies topics and to get more reading into the content areas. Because articles come in all reading levels, you can select a range of them and meet the needs of strivers. If, in the end, striving readers cannot read the article you've chosen, read it to them or have them read it with a partner. After all, it's short enough! By doing that, you allow them to participate in the discussion. But make sure they have plenty of time that same day to read a well-matched text.

Inquiry Circles

Inquiry circles are small groups of kids working together to study a common topic, investigate a question of interest, or work on a problem or an issue collaboratively. They are a lifesaver for striving readers, because they do not require adaptations. They work for all kids just as they are designed. They differentiate naturally and organically. Unlike in book clubs, kids aren't required to read the same text. So, we kick off

Steph confers with an Ancient Egypt inquiry circle.

inquiry circles by gathering texts and other resources related to the topic under study, often with the students' help. Text sets and source sets are particularly useful in small-group collaborative inquiries.

Because kids join inquiry circles based on interest, it is not the least bit unusual to find a striving reader in a circle with a reader who is two years above grade level. It is a common interest that binds them into the same tribe. Inquiry circles have the power to break the cycle of embarrassment and inferiority often felt by striving readers because those readers can participate as effectively as more developed readers. Often innately curious, strivers bring a great deal of enthusiasm and energy to inquiry circles. We can't recommend inquiry circles more enthusiastically in our pursuit of equity for striving readers as well as fun. For more information on them, see Steph and Smokey Daniels's *Comprehension, Collaboration: Inquiry Circles for Curiosity, Engagement and Understanding* (2015).

Partner Reading

When it comes to striving readers, partner reading is both a blessing and a curse. Sometimes it works wonders and sometimes it falls flat. Too often, the teacher has kids read something that is too hard for the striver. So, she pairs the striver with a thriver who ends up doing all of the reading, thereby, yet again, denying the striver reading time that he or she so desperately needs.

Or how often have you seen reading partnerships in which the two students take turns reading paragraphs—one student reads a paragraph while the other one stares off into La La Land, and then they switch and the same thing happens in reverse? To avoid this kind of behavior, we let reading partners know that it is the listener who has the biggest job. We give the listener a pad of sticky notes and have him or her jot down or draw anything he or she:

- wonders,
- learns,
- is surprised by, or
- is confused by.

When the reader is done with his or her section, the listener leads a discussion based on the notes taken during the reading. Active listening is an important strategy for all readers, especially striving readers, because it keeps them engaged and participating.

If we want striving readers to glean information from text that is above their level, pairing them with more proficient readers may work. But do it in small doses. If strivers never get a chance to read, they won't develop confidence, agency, or reading skill. You may also want to consider audio books—the listener can use the same prompts as they jot or sketch their thinking on sticky notes while listening to audio books. Reading is a social act, and well-planned, well-executed partner reading proves that. It's both collaborative and fun.

WHOLE-CLASS NOVEL VS. SOLAR TEXT READING

Nothing strikes fear in the heart of a striving reader more than the whole-class novel. Across the country, even to this date, we see classrooms full of core novels, particularly in intermediate and middle grades. Teachers usually choose a novel with the best of intentions. It may feature enduring themes and literary elements that they believe will enrich their kids' lives. It might connect somehow to the lives of the kids in their classroom. It might build empathy. It might relate to and enhance a topic they are studying in social studies or science. The teacher may love the book so much that she or he can't resist sharing it. These are all wonderful reasons to choose a core novel.

The problem, of course, is that striving readers will almost certainly not be able to read it. The truth about a whole-class novel is this: In a class of 30 sixth graders, about 10 can and want to read it; another 10 can, but don't really want to; another five would really like to, but can't (our hearts really ache for these kids); and another five can't and couldn't care less. Not hard to guess where our strivers fit. So, in the name of equity, we need to figure this out.

Solar text reading is a viable option, where the teacher reads the whole-class novel aloud because that is the only way that everyone is able to read it. The novel becomes the solar text; it is at the center of the textual solar system. As she reads, she collects related short text satellites—articles, poems, short stories, etc.—that revolve around the novel and capture its themes and content.

So, for instance, let's say the teacher is reading aloud Gary Paulson's *Hatchet*. She could bring in articles on surviving in the woods; animals of the north; Sully Sullivan, the commercial pilot who landed the plane on the Hudson; divorce; heart disease—all themes and content related to the book. These short pieces enhance the reader's understanding of the book by ferreting out interesting information and ideas simmering in the text. And they give kids much to talk about. We encourage kids to collect these satellite texts as well. No surprise, they often find the most intriguing pieces of all.

We don't reserve solar text reading merely for whole-group novel replacement. We also form book groups around it. A small group of kids may be reading a piece of literature, a picture book, or a novel, and collect the satellite texts. These texts, which relate to the themes and content, can add to their book group discussions and fuel their thinking beyond the text.

8. Share pathways to understanding through digital reading, listening, and viewing.

Digital reading, listening, and viewing allow kids to gain information in ways unimaginable only a decade ago. However, we find ourselves in the midst of a raging debate as to which is more beneficial—digital reading or print reading. Evidence is mounting that online reading is problematic for a number of

reasons, including all of the distractions that surround it (Ferlazzo, 2016). There's no doubt that clickbait and pop-ups tend to lure us away from the main text. Steph can barely resist a Nordstrom's ad for shoes at 50 percent off. Annie finds herself craving a latte when a Starbucks banner pops up. Although most studies on digital reading have been done with college students, it's not unreasonable to assume that striving readers can also be easily lured away.

However, we've found a number of digital formats that may keep striving readers focused and motivated, including audio books, podcasts, and e-books. Because, the truth is, strivers can score big in this new world of digitization if we give them the tools to do so.

Audio Books

Audio books are ubiquitous. Teri Lesesne refers to audio books as "reading with your ears." Steph adores them. So much so, in fact, that she has developed a rather bizarre affection for traffic jams since they allow her more time in the car to listen to books. When she arrives home, she often languishes in the driveway until the chapter concludes. The next morning, she jumps on the treadmill not just to get in a workout, but to savor the following chapter. But there are those who question the value of audio books, suggesting that listening to them, rather than reading a print version, is "cheating."

Daniel Willingham, the famed psychologist from the University of Virginia, states, "Listening to an audio book might be considered cheating if the act of decoding were the point; audio books allow you to seem to have decoded without doing so. But if appreciating the language and the story is the point, it is not. Comparing audio books to cheating is like meeting a friend at Disneyland and saying, 'You took the bus here? I drove myself, you big cheater.' The point is getting to and enjoying the destination. The point is not how you traveled" (2016). And we are talking about adults here! What about kids?

The good news is, audio books have a positive impact on literacy achievement, particularly with striving readers.

PROMISING RESEARCH ABOUT AUDIO BOOKS

A study from WestEd on the impact of audio books on vocabulary development, comprehension, and reading achievement of second and third graders in San Francisco showed astonishing growth. For 10 weeks, students listened to audio books, without following along with the text, three times per week for 20 minutes in school and two more times for 20 minutes at home. The treatment group grew by 58 percent of the annual expected gains in reading achievement. It also outperformed the control group by three times in reading comprehension, seven times in vocabulary, and four times in reading motivation (Flynn, Matlen, Atienza & Schneider, 2016). Listening to audio books also led to kids reading more. Stunning results, with positive implications for striving readers and their motivation to read. For more information, check out Mary Burkey's book *Audiobooks for Youth: A Practical Guide to Sound Literature* (2013), as well as her *Booklist* column, "Voices in My Head."

We generally allow kids to choose their own audio books and provide them with a pad of sticky notes to draw or jot down their thoughts while listening so they can hold them for later discussion. We also often have two kids share a headphone set and listen to an audio book simultaneously, taking time to stop and talk about it while they are listening.

Podcasts

Podcasts, too, are ubiquitous these days. High school English teacher and *Atlantic* magazine contributor Michael Godsey found that many of his kids, particularly his more reluctant readers, were struggling to read novels. Some claimed they got bored, spacing out within a few minutes of opening the book. Others just admitted they "hated to read," which is like a knife in the heart to all us teachers. But Michael's kids really enjoyed podcasts, especially the NPR series *Serial*, about the murder of a teenager, the accused killer, and a journalist who tries to solve the mysteries surrounding the case. But the game changer for his students came in *Serial's* second season, when the producers posted the transcripts of each episode online. Michael began to project each transcript as his students listened to the episode, transfixed. They couldn't take their eyes off the words. This experience jump-started all kinds of reading in Michael's classroom, including the reading of strivers and emerging bilinguals (2016). His students reported on why:

- reading along helped them focus on the content.
- reading ahead led to a more solid understanding of the narrative.
- rereading cleared up confusion.
- listening to and seeing the words helped them pronounce those words.
- listening and reading along allowed them to keep up with the pace of information.

STORYLINE ONLINE

A terrific resource, from the Screen Actors Guild and the American Federation of Television and Radio Artists, is *Storyline Online*, which provides opportunities for children, parents, educators, and anyone else interested in listening to and viewing classic children's stories read by professional actors. The collection includes over 30 books written by some of our favorite authors, such as Patricia Polocco, Tomie DePaola, Mem Fox, and Ysaye Barnwell, read by actors including James Earl Jones, Allison Janney, and Hector Elizondo, to name a few. The stories can be found at www.storylineonline.net. They can also be found on YouTube, where closed captioning is available. (Search for "Storyline Online.") Storyline Guides developed by literacy specialists accompany each book and offer suggestions for extensions, as well as information on the author, illustrator, and reader. *Storyline* adds about three or four books a year and plans to offer Spanish readings in the near future. Truly a great resource for our striving readers.

Emma Rodero, a communications professor from the Pompeu Fabra University in Barcelona, explains, "Listening, unlike looking at the written page, is more active since the brain has to process the information at the pace it is played …. Audio is one of the most intimate forms of media because you are constantly building your own images of the story in your mind" (as cited in Godsey, 2016). Many of Michael's students agree. Try Googling "podcasts for kids." You will find more than a lifetime's worth of material, but this list from NPR contains many of our favorites: www.npr.org/podcasts/2036/kids-family.

Audio books and podcasts offer kids opportunities to hear experienced readers and speakers, often professional actors, express themselves. They provide a range of entry points for striving readers that allow them to build fluency, strengthen comprehension, and engage with compelling, significant narratives, issues, ideas, and curiosities.

E-Books

Most striving readers have spent most of their short lives thinking of themselves as "bad" readers. How many times have they found themselves seated next to kids during independent reading who are reading 300-page novels, a year or two ahead of their grade level? Any drop of confidence strivers have evaporates the moment those kids pull out their books, especially if they think of the books *they're* reading as "baby books."

THE VALUE OF AUTHENTIC TEXT FOR ALL KIDS!

We think it's clear, given our passion for young adult and children's literature—and real texts of all kinds across genre—that we believe all students deserve the richest authentic texts possible. What do we mean by "authentic"? We look to a definition from 1977 to define authenticity: "A stretch of real language produced by a real speaker or writer for a real audience and designed to convey a real message of some sort" (Morrow, p. 13). In other words, authentic text is living language that serves multiple purposes (Halliday, 1973)—not contrived text written or assembled solely for the purpose of teaching skills.

A subset of contrived text is *decodable* text. It's tempting to think that because decodable texts comprise words with consistent spelling patterns such as *big, pig, wig, jig* that they are easier for kids to read. But, in fact, the language is typically nonsensical, often devoid of meaning, and, therefore, harder for kids to read and comprehend. Striving readers, who are often reluctant to read at all, deserve and need engaging text rich with meaning to lead them into the world of reading. We're not surprised that there's no independent, verifiable research to support the use of decodable text, a fact noted by the National Reading Panel (2000).

Former International Literacy Association President and Reading Hall of Fame member Richard Allington and colleague Haley Woodside-Jiron conducted an in-depth analysis of research on decodable text; they write: "We have carefully traced the research citations noted in advocacy and policy statements and were unable to locate any 'reliable, replicable research' concerning the use of 'decodable text' on which these policy decisions were based" (p. 213).

Why not invite all children, particularly striving readers who are often relegated to decodable text, to feast on the richest authentic language possible rather than give them a thin gruel of fake language?

One type of reading we have found that helps avoid that situation is e-book reading—reading on Kindles, iPads, Chromebook e-readers, and so forth. We are huge fans of print books, but can't help notice the confidence that e-reading builds in our striving readers, likely for the same reason that *50 Shades of Grey* sold so many e-book copies: *No one knows what you are reading!* And, for the time being anyway, digital devices are still pretty cool at school, which makes the reader using them cool. So we download books that striving readers can and want to read, and they can read them with confidence because their choices remain anonymous.

And it's worked! We have seen kids make a year's growth in several months when reading, without fear of judgment, on e-book readers. This is not a solution for kids who prefer print, but try it out with one child for whom you have concerns—especially a striver who is naturally drawn to technology. You may be surprised by how much more they read and how much growth they make.

Ultimately, our suggestions are about equity, giving striving readers equal access to the world of story, issues, and ideas, through listening and viewing. Above all, striving readers need time to read books that they can read and want to read every single day.

INSTRUCTION

Use these questions to teach responsive, learner-focused, thinking-intensive reading, with comprehension at the core.

Self-Questions

- Am I teaching comprehension strategies and modeling their flexible use to construct meaning?
- Have I modeled how to reread to clarify meaning?
- Am I teaching with the Gradual Release of Responsibility framework, keeping whole-class work short and explicit, and devoting most of reading instruction to guided practice?
- Am I giving students enough time to practice strategies they have learned independently?
- Am I using interactive read-alouds to provide access to all students, engage them in guided discussion, and build community?
- Am I forming small groups based on instructional need, as well as on interest and inquiry?
- Am I providing a range of entry points—videos, images, artifacts, podcasts, audio books—into information so strivers can build knowledge using texts and other sources?
- Am I giving kids plenty of time to just plain read?

Kidwatching Questions

- Is the student listening to the inner conversation to monitor comprehension?
- Is the student annotating the text in some way and leaving tracks of thinking?
- Is the student using fix-up strategies to get back on track when meaning breaks down?
- Is the student comfortable reading both in print and digitally? Does he prefer one over the other?
- Is the student becoming a more confident reader? What makes you think so?

Conferring Questions

- What are you thinking about your reading?
- What can you do when you come to a word or an idea that you don't understand?
- What strategies can you use to make meaning when you get confused?
- How can text features and signal words help you stay on track when reading is challenging?

Part III: Transform

"Education is for improving the lives of others and for leaving the community and world better than you found it."

—*Marian Wright Edelman*

scholastic.com/ThriveResources

"Want to collect data on how children are learning? Know them. Watch them. Listen to them. Talk 'with' them. Sit with them. Be with them."

—Joe Bower

Assess Readers in the Round

As Joe Bower suggests (at left), we need to assess students in a dynamic, robust way that considers the whole reader and the universe of behaviors, attitudes, and understandings that he or she exhibits. Hence, the title for our formative assessment tool: Assessing Readers in the Round! The ARR helps us determine whether our students understand that reading is supposed to make sense, to sound like cohesive language (not a grab bag of words!), and, ultimately, to be a deeply satisfying and pleasurable experience. Identifying what our strivers know about reading and what they still need to learn informs our instruction and optimizes our support. Most importantly, the ARR enables us to "table the labels" and see our students in all their capable glory—with challenges to overcome, yes, but also with many strengths that we can help them recognize, access, and learn to use more efficiently and effectively. Above all, we want our students to see themselves as readers and understand what readers do so they can track and grow their own reading success.

You can download a series of Assessment Forms for this chapter at scholastic.com/ThriveResources.

Step 1: Collect full-spectrum data on your strivers.

Use the gatefold and chapter-end ARR questions to engage in two data-collecting actions you likely already do every single day: kidwatching and conferring. Here, we take a deep dive into those two methods of data collection since they give us so much rich, authentic information. But keep in mind that we think of "assessment as inquiry," which means that the rich flow of daily classroom life offers innumerable opportunities to notice, track, and document what your students are learning about reading. "Every learning event is an opportunity for assessment" (Bridges, 1995). And then, of course, this information informs your teaching. As Mary Howard puts it, "Our best source of information is a thoughtful and skilled teacher who observes and learns from the student" (Howard, 2009). For additional guidance, see Guidelines for Collecting, Analyzing, and Sharing Data on pages 219–220. These are our suggestions for collecting data in the round, discussing with your strivers, analyzing for strengths, and working together with your strivers to determine their next-step reading and learning goals. No doubt you can add to this list!

Kidwatching

Yetta Goodman, who coined the term "kidwatching," and Gretchen Owocki explain the power of kidwatching: Rather than viewing some children as "low," "behind," or "lacking in skills," teachers who kidwatch view all children as creative, capable learners—on their way to "achieving control over the conventions of language—always in process," always moving forward (2003). Teachers who are just beginning to kidwatch are always amazed by the intellectual curiosity and learning ingenuity of their students. They learn that while every child needs support in some areas, every child also has strengths.

We can't stress enough how much we learn about kids' reading and thinking by simply listening closely to what they say. If we listen, most of them will talk. Some strivers yearn for informal conversations about their thoughts, wonderings, and interests. Others are more reticent, so we search for multiple ways into conversation.

Kidwatching in Action: Getting to Know Your Students. We capture kids' responses in writing—and encourage them to do the same. We record what kids say in class discussions on charts and/or encourage them to draw or jot their thoughts on sticky notes and place them on the chart. This makes their thinking visible and public and provides a window into their understanding. Steph takes her notes on an iPad, whereas Annie takes hers in a traditional notebook. Regardless of the kidwatching recording technique you choose, the goal is the same: getting to know your students as individuals with unique needs, interests, challenges, and strengths. For a focused look at kidwatching in action, let's zero in on fifth-grade teacher Barbara Gilbert's "Getting to Know Your Students," adapted from Donald Graves (1989) and appearing in the book *Reading Strategies for Deep Thinking* (in press) by Diane Stephens, Jean Anne Clyde, and Jerome Harste. This simple kidwatching exercise helps teachers reflect and build upon what they know about their students. It emphasizes appreciating the whole child as a unique individual, a reader, a writer, and a learner in and out of school. This includes awareness of the child's home culture (Moll & González, 2004). Additionally, it helps teachers place students at the center of learning, turning their interests and strengths into opportunities for academic success. It also demonstrates caring, one of the tenets of good teaching.

Annie's colleagues have adapted Barbara's "Getting to Know Your Students" framework to capture comprehensive data about children. Notice in the example on the next page how knowing children in the round builds empathetic relationships and informs bookmatching.

Getting to Know Your Students

Student's Name	Home and Culture	Experiences and Interests	Student as Reader	Student as Writer	Student as Learner
Brett	Takes care of his two siblings and one cousin between dismissal and when Mom returns home from work. Particularly close with his one-year-old baby brother.	Fascinated by his baby brother's language development, is a huge fan of New York Soccer Club, plays goalie on the local soccer team.	Reads to his siblings and cousin at home regularly, finds it challenging to find a quiet place and time to read independently at home.	Enjoys writing about topics he has researched (e.g., beehives, symbiotic relationships, kid inventors).	Highly organized, prefers a quiet workspace, enjoys helping his peers once his work is complete.
Marquis	Parents take turns working from home. Marquis is an only child. He is very close with his dog.	Incredibly knowledgeable about luxury cars, particularly interested in design specs and autonomous vehicle technology.	Voracious reader of joke books, compendia, and car magazines; willing to try other genres but has not yet found one that appeals to the same degree.	Keeps a notebook to record funny bits of conversation he overhears, jokes, and interesting facts; draws and labels car designs.	Takes advantage of varied seating arrangements particularly the standing table, learns best when provided opportunities to talk through his ideas with peers.
Cassie	Spends much of her free time playing with her sister who is in kindergarten. Grandma is an important person in the girls' lives and they often stay with her during the week.	Engages in elaborate inventive play scenarios with her sister. They make clothes for their collection of dolls to support the imaginary worlds they have developed.	Strong preference for magazines and graphic format fantasy novels with strong female protagonists. Beginning to show some interest in free-verse novels.	Writes extensively about the imaginary worlds she and her sister have created. Chooses to write during transitions and indoor recess.	Pushes the class to think outside the box about situations and challenges.
Joaquin	Recently joined the school community from a school in Guatemala.	Very proud of his heritage, knows a great deal about and is interested in agriculture including rearing of livestock and growing crops since he lived on his grandparents' farm in Guatemala.	Prefers reading novels in Spanish, particularly Capitán Calzoncillos and expository nonfiction in English. Recent areas of interest include natural disasters and apex predators.	Began keeping a journal when he moved to the U.S. and writes letters home to family in Guatemala regularly.	Gaining confidence sharing his thinking with the class, proactively seeks help from peers when English vocabulary presents a challenge.

From Striving to Thriving © 2017 by Stephanie Harvey & Annie Ward, Scholastic Inc.

Conferring

The most powerful way to reach a striving reader is to spend five or ten minutes engaging with him in what Annie refers to as a "reader-to-reader, heart-to-heart conference." Sometimes, discovering what a reader is thinking takes simply asking, "What are you thinking about?" or, as Carl Anderson suggests, "How's it going?" (2000). Other times our conferring prompts are more specific.

We watch kids' facial expressions closely. We notice kids' expressions and body language while they read and/or work. Hunched shoulders, a wrinkled nose, a quizzical look, a smile, or a frown can give us an indication of what a reader might be thinking.

Two assessment procedures, in particular, that will help your strivers strengthen what they are doing effectively and let go of things that are undermining their powerful reading are:

- Running Records
- Over-the-Shoulder Miscue Analysis (OTS)

Both procedures provide strivers with essential information about themselves as readers—what's working that they should strengthen and what's not working that they should drop.

Maggie conducts a running record and OTS miscue analysis.

ASSESSING YOUR STUDENTS' DEVELOPING LANGUAGE AND LITERACY ACROSS CLASSROOM, HOME, AND COMMUNITY

This list reminds us of the rich, full lives our strivers lead—not just at school but at home and in their own communities. As you engage in kidwatching at school, consider how you might tap your strivers' reading strengths at home by participating in home visits (Mapp et al., 2017) or simply talking with parents when they visit your classroom or attend student/family conferences. Wilhelm & Smith (2013) found that some students who ignored assigned reading at school were actually living rich, full reading lives at home, exclusively focused on texts of their own choosing.

Home-Based Information

1. What funds of knowledge are present in the student's home?
2. What print materials are routinely used in the home?
3. What kinds of literacy interactions and relationships does the student have with others in the household?
4. What kinds of literacy interactions does the student have with friends and family in other settings?
5. What is the student's language background?
6. What is the student's cultural background?
7. What goals and expectations does the family have for the student?
8. What do family members recall about their own experiences with language and literacy in school settings?

Classroom-Based Information

1. What topics/content/genres are of interest to the student?
2. What language and literacy practices does the student lean toward when given a choice?
3. How would I characterize the student's language and literacy identity?
4. What discourse patterns seem familiar to the student?
5. How is the student applying language and literacy practices to new contexts and settings?

From Striving to Thriving © 2017 by Stephanie Harvey & Annie Ward, Scholastic Inc.

Student-Based Information

1. What are the student's views of him/herself as a reader and writer?

2. What is the student learning/reading/writing?

3. Which kinds of reading, writing, and collaborative experiences does the student prefer?

4. What is the student learning about her/himself as a learner?

5. How does the student feel about school?

Community-Based Information

1. What family-oriented agencies are present in the community?

2. What shopping facilities and other businesses are present in the community?

3. What signs and other environmental print are present in the community?

4. What libraries, bookstores, and shops with text are available to families?

5. What places of historic interest are present in the community?

6. How diverse are housing patterns and the population in terms of age, race, ethnicity, and family structures?

(from Owocki and Goodman, 2003)

Running Records

"Listen" closely to Reading Recovery trained literacy expert Ellen O'Connor Lewis as she interacts with first-grade striver Nate. First, you'll notice Ellen's thoughtfulness and compassion, but you'll also notice her iron-clad commitment to focusing on Nate's strengths as a reader—focusing on all that he's doing right as a reader as revealed by his running records. And, equally important, helping Nate focus on his strengths so he can bolster those strategies while letting go of those behaviors, attitudes, and understandings that are interfering with his proficient reading. This is the exquisite art of teaching.

NATE'S STORY

Nate was a first grader in a Title I school in Virginia. My concerns for Nate were many. He was a native English speaker, yet seemed to struggle with the simplest sight words. He was a lively, happy child with interests in math, art, music, social studies, science, and stories—as long as they were read to him.

The literacy team invited Nate to join an intense literacy Tier 2 intervention model we called RISE (Reading Intervention Student Express) using Jan Richardson's guided reading theory and practice. We would work with him in a small-group setting for an hour every day, focusing on the four areas of literacy he needed to master to be successful. He would rotate through 15-minute stations working on new and familiar texts, guided writing, and word work. This intensity allowed us to determine what was holding Nate back from becoming a reader and help move him forward.

By using running records with Nate nearly every day on simple emergent-level text and analyzing what work he was and wasn't doing on text, I was able to assess Nate's challenges and decide where to go next with his instruction.

The first and most crucial revelation was emotional. This little guy had moved schools four times in two years. His skill acquisition was minimal. He had his alphabet in place, both letter recognition and sounds, and even had one-to-one correspondence on simple text. But Nate was afraid to make an error. He so desperately wanted to be right and fit in with his classmates, that he simply created stories around pictures or took a lucky guess using an initial letter. In short, Nate did not know what to do with words, how to solve, look for parts, or recognize blends or chunks. He needed to be taught what to do.

By using running records to focus on what he *could* do and use his strengths, I knew I could move him forward. As I shared the records with him, we became partners in his literacy journey. First, we celebrated his small victories, then we could focus on fixing up a tricky word and learning how to use that skill on another tricky word.

At Level C, we began by looking at his running records together. We acknowledged his early skills out loud, celebrating them as successes. This seemed to puzzle Nate as all he saw were the errors. We shifted that view as partners. Every conversation about his running records began with, "Look what you did so well right here." I encouraged him to tell me what he did to solve. "I used meaning there, yeah!" Thus, he became an important stakeholder in his own reading progress.

We worked on his initial skills, sight words, blends, vowel sounds, and chunks. I showed him how to use visual, meaning, and structure cues to solve. Targeted prompts that matched his needs worked for Nate. "Does it sound right?" worried

Nate because he, indeed, knew it did not sound right—but he didn't know what to do. The magic came with showing him what to do to fix his errors.

After eight weeks of the intense RISE intervention, Nate thrived and moved from level C/3 to an Instructional Level G/12. By looking at his own running records and conferring with me about what we both saw, he is ready to move ahead with a plan. Nate knows what to do, and together we will help him continue his successful literacy journey. We are both confident about his reading future. (You can see Nate's Running Records at scholastic.com/ThriveResources.)

Fiction: *Miss Blake and the Pet Snake*, Level G, Next Step Forward Reading Assessment Grades K–2, Scholastic, Inc. 93% accuracy, 1:8 sc rate, 3/4 Fluency, 8/10 Comprehension, Instructional Level

(by Ellen O'Connor Lewis, Reading Recovery Trained Literacy Coach)

Over-the-Shoulder Miscue Analysis (OTS)

Miscue analysis is a potent assessment tool that reveals how the reader is processing text; however, miscue analysis does require training, and some teachers may find it too time-consuming to manage in the busy rush of classroom life. To address that concern, literacy expert Ruth Davenport (2002) developed Over-the-Shoulder (OTS) Miscue Analysis. Anyone can learn OTS and then, ideally, develop what Yetta Goodman has termed "miscue ears." In other words, once you understand miscue analysis you will always listen to kids read aloud with appreciation for their high-quality miscues that do not interfere with meaning. Additionally, you'll understand what to do if their miscues do disrupt the flow of meaning.

The key, of course, is to help each striver develop their own "miscue ears" so when they depart from the expected response they can quickly determine if a miscue reflects or disrupts the meaning of the text.

OTS Miscue Analysis is a tool for gathering and recording essential assessment data about students, their miscues, and retellings. It allows teachers to make notes about miscues, strategies to teach, or observations to share with the reader. As literacy expert Ruth Davenport explains (2002), "Miscues provide important information about readers. We can listen to a reader who appears to be struggling with a text and realize that either she is making miscues that don't change the meaning," or she is correcting those miscues that do interfere with meaning.

The purpose of OTS miscue analysis is to provide a teaching conversation in which students are empowered as readers. This conversation helps students optimize their successful strategies and revise those that interfere with effective and efficient reading.

How to Use OTS

Using the OTS forms as a guide, follow this three-part process:

Before the Reading:

- Complete the top part of the cover page.

During the Reading:

- Record information about each miscue on the miscue page.
- Make notes in the margin of any comments made during the reading.

After the Reading:

- On the cover page, scribe as much of the teaching conversation as possible.
- On the insights page, total each column from the miscue page and record your observations about this reader.

The OTS Conference

In a one-to-one conference with the student, follow this process:

- Ask a student to join you in a reading conference and to bring any book she is currently reading.
- Talk briefly about the text and complete the cover page.
- Listen to the student read while looking over her shoulder at the text.
- Complete the miscue page during reading.
- Scribe the retelling and discussion after the reading on the cover page.

- Select and discuss several miscues that changed meaning.
- Select a strategy to introduce or review.
- Celebrate what the reader has done well.
- Complete the insights page and determine graphic similarities (after the student has left the conference).

At this point in conducting an OTS, we know a lot about our readers. We have the following:

- **Numerical information**—the percentages from each column on the miscue pages
- **Linguistic information**—by examining:
  - » *Syntax*—the relationships between the miscues and the text item: Are they the same part of speech? Did the reader substitute a past tense verb for a noun, or for a past tense verb?
  - » *Semantics*—the reader's ability to construct meaning: Did the reader lose meaning, leave uncorrected a high-quality miscue that didn't change meaning, or self-correct?
  - » *Graphophonics*—the reader's knowledge of symbol-sound relationships: Are most of the letters the same in the miscue and the text item?
  - » *Qualitative information*—by considering whether this reader is monitoring his reading and is actively involved in the process of constructing meaning or whether he needs to be more concerned with making meaning.

We can also think about other observations, such as fluency and personal connections, as shown through side comments, questions, and whether the reader is enjoying the story.

Recommendation:
- Conduct an OTS miscue analysis, if possible, every 2–3 weeks with your strivers.
- Complete the Holistic Evaluation every quarter to collect additional summative information.

You can use the forms below to guide an OTS Miscue Analysis. They are available at scholastic.com/ThriveResources.

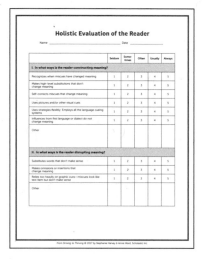

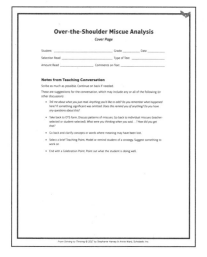

From Striving to Thriving © 2017 by Stephanie Harvey & Annie Ward, Scholastic Inc.

GUIDELINES FOR COLLECTING, ANALYZING, AND SHARING DATA

Find your own way into the inquiry process—collecting, analyzing, and sharing data in ways that make the most sense to you. Here are some ideas to help you get started.

Case Studies *include*

- Pictures of the child
- Inventories of her assets and interests
- Records of the books she's selected from preview stacks
- Reading logs
- Comments she's made about what she's reading
- Watershed books and/or series
- Teaching points from conferences and guided reading groups
- Examples of self-monitoring and risk-taking (necessary for learning)
  - » Speaking up during group discussion
  - » Offering an original interpretation of text
  - » Reading a wide variety of genre, topics, authors
  - » Skipping unknown words and reading deeper into the text to construct meaning
  - » Correcting miscues when they interfere with meaning
  - » Predicting and confirming outcomes, questioning, drawing inferences, synthesizing
  - » Writing in a variety of genres about a range of topics
  - » Approximating spelling of unknown words
  - » Awareness of self as reader, writer, and learner; setting learning goals for herself
- Dates, forms, and topics of home communication
- Parents' perspectives on her reading life
- Other data such as running records, miscue analysis, independent reading levels, fluency rates, sight word vocabulary, writing samples, and examples of invented spelling

  Assemble these chronologically and look for cause and effect. Note the impact of specific books or series and your teaching on the child's reading development.

Kidwatching and Conferring Records *include*

- Anecdotal notes from classroom observations and conferences
- Students' exact language as best you can
- Recordings of read-alouds and booktalks
- Recordings of retellings

  Does the student properly:
  - » Introduce the story?
  - » Include information about the setting, characters, plot, and more?
  - » Identify themes, problems, and solutions?

» Understand the main point of the story?

» Notice literary devices in the crafting of the story?

- Recording of Book Study Groups. Student:
  » Completes reading on time

  » Comes prepared to discuss and participate actively

  » Reflects evidence of deep engagement with the book

Record the actions you've taken based on what you've gleaned through kidwatching and conferring, and note the impact.

Reading Logs and Ladders *include the following:*

- The reading paths readers have taken from text to text
- Record of text completion and abandonment
- Reading Logs. Student writes:
  » personally significant and expressive logs.

  » entries that reflect the student's personal response to reading.

  » required number of entries.

Note patterns of student reading growth and tastes (likes and dislikes); use these to inform your book-matching efforts.

Students' Self-reflections, Written and Video *include the following:*

- The reading goals students establish for themselves: monthly, quarterly, and across the year
- Their self-analysis of their goals—did they meet their goals? Why or why not?
- Patterns of development as students' reading plans evolve

Listen carefully to each striver; kids tend to tell us precisely what they need.

Library Use and Circulation Histories *include the following:*

- Data from your library circulation system
- Data patterns from striver's school and classroom library patronage
- Student's ability to use the library and references sources on her own and with help

Note patterns of library patronage and use as an important form of self-advocacy that can be taught and tracked.

Rates of Growth Relative to District Independent Reading Benchmarks *include the following:*

- Rate of change relative to established benchmarks to gauge whether striving readers are making the accelerated progress they will need to close the gap and thrive
- Level movement (understanding that even modest gains can either be evidence of growth or reason for concern if the gap between the student's level and grade level expectations is widening)

Study rates of growth to foster an appropriate sense of urgency around striving readers' learning trajectories.

Step 2: Discuss and analyze the data with each striver.

You will read, analyze, and reflect on your students' responses—sticky notes, thinksheets, sketch notes, reading logs—always searching for evidence that readers are making meaning. We take what we learn from these responses to design next-step instruction.

Once you have a sizable pool of data (ideally, that you've gathered monthly for your records and quarterly to share with families), spend time analyzing it for the student's reading strengths and needs (ideally, with your colleagues first and then with the striver and his or her family members). As you sort through the data you've gathered, look for patterns and evidence of growth across the four principles that define reading for us: reading as a personal process, a social/cultural process, thinking, and language.

SEARCH FOR EMERGING STRENGTHS

Is the striver:

- Developing a personal relationship with reading?
- Deepening his or her social relationship with peers and books?
- Drawing on cultural background and language strengths to engage with texts in a meaningful way?
- Thinking and problem solving his or her way through a text?
- Using a range of strategies to make sense of print?
- Self-monitoring for meaning?
- Self-correcting when a miscue interferes with meaning?
- Growing more confident as a reader?
- Taking risks that propel growth, such as exploring new genres or volunteering to give a book talk?
- Developing a more sophisticated and thoughtful understanding of the place of reading in his or her life?

DAY-TO-DAY READING ASSESSMENT IN THE READING WORKSHOP

For thoughtful conference questions and so much more, from expert teacher/incoming NCTE President Franki Sibberson, order ASAP her inspired *Day-to-Day Assessment in the Reader's Workshop*. Co-authored with Principal Karen Szymusiack, these two veteran educators show you how assessment drives every instructional move and decision you make in your classroom. To help frame your analysis of assessment data, the authors suggest asking these questions:

- What are the child's strengths?
- When is the child most engaged during the day?
- What jumps out as a big goal for the child?
- Are their obvious patterns to her learning?
- Are the assessments consistent or do they tell us different things?
- How does the child's attitude about reading relate to performance?
- Do formal and informal assessments show the same things?

Once we have gathered answers to these questions, we ask ourselves the most important questions:

- What one or two goals are most critical for this child right now?
- What's next?

CAPTURE DATA WITH YOUR SMARTPHONE

We use our smartphones to memorialize important conferences, interesting book choices, text passages kids have navigated skillfully, dynamic book clubs, student-created anchor charts, reading partnerships, and anything else that strikes us in the course of a day. Photos and videos provide marvelous evidence of kids' progress to share with families electronically and/or in conferences. Many pictures in this book were snapped authentically in the moment. Of course, it's vital to have parental permission for any identifiable photos.

Step 3: Discuss and set goals in a student/family conference.

While working with the striver and his or her family, consider organizing the analysis into the Reader's Profile form on page 225, which we've framed around the four principles that define reading for us. Ideally, when possible, you will complete the form with the striver and his or her family members during Student/Family Conferences. The aim is to document evidence of reading strength—at home and at school—so you can discuss with the student and family members everything he or she is doing well as a reader and create a plan to help him or her overcome things that are still challenging.

To bolster the family partnership in your strivers' developing reading success, consider engaging your students and their families in creating "Strength-Focused Reading Portfolios."

BOOK NOTE
POWERFUL PARTNERSHIPS

Dr. Karen Mapp, one of our nation's leading authorities on family and community engagement, reminds us, "Conferences are a critical component of building strong partnerships with parents centered on their child's learning. When well planned and thoughtfully approached, these conferences are an ideal opportunity to strengthen and deepen your partnerships with parents"—especially in ways that benefit your strivers.

First and foremost, remember: Assessment is inquiry. You might think of yourself as a researcher in your own classroom, gathering data that you can use to shape your instruction and help your students see concrete evidence of their learning strengths. While below we suggest questions for Student/Family Conferences that ask the student to evaluate his or her progress over time (and, therefore, are more summative than our end-of-chapter ARR questions), feel free to ask questions that make sense to you and help guide your inquiry.

QUESTIONS TO GUIDE STUDENT/FAMILY CONFERENCES

- What have you read since we last met that you enjoyed? Tell us about your reading process and in what ways the text changed you.

- Let's discuss what you've written. What does it tell you about yourself as a reader, writer, and thinker?

- What projects have you participated in since we last met for our quarterly conference? Which ones did you most enjoy and why? What went well? What challenges did you encounter and why?

- What did you need to learn in order to complete these projects? Why is that learning valuable to you?

- Let's discuss your participation in classroom discussions. Can you tell us about the learning conversations you've had with me, your family, and your classmates and friends—at home and in school?

- How do you know when you're learning?

- How do reading, writing, and talking help you learn?

- What do you believe you're doing well? What would you like to do better?

- Let's think about the next learning goals for you. What would you like to list? (We recommend, of course, that you share your own learning goals for each striver—and invite family members to do the same.)

Reader's Profile

Evidence of _____ 's Reading Strength

(*name*)

Reading Is a Personal Process

Home

School

Reading Is a Social/Cultural Process

Home

School

Reading Is Thinking

Home

School

Reading Is Language

Home

School

Next Steps for _____ :

Teacher _____

PART III • TRANSFORM

The Strength-Focused Reading Portfolio

To bolster the family partnership in your strivers' developing reading success, consider engaging your students and their families in creating "Strength-Focused Reading Portfolios."

With your students, gather work that showcases what they can do, discuss it with them and perhaps family members, and invite them to evaluate it and use what they learn to move forward.

The ultimate goal of assessment as inquiry is to draw students into the inquiry and help them self-monitor, track, and document their own progress. What, for them, indicates reading growth and success? How might they gather evidence of their own development? One sure way to accomplish these goals and more is a strength-focused student portfolio. It's not a scrapbook, nor is it formally graded. It is a student- and teacher- (and, when possible, family-) curated selection of learning artifacts that reflect the students' learning journey.

What Goes in the Portfolio and Why

Students select entries and shape their portfolio presentation to demonstrate evidence of their strengths and learning potential. They might select:

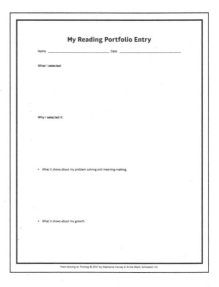

- lists of books they've read,

- reading journal entries,

- lists of favorite new words gleaned through reading,

- writing samples, or

- richly captioned photographs and video clips of science or social studies inquiry projects, class field trips, or any memorable, meaningful learning events that take place in the classroom or beyond.

Ideally, each entry is accompanied by a self-reflective note that explains why it's included in the portfolio (available at scholastic.com/ThriveResources).

From Striving to Thriving © 2017 by Stephanie Harvey & Annie Ward, Scholastic Inc.

Making Portfolios Work

Some teachers give their students time at the end of every week to think about their portfolio. It shouldn't feel like a time-draining obligation, but rather something to look forward to because it provides a moment of self-reflection on reading strengths and progress and, additionally, may invite a response from the teacher and/or peers and family members. There's no one right away to do portfolios; chart the path that makes sense to you and your students. Here is a step-by-step progression you might use to frame your portfolio process:

- Explain, discuss, and negotiate with students the goals and process of strength-focused student portfolios; in many ways, the portfolio is the ARR's physical manifestation.

- Discuss the range of entries the portfolios might showcase and the self-evaluative note each entry should include.

- Determine the criteria teachers, students, and family members will use to evaluate the portfolio, for example:

  - » evidence of effort and improvement

  - » quality of self-evaluation

  - » range of entries and overall presentation

  - » next-step goals

- Students self-evaluate their portfolio.

- Teachers review the portfolios and add their comments.

- Students present their portfolios to a wider audience including their families and peers.

Regardless of the questions you choose to ask during meetings with your strivers, you'll want to model them for all your students throughout the year. The aim remains the same: to capture the striver's strengths as a language user—a reader, writer, speaker, and listener. All language processes work together to support the striver as a successful thinker and learner who will develop a confident, capable, and fulfilling reading life.

As you collect data over time (daily, weekly, monthly, and quarterly) use the ARR (kidwatching notes and records from conferences), as well as the strivers' retellings, running records, written self-reflections, reading logs, and other sources.

Understanding Assessment as Inquiry

Assessment as inquiry informs us of the following three things:

1. **Our students' learning and progress.** By carefully watching kids, analyzing their work, and listening to what they say, we get a good idea of what they have learned and understood—or not learned and misunderstood.

2. **The direction of our future instruction.** Observation and responsive teaching go hand in hand. Based on the evidence we observe in strivers' work, we design responsive follow-up instruction—instruction that is tailored to their needs. They may need a different book, more time to read, more targeted instruction, or a needs-based small group. We plan our next steps based on what needs attention and elaboration, based on what each child is understanding or not.

3. **The quality of our past instruction.** If a striving reader isn't getting quality instruction, we need to find out why. As such, we rethink and redesign our instruction as necessary to see if another approach might work better. And in the process, we never let our strivers lose sight of their strengths as readers.

Engage in Your Own Inquiry-Based Assessment

While we want you to circle the wagons around all striving readers with a sense of urgency, you may want to identify one in particular to follow closely. Commit yourself to assessment as a process of inquiry. As the ILA/NCTE Task Force points out, once you make this commitment, your classroom becomes a "center of inquiry" (2010). You're able to embrace your role as a professional decision-maker, gather multi-faceted data, examine it on your own, discuss it with your colleagues, and share it with your students and their families. And then you can use the data to create a classroom reading community that will help all your students thrive.

You may find our recommendations in this section a bit open-ended. That's deliberate. The point is to find your own way into the inquiry process, establishing your own rhythm and routine for data collection, analysis, and conferring with your students. Ultimately, the most important thing is that you shift from a handful of summative assessments to a spectrum of formative assessments (including the ARR), learn to focus first on the child's strengths, and build from there. It's also important to work hard to help the child become an observer of his or her own reading process, learn to self-monitor for meaning, and set his or her own reading goals. The aim always is to help the striver see him- or herself as a reader with a rich reading life, plans, and goals. Finally, to the extent possible, find ways to reach out to families and involve them in the assessment inquiry process.

"To make a great dream come true, the first requirement is a great capacity to dream; the second is persistence."

—Cesar Chavez

CHAPTER 8

Advocate Tirelessly

One bright April morning, fourth-grade teacher Matt Porricelli led his class on a brisk walk to the Mamaroneck Public Library, just under a mile from school. Nasty storms had forced Matt to postpone the trip twice, but with school vacation approaching, he was determined to get there so the kids could borrow stacks of books to read over break. Matt knew that without library books, many of his students would not have access to reading material. A class survey had revealed that 17 of his students did not yet have a public library card; Matt subsequently learned that seven of his students had never been inside the library, including one whose apartment was directly across the street from the library with a view of the entrance.

Rather than waste time puzzling over why the majority of families hadn't yet tapped into this powerful local resource for their children, Matt decided to take the matter into his own hands. To families whose children did not have a card, he circulated the library's application and provided guidance until the applications were completed.

Librarians opened the library 30 minutes early and treated Matt's students like VIPs. By the end of the visit, the class had checked out 84 books. Five students downloaded the library's OverDrive app onto their personal devices, giving them access to e-books and audiobooks. On the walk back to school, kids shared their books and proudly clipped their library cards to their jackets with carabiners from the librarians. Natalia said, "I never realized how easy it is to go and get books. My babysitter and I walk by here every day!" Ashly exclaimed, "Next time, I'm going to bring a bigger bag so I can take home more books." To ensure that library patronage becomes a regular habit rather than a one-time experience, Matt is teaching kids how to reserve and renew books, skills they will practice on two more library trips before the end of the school year, with full support of school and district administrators.

All children deserve dedicated and energetic teachers like Matt. And all teachers deserve informed school leaders who encourage innovation and risk-taking, and who provide the resources necessary to bring sound ideas to fruition. It is a cruel irony that striving readers, who deserve and urgently require the greatest access to captivating books, often have the least access. It is also troubling that educators seeking to meet striving readers' needs with research-based approaches are often stymied by a lack of resources and, even worse, mandates to adopt unsound programs and fragmented interventions.

"Next time I'm going to bring a bigger bag so I can take home more books."

—ASHLY

Trying to do the right thing can be tiring and often lonely. So, we've written this chapter to put wind in your sails as you seek to get what you need for your students and for yourself. We've included a chart called "Vital Components of Reading: Research to Know" online at scholastic.com/ThriveResources. This chart boils down much of the research we've presented thus far to guide your actions and to inform others. Share it far and wide!

1. Be a literacy upstander.

An all-too-common mantra among teachers who are bombarded by unsound mandates is, "Shut the classroom door and do what works." While a closed-door approach may get you through the day, it deprives you and your students of the benefits that come from being a literacy upstander, one who actively engages colleagues in professional discourse.

For example, going against the grain on your own is expensive. Without systemic funding sources, you are likely to find yourself spending a lot of your own dollars purchasing materials and books for classroom libraries. According to *Money* magazine, most teachers spend around $500 on supplies and resources for their classrooms annually, and one in ten spends over $1,000 a year (White, 2006). While it may seem daunting to sway an administrator to prioritize independent reading, imagine the benefits of money allocated for school-wide textbooks, packaged reading programs, and/or test-prep materials being spent on authentic trade books. Depending on the level of autonomy your administrator has, he or she may appreciate your advocacy and guidance on how best to put limited resources to work.

And never forget: Research is your friend! Take the time needed to share pertinent research from the "Vital Components of Reading: Research to Know" chart with your administrators. Once your principal, for example, understands the benefits of "light reading" via comic books (Krashen & Ujiie, 1996), he or she might be more inclined to fund an infusion of graphic novels into your classroom library. And then, too, research arms you and your administrator with talking points when you encounter parents who question the appropriateness of reading graphic novels on school time.

Be a guardian of children's reading lives.

In this section, we provide "Top 10" lists for advocating with key populations like kids, families, and administrators, as well as ways to help kids advocate for themselves. By following this advice, you will truly become a guardian of children's reading lives.

TOP TEN
Moves to Advocate for Striving Readers Every Day

1. Get to know each reader in the round. Familiarize yourself with his or her family, interests, and life outside of school.

2. Use the ARR to identify and document each striver's reading and learning strengths; design curriculum and instruction that builds on what kids can do.

3. Help strivers understand their reading strengths and learn how to set goals for themselves, building on their strengths. Help kids and families understand that learning necessarily entails risk-taking and miscue-making. Help families support their strivers at home, understanding that development occurs over time.

4. Ensure each striving reader is well matched with high kid appeal and low effort-to-reward ratio books he or she can read and wants to read. Fill your room with engaging, culturally responsive books so every child can find him or herself in multiple titles.

5. BookTalk and encourage reading every day by providing ample time for kids to read in school while also encouraging reading at home. Send books home with every child every day. Limit homework; make reading the main event.

6. Teach comprehension strategies explicitly to give striving readers the tools they need to hurdle the background knowledge gap, move forward, and develop reading independence and agency.

7. Guard against striving readers being pulled out for interventions during your classroom literacy block. Interventions should supplement, not supplant, strivers' time with you and their classmates—make sure strivers who receive supplemental interventions have an active reading life that's full of real books!

8. Provide multiple entry points into reading by harnessing the full force of language: speaking, listening, and writing. Tap the meaning-making power of multimedia and the visual and dramatic arts as well.

9. Prevent a summer slide—and encourage a summer leap—by sending strivers home with books to read over long weekends, school vacations, and summer break.

10. Ensure children have unfettered access to school and public libraries all year long.

TOP TEN
Moves to Advocate for Families

1. Reach out to each family prior to the new school year. Introduce yourself and find out preferred modes of, times for, and language for communication. Get to know caregivers, siblings, and other close relatives, in addition to parents; if possible, arrange for a home visit.

2. Identify a translator if you don't speak a family's primary language. Make arrangements for oral and written communication across the year.

3. Invite parents to tell you about their child: his or her passions, hopes, fears, responsibilities, friendships, and significant life events. Ask families about their hoped-for goals for their student and share your goals as well.

4. Ask parents, grandparents, and caregivers about their occupations, hobbies, and areas of specialty. Might they share them with their child's class?

5. On back-to-school night, explain the importance of self-selected independent reading. Model how you think aloud while reading picture books, sharing questions, connections, and responses to the text. Help them understand what you believe about reading and why you teach and assess the ways in which you do. Follow up with families who aren't able to attend back-to-school night.

6. Communicate with families about the books striving readers are bringing home. You might also provide families with a list of general questions that they can use to initiate a conversation about the books their kids are reading; for example, "What surprised you about this book? How has it changed your thoughts and feelings?"

7. Urge families to provide a reliable time and calm place for students to read at home every day. Share that homework will consist mostly of reading without traditional worksheets.

8. Explain the importance of talk in children's literacy development in all primary languages—and thus, the importance of conversing at the dinner table, storytelling, sharing family lore, and talking about the texts family members are reading. Encourage family members to model their own reading lives for their children.

9. Ask families to secure public library cards for their children—and explain or demonstrate how if they're not sure.

10. Invite families to participate in family literature circles. Choose short texts such as magazine articles or short stories that are easy to read, translate as needed, and circulate electronically.

TOP TEN

Moves to Help Administrators Advocate for Students

1. Share research on reading development (summarized on pages 250–251) and the vital importance of providing children with access to books, choice of books, and time to read every day.

2. Offer to facilitate faculty workshops and parent coffees on the importance of voluminous, high-success reading.

3. Educate principals about the pernicious phenomenon of book deserts; ask for school library circulation limits to be increased or abolished.

4. Speak up if striving readers are pulled out for interventions during the literacy block. Collaborate with your colleagues to modify the schedule and propose alternative forms of instruction.

5. Invite administrators into your classroom during independent reading time; encourage them to confer with kids about what they are reading.

6. Share success stories: Provide artifacts and anecdotes of striving readers' growth.

7. Share the classroom library blueprint in Chapter 3, page 95. Request funds for books with specific examples of their appeal to striving readers.

8. Offer to organize "weed-a-thons": group time to clean out and inventory classroom libraries.

9. Stress the importance of buying new professional books so that you and your colleagues are up on the latest thinking about teaching and learning. Offer to facilitate faculty book clubs and/or faculty workshops to share key findings from those books. Make the point that reading professional books is a cost-effective and powerful form of professional development. Share pivotal professional research via social media.

10. Make administrators aware of valuable professional development opportunities (e.g., workshops and conferences). Request to take advantage of those opportunities and provide a detailed rationale.

TOP TEN

Moves to Help Students Advocate for Themselves

1. Help students understand what reading is and what readers do. Help them develop their own identity as readers, aware of their strengths and challenges with reading plans and goals.

2. Help kids develop a quiver of comprehension strategies and track their use to ensure they are constructing meaning when they read independently and come to difficult parts—and know what to do when they lose track of meaning. Understand that all readers miscue; self-monitor for miscues that interfere with meaning; otherwise, keep going!

3. Develop an intellectually vibrant classroom environment in which you honor your students' thinking; invite them to make their thinking audible and visible by routinely sharing examples of their questions, problem solving, and engagement with texts and inquiry projects.

4. Urge students to speak up for themselves. Model the language that communicates that awareness to others. Examples: "I really enjoy (specific genre) and understand how to read it, but sometimes I find (other genre) confusing. When books look really dense and long, I sometimes have difficulty getting into them."

5. Help kids develop strategies—when faced with complex text about a topic they care about or need to know about—to locate more accessible information by going online, listening to audiobooks or podcasts, viewing videos, interviewing specialists, etc.

6. Seek kids' opinions about books to procure for and weed out of the classroom library. Honor their suggestions.

7. Teach kids how to check out, reserve, and renew books from school and public libraries. Make sure they know library resources are theirs to borrow!

8. Model and teach kids how to participate in lively discussions about books and ideas; for example, how to express a different opinion using phrases such as, "I heard what _____ was saying. Here's another idea," "I beg to differ," "To me, it looks as if . . .," "I look at that a little differently . . ."

9. Create a socially/emotionally safe classroom in which students feel free to solicit help when they need it, by speaking up and using language that communicates their needs such as, "I understand how to . . . but I need a little help with . . .. Is there a time we can meet?" "I get this part, but am confused by this next part . . . " "I'm feeling a little overwhelmed; can we talk?"

10. Help students every day experience the joy and power of the Reading Zone.

In serving as the guardian of children's reading lives, your first job is to know the difference you make, even when kids are receiving interventions outside your classroom. Put another way, as Po realizes in the climactic scene of *Kung Fu Panda*, "There's no secret ingredient. It's just you." This means you must double down to provide access, choice, and time for each of your striving readers by insisting that each one has appealing independent reading books every day, whether or not he or she receives additional interventions. For example, middle school librarian Kelsey Cohen recently sent out this email, seeking a hot new graphic novel for a striving eighth-grade reader:

Subject: Reading SOS

Hi all,

Susan Hein has a reluctant eighth-grade reader who is dying to read *Dogman Unleashed*, the second book in the Dogman series. Our copy is MIA and the elementary librarians say their copies are checked out immediately upon return. Anyone happen to have a copy to share?! I'll come pick it up later today!

Thanks in advance, Kelsey

Kelsey L. Cohen
Hommocks Middle School Librarian
Mamaroneck UFSD

We often hear of "cascading disasters," in which everything that can go wrong does. Now imagine the opposite, "cascading victories," in which chains of positive events, spearheaded by committed educators, lead to highly productive outcomes for kids. The *Dogman* example is a cascading victory because:

- the striving reader knew what he wanted to read and advocated for himself. (Someone had made him aware of Dav Pilkey's new series.)

- the district recognizes humorous graphic novels as a worthwhile choice for independent reading.

- his English teacher consulted with the middle school librarian to locate a copy of the book he wanted.

- the librarian knew of this popular and highly accessible new release and had already added a copy to her collection.

- she reached out to elementary colleagues to procure an extra copy. When that didn't work, she reached out to Annie and Maggie Hoddinott, the literacy ambassador, knowing they would drop everything to track down a copy.

- Maggie had held a copy of this hot new title in reserve for precisely such a reading emergency; she delivered it to Kelsey, who put it in the child's hands by day's end.

Above all else, own the all-important responsibility of being the guardian of kids' reading lives; don't abdicate it or assume someone else is doing it.

Proactively request books.

Fortune favors the prepared. In high school, Annie's daughter Mimi would "pre-load" an electronic shopping cart with desired items from her favorite clothier, Modcloth, and forward the link to relatives seeking gift ideas for her. Take your cue from Mimi by maintaining a wish list of books so that you are poised to pounce if and when precious funds become available. Learn your school or district's approved book vendors and its required purchasing procedures. Submitting a properly formatted, ready-to-place order dramatically increases the likelihood of approval when time and resources are limited. If the answer is no, be polite but persistent and try again in a month. Then, if necessary, in another month. Gentle relentlessness keeps your needs in the forefront. Always pair requests with explanations of how specific kids will benefit.

Use the classroom library blueprint provided in Chapter 3 to weed and identify gaps in your collection. Be sure to save copies of egregiously dated and worn books to show your administrator and make a case for replenishment. Prepare to fill gaps in your collection by identifying appealing titles, using the reliable sources listed in Chapter 3. For example, to increase the number of books by Latino/a authors and illustrators, Annie's colleagues regularly request Pura Belpre Award winners or borrow them from the library. Over time, inventorying, weeding, and replenishing titles enables you to "build the library for the readers you expect."

To "customize your library for the readers you meet," particularly striving readers, find out about them! When you get a new class list, talk to the previous teachers of those kids about their interests and reading preferences. Identify books that might entice them, and have those books on hand when school opens,

From Striving to Thriving © 2017 by Stephanie Harvey & Annie Ward, Scholastic Inc.

either by ordering them or borrowing them from the library. In "With an Air of Expectancy," Katherine Bomer encourages us to build our classrooms from what we learn about our kids instead of imitating Pinterest postings, and she specifically mentions greeting children with hand-picked books: "What if our children could walk into a classroom at the beginning of a school year that said in the ways it was organized, and through the words and gestures we used, 'We are *expecting you*, precisely you'" (Glover & Keene, 2015).

2. Collect, analyze, and share data.

Although we have cited overwhelming research that voluminous, high-success reading turns striving readers into thriving readers, it's important to look well beyond test scores for evidence of that growth and to share that evidence with students, families, and administrators. Here are powerful ways to capture evidence of readers' growth:

 TIP

Middle school special educator Chrissy Alleva helps her students advocate for themselves by having them write a letter to their forthcoming teacher at the end of the school year. In these letters, students introduce themselves, detail their passions and curiosities, describe themselves as readers and writers, and offer their hopes for the year to come. Chrissy's colleagues delight in these letters, and most write back over the summer, paving the way for warm and strong relationships.

- **Case studies.** Gather items such as photographs of the child; inventories of her assets and interests; records of the books she's selected from preview stacks; reading logs; comments she's made about what she's reading; watershed books and/or series; teaching points from conferences and guided reading groups; dates, forms, and topics of home communication; parents' perspectives on her reading life; and other data such as running records, miscue analysis results, independent reading levels, fluency rates, and sight-word vocabulary.

  Assemble these items chronologically and look for causes and effects. Note the impact of specific books or series, as well as teaching moves you've made on the child's reading development. For example, fourth-grader Cassidy blossomed as a reader of graphic novels following a guided reading lesson in which her teacher taught the conventions of reading illustration frames and speech balloons. The timing of that lesson coupled with the availability of the *Lumberjanes* series resulted in accelerated growth; Cassidy's parents reported an increase in reading at home and heightened empathy for others.

- **Kidwatching and conferring records.** The notes you take on clipboards, tablets, or laptops are a goldmine. Be sure to capture kids' exact language as best you can. Record the actions you've taken based on what you've seen and heard, and note the impact.

- **Reading logs and ladders.** Following the paths readers have taken from text to text sheds light on their growth and informs your book-matching efforts with other readers. While teachers often lament when kids linger in and reread familiar series, the volume they achieve in reading those beloved books triggers demonstrable growth by other measures.

- **Students' written and videotaped self-reflections.** When we listen carefully, kids tend to tell us precisely what they need us to know. Yandel's statement in Chapter 4, captured on an iPhone during a home visit, proves it: "Teachers should ask kids what they're really interested in and try to find the books that have those things in them…. I think that would help teachers help students become better readers so they can read and learn at the same time." Giving kids opportunities to reflect on their growth fosters agency and efficacy.

- **Library circulation histories.** While reviewing data from the Follett Web Circulation System, Annie and her colleagues noted a pattern that striving readers checked out books mainly during scheduled library periods, whereas thriving readers did so not only during those periods, but also before school, after school, and at lunch. Library patronage is an important form of self-advocacy that can be taught and tracked. So, teach striving readers to avail themselves to the library whenever time allows—and track their visits and choices.

Payton has learned to self-advocate.

From Striving to Thriving © 2017 by Stephanie Harvey & Annie Ward, Scholastic Inc.

- **Rates of growth relative to district independent reading benchmarks.** In addition to monitoring students' independent reading levels at several points across the year, it's important to study the rate of change relative to established benchmarks to gauge whether striving readers are making the progress they will need to close the gap and thrive. Even when a striving reader is making modest gains (e.g., moving from a Level K book in September to a Level L book in January), he is likely slipping further behind because the gap between his level and grade level expectations is widening. Studying rates of growth fosters an appropriate sense of urgency around striving readers' trajectories.

3. Keep going and keep growing.

When Annie worked for the New York City Department of Education, her colleagues, led by Region 9 Superintendent Shelley Harwayne, organized Book Lovers' Day, an uplifting conference filled with talks from authors and literacy leaders. Annie captured, and rereads often, this nugget from Jim Burke about the importance of ongoing professional growth: "Make a commitment to nourish yourself, to bring good things in. You don't want to be an unfed pond—you need to keep things streaming in. Be a warrior; stay engaged. Create a classroom full of encounters with ideas. Fill kids with possible selves. Help them discover the lives they're trying to lead" (2004). As busy as we are attending to children's needs, we must make time for our own learning. Doing so keeps us fresh, curious, knowledgeable, and motivated.

Form a supportive professional community.

While few of us get to choose our colleagues, we can choose the company we keep at work, the stances we take, and the ways we talk about children. In 2001, researcher Donald Graves undertook a major study on the professional energy levels of educators. He conducted extensive interviews with teachers all over the country, asking three simple questions: "What gives you energy? What takes it away? And what for you is a waste of time?" Steph was lucky enough to be one of the interviewees. Don published his findings in a concise, beautiful book called *The Energy to Teach*, in which he encourages us, among other things, to seek out colleagues who give us energy and to avoid those who sap it.

We supply energy to others when we:

- Watch our language. Remove labels such as "struggling reader" and "low" from our vocabulary and replace them with constructive descriptions: "Brandon has a strong preference for nonfiction, particularly compendia. He is open to reading fiction related to television shows such as *SpongeBob SquarePants and Gravity Falls,* for which he has background knowledge."

- Know and discuss children's assets: "Brandon loves learning little-known facts and sharing them with others."

- Replace judgment with empathy: "Mom and Dad both work long hours. Brandon has witnessed some difficult situations and can be emotionally vulnerable. He thrives when I express interest in him as a person and let him know I care about him."

- Share positive anecdotes: "During indoor recess, Brandon and Kendrick pored over *Wacky Facts About the Human Body* . . . and giggled together."

- Adopt an inquiry stance. Pose genuine questions that require kidwatching and data gathering to gather answers: "I wonder whether Brandon would like *The 13-Story Treehouse*? It's fiction, but it's irreverent and cartoony. Let's see how he reacts when I book-talk it. I've noticed that he responds to social energy when books go viral."

- Help colleagues recognize and move beyond their assumptions about children and families: "I agree that the town library is a wonderful

resource, but when you say that Brandon's parents should take him there, aren't you assuming that they have the time outside of work and transportation to do so?"

As actor Alan Alda urges, "Begin challenging your own assumptions. Your assumptions are your windows on the world. Scrub them off every once in a while, or the light won't come in."

Attend to Your Own Professional Growth.

When Annie started teaching middle school English in 1988, she was fortunate to find herself among upbeat, child-centered colleagues in a district that encouraged innovation. Even so, literacy-related professional development opportunities were rare, consisting mainly of professional books that the department chair ordered. Nancie Atwell's seminal *In the Middle* introduced Annie to the reading workshop model. The following year, transcripts of Georgia Heard's wise and gentle student conferences in *For the Good of the Earth and the Sun* inspired Annie to implement a poetry unit fueled by mentor texts rather than prescriptions. Annie is grateful to her first department chair, Joyce Berrian, for throwing her a lifeline of professional texts and the educational leaders who write them.

Times have certainly changed. Whereas Annie endured long dry spells between bursts of enlightenment from new professional books, the Internet and social media now flood educators with daily streams of material that range from peer-reviewed research to inflammatory opinions. The good news is that professional development opportunities are ubiquitous, portable, and flexible; the catch is that we must identify reliable, useful, and stimulating ones. To maximize productivity, we must be discerning, disciplined consumers and responsible contributors. Mining our own habits of growing as professionals, we recommend the following actions:

Follow Reliable Blogs. How fortunate we are that so many literacy leaders generously polish and publish their thinking on blogs between conferences and professional books! Blog posts tend to be more spontaneous than peer-reviewed articles, but more substantive and well-crafted than, say, Facebook posts or tweets—a happy medium! These are a few of our favorite blogs, which are chock-full of book recommendations, wise commentary, policy updates, and advocacy strategies.

RELIABLE BLOGS

Nerdy Book Club
nerdybookclub.wordpress.com

Co-founded by Donalyn Miller, Colby Sharp, Cindy Minnich, and Katherine Sokolowski, *Nerdy Book Club* is a vast, inclusive network of book enthusiasts. The club publishes each year's Nerdy Book Award winners and an array of Nerdy Bookcasts.

The Book Whisperer
bookwhisperer.com/blog

Donalyn Miller's website includes her blog and a treasure trove of other resources, such as an archive of her *Book Whisperer* columns from *Education Week*, a lengthy "Blogroll" of recommended literacy blogs, and a repository of presentations.

The Goddess of YA Literature
professornana.livejournal.com

When she is not feverishly book-talking, Teri Lesesne is busy dispensing "Pearls from the Goddess," candid and eye-opening takes on educational topics and trends. Teri's provocative journeys of thought help readers develop and defend their own stances.

To Make a Prairie
tomakeaprairie.wordpress.com

Named for an Emily Dickinson poem, Vicki Vinton's blog is elegant and deeply satisfying. Each essay is an exquisitely crafted rumination on classroom practice, illustrated by carefully chosen student writing and artwork that deserves to be read, reread, and savored.

A Year of Reading
readingyear.blogspot.com

Franki Sibberson, 25-year veteran teacher, librarian, and 2018 President of NCTE, and Mary Lee Hahn, writer and amazing elementary teacher, maintain a blog that recommends books kids will love, suggests tried-and-true teaching strategies and techniques, and offers literacy teaching and constructivist theory and practice.

Crawling out of the Classroom
crawlingoutoftheclassroom.
wordpress.com

Jess Lifshitz's blog illustrates how her students use books to explore social justice, identity, and diversity and pursue compelling inquiry projects.

Brain Pickings
brainpickings.org

Maria Popova's posts appear on Sunday mornings—sumptuous ideas to be enjoyed over coffee. Maria's carefully curated book reviews are generously laced with quotations and illustrations.

From Striving to Thriving © 2017 by Stephanie Harvey & Annie Ward, Scholastic Inc.

Open Culture OpenCulture.com	Founded by Dan Coleman, Associate Dean of Stanford University's Continuing Studies program, this blog is one of the best sources of free cultural and educational information on the Internet. Delving into a wide range of historic, scientific, social, literary, and artistic topics daily, *Open Culture* never ceases to feature intriguing stories, topics, and issues for further investigation.
Watch. Connect. Read. mrschureads.blogspot.com	Children's librarian John Schumaker's (a.k.a. Mr. Schu) appetite for great children's books is exceeded only by the energy with which he shares them. As a blogger, his mission is to "explore children's literature through book trailers." To scroll through Mr. Schu's posts is to encounter a rollicking parade of irresistible books and author commentary.

Tune Into YouTube. Once lauded by *Entertainment Weekly* for "providing a safe home for piano-playing cats, celeb goof-ups, and overzealous lip-synchers" (2009), YouTube has become an empowering, go-to resource for people looking to learn just about anything, including how to meet the needs of striving readers. Publishers and professional organizations post book trailers and workshop videos, and many literacy leaders maintain their own YouTube channels to make their ideas widely available. For example, Teri Lesesne and Karin Perry post lively, informal book talks on their YouTube channel, *Professors Providing Professional Development* (PPPD): youtube.com/channel/UCSaYxeoQmxa8ECTkGO7TfOg. Annie likes to prop up her phone on the kitchen counter and take in Teri and Karin's recommendations while she's cooking dinner!

Let a Little Birdie Tell You. Like YouTube, Twitter has also morphed as it has grown. Co-founder Evan Williams notes its transformation "from a social network to an information network," meaning that people are using it less to share breakfast choices and more to share professional information (Lapowsky, 2013). Unaware of its capacity as a professional development tool, Annie was mightily surprised when Steph raved about Twitter during a visit to Mamaroneck and invited her to peer into her phone. As Steph scrolled through tweets with links from influential figures such as Sir Ken Robinson and Yong Zhao, Annie realized that the 140-character limit is the tip of the iceberg and that the linked resources are a professional gold mine.

Many literacy leaders who actively blog also tweet, providing a real-time reflection of their latest thinking. Here is a list of some of our favorite tweeters.

Our Favorite Tweeters

Nerdy Book Club @nerdybookclub	Stephen King @StephenKing
Donalyn Miller @donalynbooks	Stephen Krashen @skrashen
Teri Lesesne @professornana	Kylene Beers @KyleneBeers
Mr. Schu @MrSchuReads	Cornelius Minor @MisterMinor
Penny Kittle @pennykittle	Nell Duke @nellkduke
Kelly Gallagher @KellyGToGo	Carol Jago @caroljago
Maria Popova @Brainpicker	Chad Everett @chadeverett
Mary Howard @DrMaryHoward	*And don't forget about the two of us!*
Colby Sharp @colbysharp	Steph @stephharvey49
Valerie Strauss @valeriestrauss	Annie @annietward

In addition to following individual literacy leaders, it's exciting to participate in Twitter chats and conferences via hashtags. For example, #TitleTalk is a Sunday night Twitter chat that's moderated by Donalyn Miller and Colby Sharp. As you try to keep up with the dynamite book recommendations flashing across your screen, you'll feel like Lucy and Ethel in the chocolate factory! At the start of most chats and conferences, organizers specify a hashtag for participants to use as they tweet about sessions. This means you're never closed out; following the hashtag enables you to tap into photos, quotes, presenters' slides, and handouts, whether physically or virtually present. Annie has "attended" several Boothbay Literacy retreats this way, almost smelling the Maine salt air.

Journal Tracking. We recommend making a habit of reading educational journals such as *The Reading Teacher, Language Arts,* and *Educational Leadership,* which offer a window into what's new in classroom practice, where we are headed, and how educational research is impacting our work. Let's face it, teaching every day and thinking about how to best support our students takes a lot of time. Our nightstands are piled high with reading material we keep hoping to get to. To ensure that we are getting to this information and reading the research, Steph suggests a process called journal tracking. Here's how it works: Your principal orders a range of journals—on teaching reading, science, social studies, math, and so forth. Teachers from each grade level choose to read one of the journals thoroughly each month. So perhaps the third-grade teachers are responsible for *The Reading Teacher*. Those teachers divvy up the articles and carefully read them, identifying ones that would be a good fit for a particular grade level or specialty and making sure those articles go to the educators who will benefit most from them. The administrative staff chooses a journal too, often *Educational Leadership*, and follows the same procedure. This process builds a more collaborative school community because staff members are engaged, take responsibility for their journal assignment, and think about other teams, other teachers, and their needs.

Network and Affiliate: Advocate for Your Professional Learning. For teachers of reading and lovers of literacy, our "mother ships" are the National Council of Teachers of English (NCTE), the International Literacy Association (ILA), and the American Library Association (ALA). Membership includes the must-read professional journals we cite above, as well as *Voices from the Middle* and *Literacy Today*. The annual conventions of these organizations provide transformational professional development opportunities. Applying for district sponsorship to attend is well worth the effort. The NCTE, ILA, and ALA websites contain powerful professional resources. For example, NCTE publishes pithy, research-based position statements that can be used to defend instructional approaches. Finally, these leading organizations have state and regional affiliates that offer many professional development opportunities, including local conferences.

VITAL COMPONENTS OF READING: RESEARCH TO KNOW

Components That Support Reading Development	Key Research
Relationships Children put forth effort when they sense their teacher knows, respects, and values them. Strong and supportive relationships between teachers and students are the bedrock of all learning, including learning to read.	• Stipek, D. (2006). "Relationships Matter." *Educational Leadership, 64* (1): 46-49. • Pianta, R. C. (1999). *Enhancing Relationships Between Children and Teachers.* Washington, DC: American Psychological Association.
Growth Mindset All children have the capacity to read capably and voluminously. It is harmful to label some children "high flyers" and others "strugglers." Striving readers thrive under the right conditions, and it's our job to create those conditions.	• Dweck, C. S. (2007). *Mindset: The New Psychology of Success.* New York: Ballantine Books. • Johnston, P. H. (2012). *Opening Minds: Using Language to Change Lives.* Portland, ME: Stenhouse.
Access Readers need abundant, daily access to appealing texts. Be aware, though, even when they are surrounded by books, striving readers find themselves in de facto book deserts if they can't read those books. Children living in poverty typically have far fewer books in the home and have less access to public libraries.	• Elley, W. B. (2000). "The Potential of Book Floods for Raising Literacy Levels." *International Review of Education, 46* (3-4): 233-255. • Worthy, J. & Roser, N. (2010). "Productive Sustained Reading in a Bilingual Class." In E. H. Hiebert & D. R. Reutzel (Eds.), *Revisiting Silent Reading: New Directions for Reachers and Researchers.* Newark, DE: International Reading Association. • Alexander, K. L., Entwistle, D. R. & Olsen, L. S. (2007). "Lasting Consequences of the Summer Learning Gap." *American Sociological Review, 72* (2): 167-180. • Neuman, S. B. & Celano, D. C. (2012). *Giving Our Children a Fighting Chance: Poverty, Literacy, and the Development of Information Capital.* New York: Teachers College Press. • Neuman, S. B. & Celano, D. C. (2012). "Worlds Apart: One City, Two Libraries, and Ten Years of Watching Inequality Grow." *American Educator, 36* (3): 13–23. • Wong, A. (2016). "Where Books Are All But Nonexistent." *The Atlantic,* July 15.
Choice Choice is primal and motivating. The bulk of reading children do needs to be reading they have selected themselves.	• Guthrie, J. T., Wigfield, A. & Klauda, S. L. (2012). "Adolescents' Engagement in Academic Literacy." Retrieved from http://www.cori.umd.edu/research-publications/2012_adolescents_engagement_ebook.pdf • Allington, R. L. (2011). *What Really Matters for Struggling Readers: Designing Research-Based Programs.* Boston: Pearson. • Wilhelm, J. & Smith, M. (2013). "The Most Important Lesson Schools Can Teach Kids About Reading: It's Fun." *The Atlantic,* November 11.
Engagement Engaged reading is linked to every positive outcome imaginable—including a longer life! It's important to make sure that what children are reading is compelling to them. This can best be determined in reader-to-reader, heart-to-heart conferences, rather than by posing traditional comprehension questions.	• Sullivan, A. & Brown, M. (2013). "Social Inequalities in Cognitive Scores at Age 16: The Role of Reading." London: Centre for Longitudinal Studies. • Bavishi, A., Slade, M. D. & Levy, B. R. (2016). "A Chapter a Day: Association of Book Reading With Longevity." *Social Science & Medicine. 164:* 44–48. • Kittle, P. (2012). *Book Love: Developing Depth, Stamina, and Passion in Adolescent Readers.* Portsmouth, NH: Heinemann. • Wilhelm, J. & Smith, M. (2013). *Reading Unbound: Why Kids Need to Read What They Want—and Why We Should Let Them.* New York: Scholastic.
Time Children need copious amounts of time to read in school, particularly because we cannot assume that they are given that time at home nor an environment that's conducive to reading.	• Allington, R. L. (2011). *What Really Matters for Struggling Readers: Designing Research-Based Programs.* Boston: Pearson. • Anderson, R. C., Wilson P. T. & Fielding, L. G. (1988). "Growth in Reading and How Children Spend Their Time Outside of School." *Reading Research Quarterly, 23* (3): 285–303. • Beers, K. & Probst, R. E. (2017). *Disrupting Thinking: Why How We Read Matters.* New York: Scholastic. (See page 136 on the benefits of an extra ten minutes of reading a day.)

From Striving to Thriving © 2017 by Stephanie Harvey & Annie Ward, Scholastic Inc.

Components That Support Reading Development	Key Research
Volume All readers develop through voluminous reading—by turning page after compelling page. Children need to read a *lot* in school and at home.	• Anderson, R. C., Wilson P. T. & Fielding, L. G. (1988). "Growth in Reading and How Children Spend Their Time Outside of School." *Reading Research Quarterly, 23* (3): 285–303. • Miller, D. (2015). "I've Got Research. Yes, I Do. I've Got Research. How About You?" Book Whisperer blog, February 8. https://bookwhisperer.com/2015/02/08/ive-got-research-yes-i-do-ive-got-research-how-about-you/
Success All readers develop through "high-success" reading, meaning pleasurable, easy reading. They need to be reading highly accessible, appealing texts most of the time.	• Allington. R. L. http://www.teachersread.net/papers-and-articles • Krashen, S. http://www.sdkrashen.com/
Growth When readers are on an upward developmental spiral, they naturally grow into and outgrow their reading tastes and preferences. Copious amounts of "narrow reading" within a single series, genre, or topic of interest lay the foundation for readers to tackle incrementally more complex texts.	• Krashen, S. (2004). "The Case for Narrow Reading." *Language Magazine, 3* (5): 17–19. http://www.sdkrashen.com/content/articles/narrow.pdf • Lesesne, T. (2010). *Reading Ladders: Leading Students From Where They Are to Where We'd Like Them to Be.* Portsmouth, NH: Heinemann. • Atwell, N. & Merkel, A. A. (2016). *The Reading Zone: How to Help Kids Become Skilled, Passionate, Habitual, Critical Readers.* New York: Scholastic. (comes with rich embedded videos)
Year-Round Support Allowing children to choose and keep 12 to 15 high-interest books for summer reading has been shown to minimize the "summer slide," more so than traditional summer school. This is especially true for children living in poverty.	• Cahill, C., Horvath, K., McGill-Franzen, A. & Allington, R. (2013). *No More Summer-Reading Loss.* Portsmouth, NH: Heinemann. • McGill-Franzen, A., Ward, N. & Cahill, M. (2016). "Summers: Some Are Reading, Some Are Not! It Matters." *The Reading Teacher, 69* (6): 585–596. • Dunagin, J. (2017). "New Research from Public Education Partners and Scholastic Confirms Positive Impact of Supporting Summer Reading for K–5 Students in Greenville, SC." http://publicedpartnersgc.org/make-summer-count-press-conference-2017/

Components That Do Not Support Reading Development	Key Research
Incentives and Extrinsic Rewards While many teachers report short-term gains from incentives to read (e.g., stickers, prizes, pizza) and extrinsic measures (e.g., Accelerated Reader), these "rewards" do not lead to long-term gains and, in fact, may be detrimental. The best incentive to read is a compelling, just-right book.	• Kohn, A. (1994). "The Risk of Rewards." http://www.alfiekohn.org/article/risks-rewards/ • Krashen, S. (2003). "The (Lack of) Experimental Evidence Supporting the Use of Accelerated Reader." *Journal of Children's Literature, 29* (2): 9, 16–30. • Marinack, B.A. & Gambrell, L. (2016), *No More Reading for Junk: Best Practices for Motivating Readers.* Portsmouth, NH: Heinemann.
Phonics-Based Interventions After First Grade Although decontextualized, explicit, multisensory phonics intervention programs have been shown to be somewhat effective in the primary grades, there is no evidence pointing to their effectiveness beyond those grades. The primary, most reliable intervention for intermediate kids is a stream of good books.	• Allington, R. L. (2009). *What Really Matters in Response to Intervention: Research-Based Designs.* Boston: Pearson. • Allington, R. L. (2011). *What Really Matters in Response to Struggling Readers: Designing Research-Based Designs.* Boston: Pearson. • Allington, R. L. (2014). *What Really Matters for Middle School Readers: From Research to Practice.* Boston: Pearson. • Ivey, G. & Baker, M.I. (2004). "Phonics Instruction for Older Students? Just Say No." *What Research Says About Reading, 61* (6): 35–39.

Closing Thought

"The best part of life is not just surviving, but thriving, with passion and compassion and humor and style and generosity and kindness."

—MAYA ANGELOU

PRACTICES AND LESSONS

Embracing Mistakes Through Story

Share stories about innovations and successes that have come from mistakes, repeated attempts, and frequent failures, as well as simply by accident.

 WHY

It's tough to convince strivers that mistakes lead to innovation and success because most of them have spent too much time feeling embarrassed and ashamed for making them. So they may not believe that mistakes should be valued. To counter that, we share stories of amazing accomplishments that have been made by people who haven't let failure stop them. We also point out accomplishments that have emerged entirely by accident. We need kids to understand that successful people rarely get it right the first time; to be successful we have to have confidence in ourselves, make an effort, and keep trying until we get results.

 WHEN

Share these stories throughout the year, but especially right from the start to nip kids' misconceptions about mistake-making in the bud.

 HOW

Many great successes began as failures. Stories abound of extraordinary people who embraced mistakes, learned from them, and went on to change the world. Here are a few to share with your students.

1. Innovator, entrepreneur, and inventor Elon Musk started SpaceX, the first private company to transport cargo—and likely people one day—through space. The company began with one failure after another. The rocket exploded in each of the company's first three transport attempts, in 2006, 2007, and 2008, with several more

calamitous explosions as recently as 2016. Musk views these failures as a necessary part of innovation. Check out this website to see some of the explosions: timeline. com/spacex-musk-rocket-failures-c22975218fbe. Kids will be enthralled. In 2015, SpaceX reached one of its most important goals: safely returning a vertical rocket to the ground. As of this printing, the company has had a number of exciting and successful launches. From each launch, the SpaceX team has learned something to improve the next one. Musk says, "When something is important enough, you do it even if the odds are not in your favor."

2. Henry Ford went bankrupt five times before inventing the internal-combustion engine and successfully manufacturing the Model A car.

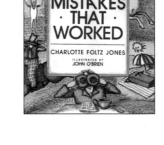

3. When working on the light bulb, Thomas Edison famously said, "I haven't failed. I just found 10,000 ways that didn't work."

4. In his book *Mastery* (2013), Robert Green says, "Think of it this way: There are two kinds of failure. The first comes from never trying out your ideas because you are afraid, or because you are waiting for the perfect time. This kind of failure you can never learn from, and such timidity will destroy you. The second kind comes from a bold and venturesome spirit. If you fail in this way, the hit that you take to your reputation is greatly outweighed by what you learn. Repeated failure will toughen your spirit and show you with absolute clarity how things must be done. In fact, it is a curse to have everything go right on your first attempt. You will fail to question the element of luck, making you think that you have the golden touch."

Kids love stories of innovations that resulted by sheer accident: Post-it Notes, champagne, the Slinky, Silly Putty, Coca-Cola, and others. Choose those you would most like to share. For more stories of interest to kids, check out *Mistakes That Worked* by Charlotte Foltz Jones.

Textual Lineage

Create your textual lineage (Tatum, 2008) to share the impact of reading on your identity and life, which serves as a model for students to create their own textual lineage.

✷ WHY

Many striving readers simply don't see the value in reading. We share our textual lineage—our own literate lives—with them so they can see the impact reading has had on us and the potential it has to transform them. We present a variety of genres and text types—books, magazines, essays, comics, graphic novels—so strivers get the message that, as literacy advocate and former principal Shelley Harwayne says, reading "widely and wildly" can change us. We want striving readers to understand that, in many ways, we are what we read!

✷ WHEN

Creating a textual lineage takes time. In fact, it is a never-ending process. We often begin the exercise during the summer or on the weekends, when we have time to seriously consider what to include. Early in the year, before we introduce our textual lineage, we share with students one important book that has influenced us and explain why. Later in the fall, we share our textual lineage over several days (see page 57). Then, whenever we read a book that has a major impact on us, we let kids know it (*"Wow I just read a book that really changed me, let me tell you about it . . ."*) and add it to our textual lineage.

✷ HOW

To build community and common understanding, we share our textual lineage in the whole-class meeting space. If we have access to all the texts that we have included, we bring them in. Holding them up, paging through them, and sharing the stories behind them has a big impact on striving readers, particularly if some of the books are from our childhood. If we don't have copies of the books, we share images of the covers.

Here's a transcript of Steph sharing her childhood textual lineage:

A Hole Is to Dig by Ruth Krauss is the first book I remember. I scribbled on it with purple crayon, and my mom scolded me. But I was trying to replicate writing, probably my first recognition that the words we read represent the language we speak. And there is a line in the book that says, ". . . mashed potatoes are so everybody has enough." Being one of five kids, I can relate, and I still love mashed potatoes!

The Sailor Dog by Margaret Wise Brown begins, "Born at sea in the teeth of a gale the sailor was a dog." I loved that lead so much; all I wanted to do was sail around the world with Scuppers. I loved the people he met in his travels and their exotic clothes. This book is probably one of the reasons I love adventure travel to this very day.

"If I ran the zoo," said young Gerald McGrew, "I'd make a few changes, that's what I'd do." My husband says Dr. Seuss's *If I Ran the Zoo* represents the control freak in me, always wanting to take control and change things. Who knows? Could be.

The Nancy Drew books were the only books I read growing up where girls could do the kinds of hair-raising, adventurous things normally reserved for boys. I was mesmerized by Nancy's confidence, skill, and power. I loved every book in the series and was forever drawn to series books because of her.

Classic Illustrated Comics made me a reader. They cost 15 cents, and I got an allowance of 25 cents a week, so I bought one every week and had ten cents left over for candy. I now collect them on eBay. They tell classic stories, swashbuckling adventures, and fairy tales in graphic form. I knew all of Shakespeare's plays before having read them in their original form. I had tons of background knowledge for classic novels because I read them as comics, and the stories were and are amazing.

• • • • •

The next step is for our students to create their own textual lineages, keeping in mind that striving readers may not have the history of texts necessary to do that. Often they have not had the rich reading experiences that thriving readers have. So we read aloud many books early in the year, which might give strivers some possibilities for their own lineage. We also search for books at their level on topics they're interested in and care about, and invite them to read those books, and decide whether to include any of them in their lineage.

Areas of Specialty: AOS

Recognize that every person in the school has an area of specialty—something he or she knows and cares about deeply. Establish AOS with students and share them throughout the school.

 WHY

Everyone has a specialty. Ricardo loves black holes. Suzanna knows a ton about dinosaurs. We have never met a child who doesn't have at least one interest. Although striving readers may not be crazy for reading when we first meet them, they are rife with interests—sports, skateboards, video games, animals, and so forth. We want all kids to recognize that they are specialists in something, so we establish a way for them, as well as adults in the school community, to share their specialties far and wide.

 WHEN

We begin to establish Areas of Specialty, or AOS, at the beginning of the year. That way, no child goes long without knowing that he or she has a specialty and can make a unique contribution. Everyone in the school, children and adults alike, participate in the AOS project.

 HOW

Every single person in the school is a specialist in something, be it cooking, painting, rock climbing . . . whatever! We begin by sharing what a specialist is. A specialist is someone who

- knows a lot about something,
- cares a lot about something,
- wants to learn more about it, and
- wants to teach someone else about it.

Then, to model, the teacher shares three things that he or she specializes in, based on that criteria. For Steph, these might include

- teaching literacy
- hiking in the mountains
- women in politics

Next, the teacher shares what she knows about these topics, why she cares about them, and what more she would like to learn about them.

Finally, she asks that kids jot at least three things they specialize in. Donald Graves believed that if you ask kids for at least three things, you will most certainly get at least one. Whereas when you ask for only one, too many kids come up with none. This is particularly true of strivers.

Once kids have jotted their specialties, we have them turn, talk, share, and choose one they most want to learn more about. We interact with kids to support them to come up with their specialties. Some do so before we even confer with them; others need more support. Strivers, in particular, may not believe they know enough about anything to be a specialist. So we confer with them and assure them that they do have a specialty, one that is every bit as important as anyone else's in the class.

During the next month, kids research and learn more about their chosen specialty. They write informational books complete with graphic features that contain at least three things they know about their specialty, three things they care about related to their specialty, and three things they learned through research. These books are housed on an AOS classroom library shelf, or in an AOS basket or niche in the room.

Additionally, we display a chart with all kids' names, photos, and their specialties so that each child is recognized and valued for his or her own specialty. Similar charts are placed in the front hallway or posted on the school website, so everyone knows who to consult to get information on a particular specialty. This public acknowledgment is particularly efficacious for striving readers.

The AOS project can go many directions. Kids and teachers can offer afterschool classes on their AOS. The teacher can arrange a time during the day for kids to teach their AOS and learn from others. The school can host an AOS day where kids and teachers both share their AOS and learn from one another. Or, more informally, kids can chat with one another and other adults in the school if they need advice from a specialist on a particular topic. As the year progresses, kids and teachers continue to share their AOS and learn from each other.

Read, Synthesize Important Information, and Jot Down Thinking

When reading, kids need to merge their thinking with the text information. At the same time, they need to separate their thinking—their own ideas—from text information. We share an article written for upper-elementary and middle-school kids called "You Can Grow Your Intelligence" (mindsetworks.com/websitemedia/youcangrowyourintelligence.pdf) and model our thinking in an interactive read-aloud.

Preparation
We hand out a copy of the article to each student, along with a two-column thinksheet titled "What the article is about/What it makes me think or wonder about," a clipboard, and a pencil.

① Connect and Engage

Introduce the idea of fixed and growth mindsets by, perhaps, telling a quick version of "The Tortoise and the Hare." Explain that scientists talk about the brain as elastic; they use the term *brain elasticity*. Have kids turn and talk about what that might mean.

② Model

Share the thinksheet. *When readers read, they need to merge their thinking with the information to better learn, understand, and remember the information. But it is important to separate our thoughts and ideas from the writer's information. As I read, I'm going to sift through the most important information and jot that down in the left-hand column. That way, we are sure to get the information as the writer intended. In the right-hand column I will jot down my thinking about the information.*

Share the article and have students preview it and talk about what they notice.

Okay, I am going to read a bit of this article on growth mindset and show you how I write down what the article is about and what it makes me think about.

I read the first paragraph, which explains that many people think intelligence is fixed and that people are born either smart or dumb.

Whoa, I have a lot of thoughts about that. I am not comfortable with what this says.

Write: "Many people think we are born either smart or dumb and stay that way forever." in the left column.

Now I'm going to write my thoughts about that on the right-hand side.

Write: "Why even go to school if this were true, I don't believe it. I've seen so many kids grow really smart by reading and thinking and working hard." Have kids turn and talk about what they think about this so far.

③ Guide

Now let's do this together. Jot down what you learned so far in the left-hand column and any thoughts, questions, or reactions you have on the right-hand side.

Keep reading and reasoning through the article for another page while the kids jot their thinking and turn and talk about the information on cue.

④ Practice

Okay, now it's time for you to partner up and continue to read, reason through the text, talk about the information, and jot the information and your thinking on the thinksheet. Take turns reading after each section. And remember to be an active listener. Jot down your thinking while your partner is reading and then talk about it.

⑤ Share

Invite kids back to the circle and have partners share one example of the information they recorded in the left-hand column and one example of the thinking they did on the right. This way they both get a chance to share. After hearing from three or four partners, since time is short, have remaining partners pair up to share. That way everyone can express his or her voice.

Great thinking today, friends. You did a nice job of recording the writer's ideas and your own thoughts about the information. We will be thinking about how to grow our brains throughout the year. This article gives us a pretty good idea of how the brain works when learning. All of us can grow more knowledgeable and thoughtful by reading, writing, and working hard. Thanks so much.

Wonder Walls, Wonder Books, and Wonder Boxes

Create structures to hold thinking, make wonder visible, and encourage collaboration with others.

❋ WHY

We build in time to capture and hold kids' wonderings because, again, curiosity is contagious! When we make kids' questions audible and/or visible for all, curiosity spreads unfettered. Kids ask questions and research is not far behind.

❋ WHEN

We launch Wonder Walls with the whole class early in the year, perhaps even on the first day of school. We build in time every week, perhaps 20 minutes a day, for kids to discuss their questions and research them. Maybe it's the last hour of the day on Friday. Some teachers build in an hour a day for this research. In addition, kids also investigate their questions during free time any day of the week. A bit later in September, we bring in our own Wonder Boxes (for younger kids) and our own Wonder Books (for older kids) and model how to use them to hold our thinking, share our questions, and do research. We build in time daily for kids to write in their boxes and books. Teachers often use Wonder Walls in conjunction with Wonder Boxes or Wonder Books for more extended writing and investigation.

❋ HOW

Wonder Walls. We gather kids together and write questions on sticky notes, placing a few notes on a dedicated wall titled Wonder Wall. After seeing the modeling, we invite kids to jot or draw their own questions on sticky notes and place them on the wall. We review their questions and point out the variety. We look to see if any questions are linked by topic, theme, or issue. If so, we group them together on the wall, perhaps encircling them with yarn to encourage kids with similar queries to collaborate. Wonder Wall questions fuel classroom conversations. Going forward, Wonder Wall questions may focus on curricular topics and spur research in science or social studies. But we never forget to make time for open wondering throughout the year.

Wonder Books. We keep our own research notebooks that we call Wonder Books. We use our own to model how to use these books so kids can create their own. Wonder Books give us a place to hold our questions, observations, thoughts, and interests. Kids write and/or draw questions they want to research and inquiries they want to pursue—Wonder Books contain questions and inquiries related to topics in the curriculum, as well as anything under the sun that kids are curious about. We assure them that these precious books are theirs alone. We don't value writing over drawing. The books will not be graded. This alleviates pressure on striving readers who are used to feeling judged at every turn. Wonder Books remind strivers that schooling is not merely about evaluating and grading, but is also importantly about learning and expressing one's thoughts, ideas, opinions, and questions. See the lesson "Keeping a Wonder Book" on page 266.

Wonder Boxes. We provide young children with recipe boxes full of index cards and alphabet tabs. They jot down or draw topics that intrigue them and any questions they have. If they wonder about puppies, they write *puppy* on the card along with a question about puppies and place the card behind the P tab. They go on to research their questions and write the information they find on the index card. Whenever we can seamlessly weave the phonemic side of reading into the meaning-making side, our striving readers benefit.

Close Viewing

Use images to spur curiosity, make inferences, and gain information.

 WHY

Our students get and will continue to get much of their information visually. Although textual literacy remains critically important, gleaning information from images is essential in the 21st century. So close viewing is just as important as close reading. This is great news for striving readers, because images offer an accessible entry point into information. The more we use images to build background and curiosity, the more our striving readers will learn and the more confident they will become.

WHEN

We begin the year using images in a variety of ways—to spur curiosity, make inferences, and gain information. We continue this practice throughout the year to fuel inquiry-based learning, build background for content areas, and continue to encourage curiosity.

HOW

Intriguing Images. Start the day several times a week by projecting an intriguing image that is likely to excite kids and draw them in. These images abound in newspapers, magazines, online, and so forth. Be on the lookout for them. Put one up on the screen and simply ask kids to turn and talk about what they wonder or what they think. Steph's colleague Anne Goudvis found a photo of a large black bear falling from a tree in downtown Boulder, Colorado, almost looking as though it was flying! Kids were enthralled. Questions cascaded out of them: "Is it real?" "Is it a costume?" "What is happening to it?" It takes only a few minutes, is great fun, and fosters curiosity. Encourage kids to hunt for their own images and bring them in to share with the class.

See Think Wonder (STW). See Think Wonder is a thinking routine for exploring images, objects, and artifacts. It is a process for constructing meaning by viewing, thinking, and wondering. It is more formal and purposeful than simply projecting images. You might use

STW to launch a content unit or a collaborative inquiry. Project an image, a photograph, a piece of art, or share an object, and ask students to do three things:

- Observe it closely—truly **see** the image or object.

- **Think** about and discuss what might be going on, what is happening, what the image is about, and so forth. Encourage them to back up their thinking with evidence from whatever it is they're viewing.

- Share what they **wonder** about the image or object and questions they have.

You can cover all three of these steps in a single lesson or you may find it helpful to cover them in two or three lessons. Once kids have been taught this process, it can become a regular practice for exploring in all content areas. STW provides striving readers with a very accessible entry point because it is all about making meaning through viewing. And, of course, it is a terrific way to fan that curiosity flame. For more information, go to visiblethinkingpz.org.

Close Viewing of Images in Quadrants. Choose an image and divide it into quadrants. Photocopy enough of the quadrant images so that groups of four can each share one. Depending on the size of your class, several groups may each have the same quadrant. Ask group members to view the image closely and discuss, think, and wonder about it. Then project the entire image and have kids discuss it. From there, remove the entire image and ask each group to report on what its members saw in their quadrants. Then project the entire image again and notice the discussion. It is likely to be far deeper and more expansive than discussions that emerge from viewing the entire image alone (Daniels & Steineke, 2011).

Viewing and Inferring From Content-Area Images. Gather and print out images related to an upcoming content unit. For instance, if you are going to be studying the Civil War, you might find images of slave auctions, battles, Ford's Theater, shackles, and so forth. Have kids meet in groups of four and discuss each image, jotting down what they wonder and what they infer on sticky notes labeled with their initials. Pass the images around so kids have lots of opportunities to respond to a wide variety. Then, collect the sticky notes to determine students' background knowledge about the upcoming unit. It is critical, particularly for striving readers, to have a good idea of what they know or don't know before starting a unit. Once you have that information, spend some time building background for kids who need it. This supports striving readers as they begin to read in the content area because the number-one way to make sense of new information is to connect it to what they already know.

Keeping a Wonder Book

Model your own curiosity: Ask authentic questions and jot them down in a Wonder Book.

Preparation

Before the lesson, buy a small notebook—or "Wonder Book"—for each student or make one by folding, cutting, and binding sheets of notebook paper. Also, be prepared to write questions in your own Wonder Book as part of the lesson.

1 Connect and Engage

Gather kids in front of you on the floor, in a comfortable space. Then you might start with, *How many of you wonder about things? I thought so; well adults do too, every single day. As a matter of fact, the more we learn, the more we wonder, so we adults actually spend more time asking questions than having the answers. Did you know that? Turn and talk about it.*

2 Model

Share an example of a question. *Well, I've been wondering about something. My granddaughter, Riley, only likes sugary cereal—but, as you probably know, that kind of cereal is not good for her or any of us. So how can I find a healthy cereal Riley will eat? I'm going to see if I can find information on cereals that are healthy. I'm going to start by asking a few of you for any ideas about cereals that you like that are healthy. Then tonight I will go online and I will probably go to the store and see what I can find. I'll never figure this out without doing the research. Talking to people, going online, and going into the field are all good ways to do research.*

Show your research notebook. Explain that most researchers have notebooks—or, as you call them, "Wonder Books"—in which they jot down their questions and any information they gather as they attempt to answer those questions. *I am going to jot down this question and several more that I have been wondering about here in my Wonder Book. A Wonder Book is a place to hold questions and thoughts so we don't forget them. Remember this: Nothing matters more than your thoughts and questions!*

Jot down and/or illustrate the questions in your Wonder Book. Share your questions and put a star next to the one that you are going to investigate first.

3 Guide

I'm going to research the question about a cereal for my granddaughter. That's the one that I care about most right now, but I will go back to the others when I have researched and answered the cereal question. Have kids turn and share some things they wonder. Then hand out a blank Wonder Book to each student.

4 Practice

Send kids off to collaborate or work independently to jot down at least three questions of their own in their Wonder Books. Encourage them to think of ways to research answers to their questions.

5 Share

Bring kids back together in a sharing circle. Ask them to review their questions and place a star next to the one that matters most to them. Then invite them to share that question with you and their classmates.

Because we rarely have the time to hear from everyone in the group, once several kids have had a chance to share, we have the kids turn to the classmates next to them and share their most important question.

Great work today. Tomorrow we will take some time to address our questions. I can't wait to see what you will find out!

Things I Wonder

How can I find a healthy cereal that Riley will eat?* 	Why is the ocean salty and lakes are not?
Why do dogs and cats seem to fight more than get along?	What is the best kind of dog for our family? 

> 🌿 **TIP**
>
> Questions and thoughts are like popcorn. They spread quickly around the room as kids talk. More reticent kids are likely to pick up an idea from hearing someone share with the whole group or talking to someone next to them.

Weeding Your Classroom Library

Keep your collection fresh, inviting, and navigable by removing unappealing, inaccurate, and unpopular books.

 WHY

Tending your classroom library is like gardening. Pruning and weeding your collection is as essential to its vibrancy as is planting fresh new titles! While we understand the tendency to hoard books for the illusion of a robust collection, doing so actually makes it harder for readers to find appealing titles when they are lost in the weeds. Less is indeed more! Here are some benefits of weeding:

- **Saving space:** With physical space at a premium in classrooms, it is better to have fewer books displayed enticingly with their covers visible than more books crammed into bins and shelves.

- **Saving time:** Weeding prevents the selection fatigue that often afflicts striving readers by enabling them to shop for books efficiently in uncluttered bins and shelves. It also enables teachers to assemble preview stacks more quickly.

- **Making the collection more appealing:** Weeding boosts the library's "cred" among kids as a reliable source of reading material. According to the weeding authority, the Texas State Library and Archives Commission (TSLAC), patrons often assume new books have been added to collections when all librarians have done is to weed thoroughly!

WHEN

Like any maintenance project, it's best to make weeding an ongoing practice. The gold standard of weeding is the CREW method developed by TSLAC, which stands for **C**ontinuous **R**eview, **E**valuation, and **W**eeding. Getting in the habit of reviewing a couple of bins a week is a good way to maintain your collection over time. Involve kids by creating a bin for them to place books they think should be culled; follow up to find out why.

Alternatively, you could organize a major "weed-athon" for spring cleaning or before packing up your classroom for the summer. Involve colleagues to build camaraderie and share the most glaring examples with each other! (For inspiration, follow the "Awful Library Books" blog (awfullibrarybooks.net) by Michigan public librarians Mary Kelly and Holly Hibner. Under the motto "Hoarding is not collection development," this duo posts the most excruciating examples they find. (And they take submissions!)

❊ HOW

Aptly, TSLAC recommends weeding books that are **MUSTIE**:

- **M**isleading and/or factually inaccurate
- **U**gly and worn
- **S**uperseded by a new edition or better book on the subject
- **T**rivial or no longer of interest
- **I**rrelevant to the needs and interests of your students
- **E**lsewhere (e.g., available in the school library)

In our experience, the easiest to spot (or sniff out) are outdated books that meet several MUSTIE criteria. Physically, they are damaged, tattered, missing pages, yellowing, and, to quote the kids, "smelly!" The content of these oldies is often troubling as well. In nonfiction books, the information may be inaccurate or antiquated, and in fiction the characters and plots may be clichéd or, worse yet, stereotypical. Discard these books right away!

You are also likely to find high-quality books that have not been circulating. Consider the following:

- Are they worth promoting by displaying more prominently, book-talking, or offering in preview stacks and conferences? Perhaps they were simply buried and will move now that you've weeded.

- Are they mismatched to your students (most likely too challenging)? If so, donate them to colleagues on the appropriate grade levels or organize a school-wide book swap.

- As much as you love them, is it possible that they no longer appeal to kids? If so, put them in your own collection for sentimental reasons but remove them from valuable library real estate.

Finally, a caveat: Not only must we fight our hoarding tendencies; we must also curb the impulse to donate MUSTIE discards to families we think could use them. Instead, we must work to acquire and maintain the freshest collections we can and to ensure that striving readers, particularly those from low-income homes, have access to the juiciest and most compelling books from our classroom and school libraries. They deserve nothing less!

Here are weeding guidelines adapted from the CREW method, Texas State Library and Archives Commission: tsl.texas.gov/sites/default/files/public/tslac/ld/pubs/crew/crewmethod08.pdf.

Book-Talking

Whet kids' appetites for reading by giving them daily tastes of the most appealing books you can find.

✳ WHY

One of the best things you can do to promote reading volume is to deliver daily, brief, enthusiastic book talks. Linda Gambrell, an authority on kids' motivation to read, says that the teacher's "blessing of the book" is the single most powerful way to get kids to pick it up (1996). The benefits of book-talking include:

- **Efficiency:** In a matter of minutes, a well-delivered book-talk typically inspires many children to read it.

- **Exposure:** Over time, book talks make kids aware of the vast universe of books, spotlighting diverse genres, formats, lengths, topics, structures, and themes.

- **Inclusivity:** When you mindfully book-talk a wide range of titles, including those at which some might initially look askance, you promote respect for all readers' tastes and capabilities and diminish the perception that "harder is better."

- **Social Energy:** Book talks get kids buzzing about books! Those who have read the book chime in, fostering others' interest in getting their hands on it.

- **Modeling:** Book-talking is a low-key, conversational way for you to share your own reading life, broadening kids' understanding of what it means to be a reader.

- **Commitment:** Scheduling daily book talks is a great way to hold yourself accountable for rooting out exciting new titles to share.

✳ WHEN

Ideally, book talks happen daily, a ritual that kids look forward to and come to expect. Snack time is a perfect opportunity because kids are relaxed and receptive. Prior to long weekends and school vacations, highlight several books in order to provide kids with options and underscore the importance of reading over the breaks. Penny Kittle delivers sparkling book talks every day to her high school students. In *Book Love* (2012), she says that she usually talks about 4–5 books a day during the first week of school because she wants to "put a lot of titles out there."

✷ HOW

To bless a book effectively, do the following:

MHS campus supervisor and voracious reader Gigi Rothweiler shares her latest picks.

- Hold the book up—let kids see it. Show the cover; flip through the pages. Point out any interesting features (e.g., endpapers, maps, photo inserts).

- Describe its genre. ("*Chains* by Laurie Halse Andersen is historical fiction, but it feels more like realistic fiction because it utterly transports you back to lower Manhattan in the 1700s.")

- Relate it to books kids are already familiar with. ("If you liked *Because of Winn-Dixie*, you're going to love *Rain, Reign* with its equally lovable dog . . .")

- Read a well-chosen passage aloud. It's important for potential readers to hear the "voice" of the book to see if it appeals to them.

- Provide a concise, spoiler-free plot summary.

- Invite kids who've read the book to further endorse it and build social energy.

- Pass the book around and/or leave it out and accessible so kids can have a look at it right away.

Armed with credible reviews, you are perfectly capable of book-talking books you haven't read. Just make sure to preview the book and select appealing pages to display and read. And be honest; tell kids, "I haven't read this yet, but I know you fantasy lovers are going to want to get your hands on it right away. You can tell me about it after you've devoured it!"

Book-talk authors with multiple books, with whom a reader can grow. Authors Kevin Henkes, Jacqueline Woodson, and Kate DiCamillo have written picture books, chapter books, and novels.

It's vital to bless books from a wide range of genres and levels of complexity to include readers of all stripes. Penny Kittle suggests keeping a running list of titles you've book-talked. Not only does this provide kids with a resource to refer back to, it helps you create balance over time.

Invite guest book-talkers to share their favorite titles: fellow teachers, custodians, secretaries, lunch monitors, bus drivers, administrators, and so on. Of course, include the school and community librarians. Guest book-talkers are a wonderful way to capture the vibrancy of a community of readers. People read an astonishing range of things in an astonishing variety of ways. See sample book talk on page 115.

Celebrating New Arrivals and Highlighting Hidden Gems

Stoke kids' interest in the classroom library by introducing new books and reintroducing buried treasures across the year with pomp and circumstance.

✳ WHY

It's important for kids to know that the classroom library is dynamic rather than static. Like any "garden," it needs to have eye-catching features that bloom continuously across the year. Novelty sparks curiosity and motivation to read. Refresh your library regularly across the year by bringing in and showcasing new titles—either by purchasing them or borrowing "satellite collections" from colleagues and/or libraries. Create new bins and timely displays: Pair new books with existing ones in novel ways to stir interest and promote circulation.

✳ WHEN

We recommend updating the collection, tweaking its arrangement regularly, and drawing students' attention to the changes at least monthly. If you have a mechanism in place to order books across the year, then it makes sense to showcase them as they come in. It's also fun to create dramatic rituals around new arrivals—the possibilities are endless! If your resources are limited, it's even more important to reconfigure your collection regularly and spruce it up with borrowed items to prevent staleness.

✳ HOW

Get kids fired up about new books and rekindle their interest in the existing collection by:

1. **Creating new and timely book bins.** Let kids' passions, the time of year, and current events inspire you to group books temporarily. Involve kids in curating and naming bins. For example, when the weather finally turns, a "Suddenly Spring" basket could include the new nonfiction books on baseball and gardening you ordered,

grilling cookbooks borrowed from the library, oldies you've plucked from your collection like *Clifford's Spring Clean-Up* and *Planting a Rainbow*, and Marie Kondo's *The Life-Changing Magic of Tidying Up*, which you brought in from home.

2. **Celebrating new arrivals**. Designate and have kids decorate a special bin or basket for new books. Create a suspenseful unveiling ritual. For example, one teacher we know invented a Book Stork who leaves new books in a wicker bassinet every so often, wrapped in a baby blanket. It sounds hokey, but the kids love it! Or create a "Reading Fairy" or "Book Wizard" who comes at night either spontaneously or—even better—in response to compelling letters kids have written with requests.

3. **Borrow satellite collections from the school or community library.** Invite librarians to draw from their collections books you think will appeal to your students, and ask them to come in and present them. In Mamaroneck, community librarians make a "Winter Blues Tour" in which they visit the elementary schools with bundles of new books. Kids love these visits and benefit from the direct connection to the libraries. Mamaroneck middle and high school librarians Kelsey Cohen and Tina Pantginis regularly wheel carts of tempting titles to middle and high school English classrooms, book-talk them, and leave the carts in place as satellite collections for a time to augment teachers' libraries.

Choosing a Just-Right Book

Model how you ask questions to choose a text that is a good fit for you.

Book choice matters, more than just about anything when it comes to helping kids make gains in reading. Teaching strivers how to choose books independently sews fertile ground for reading growth and enjoyment.

Preparation. Before the lesson, choose a book you are currently reading that is a great fit for you, meaning you are interested in it, it provides just the right amount of challenge, and it gives you something to talk and think about. Also, choose another book that you are considering reading. Prepare a blank chart titled "How to Choose a Just-Right Book." Kids will need sticky notes, clipboards, and access to many books from which to choose.

1 **Connect and Engage.** Gather the kids in front of you. Share that you have brought two books: one that you are reading right now and just can't put down and one that you haven't read, but think you might like to. Ask kids to turn and talk about whether they are currently reading a book that is a good fit for them and, if so, what makes it a good fit. Also ask if they have any idea of a book they might read next. After they have discussed, invite them to jot on a sticky note one thing that makes a book a good fit for them. Then have several students share out their thoughts.

2 **Model.** *I am currently reading a book about education called* The Teacher You Want to Be *(Keene & Glover, 2015). It is a perfect book for me, because I'm an educator so I'm always eager to learn more about teaching and learning.*

You know the story "Goldilocks and the Three Bears," right? How Goldilocks always liked baby bear's stuff because it was just right for her, mama's soup was too hot, papa's bed was too hard, but baby's soup and bed were just right? When it comes to books, that's what I try to do: pick ones that are just right for me. To do that, I have to be interested in the book, be able to read and understand most of it, and be sure it gives me something to think and talk about.

I have also brought a book that my husband is reading. He is an economist and really into this book called Capital in the Twenty-First Century *(Piketty, 2015), which is about the inequality of wealth in the United States, and how a few rich people have most of the money in the world and why that's a problem. I would like to learn more about this, too, because I agree that it is a big problem.*

One important reason to choose a book is interest—and I am interested in both of these books. When I'm choosing a book, the first question that comes to mind is, "Does this book interest me?" I'll jot that question on the anchor chart.

Explain that while interest is the most important consideration when choosing a book, so is its difficulty level. If you don't understand many of the ideas and aren't familiar with a number of the words, the book probably isn't the best choice yet.

As I flip through Capital in the Twenty-First Century, *I realize I don't comprehend quite a few of the ideas and, even though I'm an adult reader, there are words I have never seen and don't understand. So even though I am interested in the topic, I do not have enough background knowledge about it to really understand the book. It probably is not the best fit yet. I'll add this question to the chart: "Can I read and understand most of the words and ideas?" But I'll keep in mind that, down the line, I may read this book when I know and understand more about the topic, assuming I am still interested in it.*

3 **Guide.** Engage the kids in the process by having them jot on sticky notes reasons they might choose a book. When they're finished, invite volunteers to place their sticky notes on the anchor chart. Then have kids turn and engage in spirited conversation about the books they're currently reading and what those books make them think about.

From there ask, *Who would like to share what you talked about?* Some kids may share out. Others may not. Note who doesn't share as it may be an indication that his or her book is not the right fit. *Listening to you all speak makes me realize that there's something else we know about a just-right book: It give us something to talk and think about. So I'm going to add this question to our chart: Does the book give me something to think and talk about?*

4 **Practice.** Display the chart so all can see the three questions. *Am I interested in the book? Can I read most of the words and understand most of the ideas? Does it give me something to think and talk about?* Send kids off to read as you confer with individuals about book choice.

5 **Share.** Invite kids back to share about the book they are reading and whether it's a just-right book or not. Guide a discussion about how, as readers, we need to remember to ask ourselves all three of these questions when we are choosing books independently. Remind kids about your own experience choosing a book that might have been too hard.

So choosing a book that interests you is very important. But if you can't understand the ideas and words well, as I couldn't in that economics book, you probably need to hold off on that book for a bit. And a book is probably not worth choosing if it doesn't give you something to think about and talk about with someone else. So keep those points in mind when you are choosing books. And remember, above all, just because we can't read something yet, doesn't mean that we won't be able to read it soon. That's what's cool about reading, the more we read, the better we read. So keep on reading and you will all grow as readers! (Adapted from *Reading With Meaning* by Debbie Miller.)

TIP

Consider using a different metaphor with older students. For example, you may prefer to talk about certain items of clothing such as jeans that have a "just-right" fit.

Conferring for Engagement: Reader to Reader, Heart to Heart

Check in frequently with striving readers to ensure they are well matched to the texts in their hands.

❋ WHY

When a striving reader is enthralled with a book, all kinds of benefits ensue. It follows that monitoring his or her level of engagement without disrupting it is vital. To assess whether rich meaning-making is occurring, we must get into "the room where it happens": the mind of the reader. A reader-to-reader, heart-to-heart conference is the best way to verify that a well-chosen book is working its magic.

❋ WHEN

Engagement is tenuous for a striving reader in the early pages of a book. Initial disorientation is frustrating and may lead to abandonment. It's important to confer at the outset to make sure he gets into the book and derives pleasure right away. Once reading is underway, it's important to check in if you notice signs of disengagement:

- Decline in reading volume (few pages read, bookmark not moving)
- Distraction (staring into space, roaming around the room, going to the bathroom)
- "Forgetting" the book at home or in his cubby or locker

If the striving reader is well matched and progresses through the book, it's important to confer toward the end of his reading experience to help him synthesize ideas and to identify next-up books.

❋ HOW

Steph emphasizes that classroom discourse should sound conversational rather than interrogational, and that's particularly true of conferences. Consider what you know about the child, his reading behaviors, and the book he has chosen, and gauge the extent of the conference accordingly. For example, if a student is hunkered down with the third book in a series he loves, he probably needs little from you other than ample reading time. If, on the other hand, he's chosen a book that you know to be complex, he will likely benefit from a brief orientation. Pose open-ended questions and take your cues from the reader:

- How is the book so far?
- How are you getting into the book?
- What is the book making you think about?

Sample Conference 1

Vicki had read the first chapter of *Pax* by Sara Pennypacker when Annie asked, "How's the book so far?" "It's good but confusing," Vicki said. "I can't figure out who's talking. It seems like it's Pax because we hear his feelings, but it says 'he' instead of 'I'." Annie commended Vicki's observation and question about the narrator and suggested that they look at the text together to figure it out. As Annie studied the first page, she saw that it was a third person omniscient narrator—precisely what Vicki had noted without having a term for it. She also noted that the focus alternated chapter by chapter from Pax to Peter, signaled by a silhouette of a fox or boy around the chapter numeral. Annie explained that the narrator is all-knowing—that he describes both Pax's and Peter's feelings, and that he tells their stories separately chapter by chapter. Vicki was highly motivated to read *Pax* because her friends were reading it. Once her impressions of the narrator were validated and explicated, she was off and running.

Sample Conference 2

Annie had been watching fifth grader Diego read *James and the Giant Peach* for several minutes, pleased that the classic still circulates but curious whether it would hold a contemporary reader's attention. Diego's eyes came out of the book and his gaze went to the window. Suspecting disengagement, Annie pulled alongside him and asked gently, "It looks like you're taking a break from reading. What is the book making you think about?" Diego replied, "I just don't understand how James's aunts can be so mean." Annie realized that not only was Diego highly engaged, he was so moved that he needed to come out of the book temporarily to ponder the weight of the characters' cruelty. Annie spent a few minutes processing the aunts' bitterness with Diego before he resumed reading.

There is an art to these conferences: Too much direction is stifling and deprives the reader of his independence; too little direction in a complex text may cause a loss of confidence and faltering.

What Is the Reading Zone?

One of Nancie Atwell's students coined the phrase "the reading zone" to describe the psychological space a reader enters when productively lost in a book. While thriving readers are frequent flyers to the reading zone, all children need to learn the route there.

Preparation. Take photos of yourself and a few kids in favorite reading spots with enthralling books. Confer with those kids so they're ready to describe their journeys to the reading zone. On a piece of chart paper, write Emily Dickinson's poem "There Is No Frigate Like a Book," with definitions or illustrations of challenging words (e.g., *frigate, courser, chariot*). On another piece of chart paper, write "Directions to the Reading Zone" at the top.

1 Connect and Engage

Gather the class and ask this question: How is a book like a ship? Let kids think about it and then share ideas. Elicit and chart responses such as:

- It takes you on a journey.
- You may have rough seas (i.e., reading challenges).
- You may be comfortable, like being on a cruise ship.
- It takes you to beautiful destinations.
- It's handmade—someone builds it, or publishes it, and someone else sails it, or reads it.

Turn chart paper to reveal "There Is No Frigate Like a Book," read the poem aloud, and explore its meaning with the kids.

Show the photo of yourself reading a great book in a favorite spot. Describe the journey you are taking: *Here I am on the warm beach of Great East Lake in Maine. The book in my hands,* Maybe a Fox, *is a frigate that transports me to the snowy Vermont woods, where I'm with Jules, whose sister has just disappeared into an icy river. My summer surroundings fade and I feel the chill of the winter air . . .*

Show the photos of students reading and ask those kids to describe the journeys they are taking. For example, while Shyla's head rests on a roll of paper towels on the classroom carpet, *Poached* sweeps her away to FunJungle, a zoo and theme park. Have kids turn and share reading journeys.

② Model and Engage

Being inside the world of a book is a wonderful place called "the reading zone." Explain that learning routes to the reading zone and ways to overcome roadblocks help us travel there again and again. Share a few common roadblocks (e.g., fatigue, lack of interest) and how you overcome them. Invite kids to share successful and unsuccessful journeys to the reading zone.

Show the "Directions to the Reading Zone" chart. *Today we're going to pool our experiences and create a set of directions for getting to and staying in the reading zone. The first step is to choose an appealing book.* Model and record a few strategies. *For example, one way I choose an appealing book is to look at the titles on my next-up list.*

③ Guide

With kids still on the carpet, have them start recording on paper or in notebooks their best strategies to enter and stay in the reading zone. Elicit a few and share them with the class: *"Shyla says one of her best times to read is when her baby sister is napping. She wrote, 'If you have siblings, find time when they won't distract you.'"*

④ Practice

Send kids off in pairs to come up with "Directions to the Reading Zone," including strategies for overcoming roadblocks. Kids usually come up with points such as the following:

1. Choose an appealing book.
2. Orient yourself to the book; get your bearings.
3. Find a good time and place to read uninterrupted.
4. Read the book! Give it a chance.
5. If you get lost, use strategies and/or ask for help.
6. Enjoy your stay in the reading zone!

TIP

It's important to share examples of striving readers' journeys to the reading zone so they don't feel it's an inaccessible phenomenon.

⑤ Share

Call kids back to the meeting area. Have each partnership star a few effective strategies to share first. Pool ideas and create a class anchor chart. *Great job today! I'm going to print these directions on bookmarks so that you'll always have them handy when you read.*

Going the Extra Mile to Put the Right Book in a Striving Reader's Hands

Leave nothing to chance: When a striving reader is primed to read a particular book, do whatever it takes to get it to him.

✳ WHY

A striving reader's interest in a particular book is a call to action! Whether sparked by a read-aloud, a book-talk, a friend's recommendation, or a rave review, the child's desire signals an immediate but fleeting book-matching opportunity. Going out of your way to track down a copy of the book he wants not only sets the striver up for a successful reading experience; it shows him the depth of your care and commitment.

✳ WHEN

Invest extraordinary effort when a striving reader:

- has read the first book(s) in a series and is eager for the next one.
- advocates for himself; asks for a copy of something he's heard about.
- expresses enthusiasm based on a book review. ("This sounds like something I'd like to read.")
- will soon have ample reading time (e.g., a long weekend, a school vacation).
- has been in a reading slump and demonstrates notable interest.

✳ HOW

The strategies aren't complicated; they simply require time and effort. Assuming you don't have a copy of the desired book in your classroom library, do the following:

- Email your colleagues to see if anyone has a copy (see an example of such an email on page 239). If so, dash to retrieve it.

- Check school and public library collections; put the book on hold and go get it.

- Buy the book yourself. Present it to the child as a gift to keep.

Above all, strike while the iron is hot! Do what it takes to put the book in the child's hands as quickly as possible. Don't rely on other people or interoffice mail; do it yourself, and do it right away.

These extraordinary measures aren't sustainable for an entire class, but they don't have to be. Thriving readers tend to acquire books readily by multiple means, but striving readers need us to go to bat for them.

MILDRED GRADY: EXTREME BOOK-MATCHER

In 1957, Olly Neal was an at-risk high school senior in Arkansas. One of 13 children in a house with no electricity, Olly didn't care much for school and frequently antagonized his teachers. One day, he cut class and strolled into the library where he came upon *The Treasure of Pleasant Valley*, a risqué book written by African American author Frank Yerby. Intrigued but unwilling to be seen checking out a book, Olly stole it. He read the book quickly and smuggled it back to the library, whereupon he was pleased to find another Yerby book in its place on the shelf. He stole that one, too—and ultimately read four pilfered books that semester. "Reading got to be a thing I liked," Olly later commented. He went to college and later to law school, eventually becoming an appellate court judge.

At a high school reunion, Olly met up with Mildred Grady, the librarian. It turned out that she had seen him steal the original book. Rather than reprimand him, she empathized. She resolved to seek out more of Yerby's books for him on the sly. This entailed making a 70-mile drive to Memphis each time because books by black authors were not widely available in 1957. Olly credits Mildred Grady with saving his life by turning him onto books. At her funeral, Grady's son invited Olly Neal to tell the story of his mother's remarkable efforts and their impact. "I credit Mrs. Grady for getting me into the habit of enjoying reading, so that I was able to go to law school and survive," Olly Neal eulogized.

(Read more about Mildred Grady and Olly Neal at http://www.nytimes.com/2012/01/22/opinion/sunday/kristof-how-mrs-grady-transformed-olly-neal.html and http://www.npr.org/templates/story/story.php?storyId=113357239.)

Making a Reading Plan

Thriving readers plan their reading lives. They capitalize on vacations by stocking up on reading material and setting aside blocks of time to read. Engage kids in plotting some extended reading times on a calendar and identifying what they will read.

Preparation

Teach this lesson several days before a school vacation to give kids time to enact their plans. For modeling purposes, figure out what you will read during break.

❶ Connect and Engage

Gather kids around you comfortably. Project a quote about planning as a springboard for discussion, such as, "Fortune favors the prepared mind" (Louis Pasteur) or "It takes a lot of unspectacular preparation to get spectacular results" (Roger Staubach). Ask, "Why is it important to make plans? What kinds of things do you plan for, and why?" Elicit examples and share your own. Last-minute holiday shoppers are plagued with full parking lots, long lines, and meager selection; successful dieters slice and bag healthy fruits and vegetables, etc.

❷ Model

Like all healthy habits, reading needs to be planned for and scheduled. One of the things I love most about being in Maine over the holidays is the chance to read by the fire with no interruptions. Just as we plan our meals in advance and take special foods with us because there's no grocery store nearby, we plan what we're going to read and make sure we have copies so we're not empty-handed in prime reading time!

I usually choose books for work and for pleasure. (Although to me, professional reading is pleasurable!) I include magazines so I have choices depending on my mood and energy level. Hold up and describe your selections. *My daughter wants me to read her favorite series, and she's lending me the first book,* A Court of Thorns and Roses. *I got the second book from the library in case I finish the first. I'm excited to read the new edition of a favorite professional book,* The Reading Zone, *and I've downloaded it on my iPad since I'm trying to read e-books. I subscribe to* Bon Appetit *and* Food and Wine, *and I've set aside the latest issues for the trip.*

Project and mark up the reading calendar to show the specific times during vacation that are ripe for reading and those that are too busy. *We're driving to Maine on December 27, but since I can't read in the car without getting carsick, that day is a wash. We'll be by ourselves on the 28th and the 29th, so that's when I'll dig into the fantasy series. Relatives come for my birthday dinner on the 29th, so realistically I won't get any substantial reading done until they leave on the 31st.*

3 Guide

Have kids refer to their next-up lists and chat with partners about what they are excited to read and how they'll procure copies. Ask a few partnerships to share their selections and sources. List sources on the board as kids mention them: classroom library, school library, public library, borrow from friend, bookstore, download, and so on.

4 Practice

Hand out blank calendars (you can find a blank template at scholastic.com/ThriveResources) and give kids time to plot their vacation schedules and reading plans. Prompt them to schedule trips to the library if they plan to borrow books. Circulate, confer, and note intriguing examples.

5 Share

Invite kids to share their plans, making sure to include kids who aren't traveling to glamorous destinations. If kids don't mention sources of reading material, be sure to elicit suggestions from the class. *Jason would like to read* The Trials of Apollo, *but he doesn't have a copy. Does anyone have one to lend?* Make this lesson fun and festive.

Vacation Reading Plan

I plan to read . . .

Text	Source	Notes
The Court of Thorns and Roses (Maas)	Mimi lending to me	Since fantasy is a new genre to me, I need to give myself a big block of prime reading time to get into it.
A Court of Mist and Fury (Maas)	Mamaroneck High School library	I checked this out in case I love the series (but if not, I can return it without losing an investment).
The Reading Zone (Atwell and Merkel)	Purchased online	I'm excited to see the new edition. I'm going to practice reading and annotating electronically.
Bon Appetit, Gourmet	I subscribe	Magazines are my guilty pleasure. My sisters and I swap and read each other's at the cabin.

Vacation Calendar With Reading Moments

Monday	Tuesday	Wednesday	Thursday	Friday	Saturday	Sunday
20 Make reading plans with students	21 Class meets in library	22	23 Last day of school	24 Christmas Eve—cook and wrap!	25 Christmas	26 Organize, shop for food, and pack. Get videos from library.
27 Drive to Moose Lodge.	28 Stack firewood on porch. Begin *Court of Thorns and Roses*	29 My birthday! Read *Court of Thorns and Roses*. Make lobster mac and cheese for family dinner	30 Family time. Ski, snowshoe, hike	31 Family departs. Clean up. Read *The Reading Zone*. Practice electronic annotations. Happy New Year!	1 Sleep in. Make big brunch. Hike, then read by the fire. Begin packing up.	2 Drive home. Get organized for tomorrow.
3 Back to school						

Source Sets

Use source sets in a curriculum unit to engage all kids and provide a range of entry points for accessing information.

 WHY

We believe that all kids should learn and enjoy the compelling content offered in social studies, science, and language arts. Striving readers need and deserve to have equal access to that content. Source sets—multi-level, multimedia, multi-genre, multi-perspective, multi-cultural collections of information on a common topic—ensure that. Filled with artifacts, videos, and images as well as text, they are highly engaging and interactive—and offer the widest range of entry points for accessing information, making them perfect for striving readers.

 WHEN

We use source sets in curriculum units, introducing them at the start of the unit and adding to them throughout the unit. Source sets are appropriate for any topic, but we find they lend themselves especially well to habitats, space, transportation, animals, weather, immigration, and culture studies. You may want to start with a unit on one of those topics. One source set for the entire class can work, but it may become unwieldy. So we suggest multiple source sets on subtopics of your main topic—perhaps one that will accommodate four or five kids at a time in inquiry circles. When studying a specific culture, for instance, you may have a source set for education, history, science contributions, famous monuments, and so forth.

✳ HOW

Images and videos abound on the Internet, and most are free. The classroom libraries we describe in this book should be rife with all kinds of texts at multiple levels. Teachers are the most creative folks we know when it comes to gathering artifacts. Once you've thought about your unit topic, look for objects at stoop sales and garage sales. Check out sale items in stores throughout the year. Invite people in the community who have expertise in the topic under study to come in and share with the class. And most importantly, once source sets take hold in your room, recruit your students to help you gather materials!

Source set materials include but are not limited to:

- picture books, chapter books, graphic books, novels, short nonfiction, long nonfiction, short stories
- magazine, newspaper, and Internet articles
- brochures and catalogs
- poems
- images, graphics, videos
- maps
- artifacts, realia, toys
- websites, web cams
- editorials, essays, interviews, press releases
- posters
- recordings of music, speeches, public service announcements

Striving Readers and Fluency Development

✳ WHAT

The Fluency Development Lesson (FDL) is a 20-minute intensive and intentional instructional protocol. The goal is for students to be able to read a new, relatively brief text with fluency and comprehension by engaging in the key components of fluency development: hearing fluent texts, reading with partners, doing repeated reading, performing for an audience, and participating in follow-up word study. Several studies suggest that the FDL is highly effective in improving fluency, comprehension, and overall achievement of striving readers.

✳ WHY

Research has indicated that reading fluency, the ability to read texts with appropriate expression and confidence, is critical and necessary for proficient reading.

✳ HOW

Begin the FDL by selecting a short text and making two copies for each student. Poems and other rhythmical texts are good choices because they often contain rhyme, which enhances their readability, and are meant to be performed orally for an audience.

- Read the text to students several times as they follow along silently.

- Discuss with students the content of the text and your reading.

- Engage students in choral reading of the text several times.

- Have students work in pairs or small groups to continue their rehearsal of the text. Circulate and provide formative feedback to them.

- If students are able to read the text with fluency, invite them to perform it for an audience—even an audience of one, such as a parent volunteer who is willing to listen to individuals or groups.

- Engage students in a brief word study activity, using words from the text.

- Invite students to take one copy of the text home and perform it for family members and others. The other copy should remain at school for further practice and performance (e.g., Poetry Slam every Friday).

- Repeat this protocol on following days, using new texts.

With each FDL, students should approach the fluency of proficient readers. You'll likely notice that the fluency students achieve eventually transfers to other texts, such as those they're reading independently.

By Timothy Rasinski, Professor of Education in the Reading and Writing Center at Kent State University, Kent, Ohio.

• • • • •

To learn more:

- Rasinski, T. (2010). *The Fluent Reader: Oral and Silent Reading Strategies for Building Fluency, Word Recognition, and Comprehension, Second Edition.* New York: Scholastic.

Monitoring Comprehension: Following the Inner Conversation

Listen to your inner voice and leave tracks of your thinking.

Many striving readers think reading is simply about sounding out the words and calling them. So it is imperative that they learn that reading is truly about thinking. This monitoring lesson is a first step in that direction.

Preparation. Choose a compelling piece of short text, a picture book, or a nonfiction article—a text that students can really sink their teeth into. Read it before the lesson and notice what you think about, your connections, questions, inferences, and so forth, and mark them so you remember them in the lesson. Each student needs a pencil and clipboard with a piece of paper and six 3" x 3" sticky notes attached to each side of the paper.

1   **Connect and Engage.** Gather the kids on the floor in front of you. Make sure each one has a partner for turn and talks throughout the lesson. *Today I brought this book called _____. This story is about_____. Has anything like this ever happened to you? Turn and talk about that.* Invite a few volunteers to share. *When readers read or listen to and think about the words, they carry on an inner conversation with the text. They have an inner voice that speaks to them as they read. They might have a connection, a question, or a reaction. They might be confused. Readers talk back to the writer when they read. Have you ever noticed a voice in your head speaking to you as you read? Turn and talk about that.* Some students may relate immediately, others may not. *Well, today I am going to read this book aloud and stop and share my thinking as I read. I'm going to share my inner voice so you can see how I think when I read and notice how I follow an inner conversation with the text when I read. Then you will have a chance to try it. You need to remember that nothing is more important than your thinking when you read. You see, reading is thinking!*

2   **Model.** Take no more than seven minutes to read a page or two of the text, share your thinking, and jot down thoughts on sticky notes. *Let me read a little, and as I read, I will share my thinking out loud. I am going to leave tracks of my thinking on sticky notes. Just like* *animals leave tracks in the snow after a snowfall, you can tell which animals were there the night before from the fresh tracks. The sticky note tracks are a place to hold my thinking so I don't forget it. And I can see them even after I've finished reading.*

*Right here, I have a question. I wonder . . . I'll code it with a **?** on the sticky note. Here I have a connection, which I can code with an **R** for reminds me of . . . Here my inner voice said, "Huh, I don't get this part . . . ." Sometimes I get confused and need to reread or read on. But I don't write all of my thinking down or I'd never get through the text. So I need to think about what is really worth writing down.*

Stop reading for a minute and ask students to turn and talk about what they notice you doing as you read. To assess whether they understand the strategy, listen in on their discussions. This is an opportune time to invite a striving reader to share out the wise things he or she notices such as you jotting, you asking questions, things you were reminded of, and points that confused you. If that student is reluctant to speak, share for him or her, with permission. Write what they share on an anchor chart titled The Inner Conversation for all to see.

3 **Guide.** Hand out the clipboards and sticky notes and have kids try what you just modeled. Continue to read slowly and ask them to jot down their thoughts—their connections, questions, reactions, and confusions—and then discuss their ideas. Invite a few kids to share their sticky notes and turn and talk throughout.

4 **Practice.** Have kids practice the strategy in small groups or pairs, continuing to jot down on sticky notes what their inner voices say and talk to each other, just as they did during the Guide portion of the lesson. They can continue with the text you were reading or they can choose a text of their own. Explain that as they work, you will be moving around the room, conferring with small groups, pairs, and individuals as they jot down their inner voices and talk with each other.

5 **Share.** Call kids back to share their sticky notes and to share what they learned in their discussions. Ask, *What did you notice yourself doing as you were reading?* Add to The Inner Conversation anchor chart, recording their answers on it. They will likely say they asked questions, made connections, noticed surprising information, and so forth. Keep the chart posted. As kids continue to embrace the idea that reading is about many different kinds of thinking, they can add to it. *Wow, great work today! This chart is an important record of the kinds of thinking you do when you read. All of these ideas came from you. You learned so much about yourself as a reader and you also learned so much from the reading itself. When we take our inner conversation public with each other, we all learn and understand more.*

Using Fix-Up Strategies

Notice when you stray from an inner conversation with the text. Use fix-up strategies to get back on track.

One of the biggest problems facing strivers is their tendency to space out when reading and lose track of meaning. They run their eyes over the words, but don't think about them. Strivers also tend to lose their way when the text is too hard. So, after we have taught them to construct meaning by listening to their inner voice while reading, we teach them to notice when they stray from meaning and how to "fix up" the problem and reconstruct meaning.

Preparation. Choose a text that you are currently reading, one written for adults, so that you can share your own process with the kids. Create a two-column think sheet with "Problem" at the top of the left-hand column and "Fix-Up Strategy" at the top of the right-hand column. Each student needs a pencil, a clipboard, and a copy of the think sheet.

① Connect and Engage

Gather the kids in front of you, on the floor. *Today I have brought in a book that I am reading at home.* Page through the text, share the cover, mention what the book is about, and so forth. *This book has been a bit hard for me. You might be surprised by this, but even adults get confused when they are reading. Sometimes reading goes well and other times, not so much . . . .*

Share how sometimes you space out when you read; for example, when you are reading at night in bed. *Sometimes, I'll read my book, put my bookmark in, and go to sleep. The next night when I go back to my reading, I go to where I left off, but I may have no idea what I was reading. So I need to go back to a slightly earlier spot and start from there. In this case I think I lost track because I was too tired to keep reading the night before.* Jot down the reason you strayed from meaning and share it. Explain how you "fixed up" the problem by rereading the text the next night. Jot down the problem you had on an anchor chart and what you did to fix it. *Has anything like this ever happened to you? You are reading along and then have no idea what you are reading?* Have kids turn and talk.

② Model

Okay, I am going to read a few paragraphs from this text and stop and share with you when I am no longer making meaning, not listening to my inner voice, or when the text is too hard and I am confused. I will try to fix up the problem if I can. Read a paragraph aloud and stop at a spot to make a connection. Share that connection enthusiastically and then keep reading. Stop at the end of a subsequent paragraph and explain that you have no idea what you read in that paragraph because you were thinking about your connection. *Connecting to the text is a good thing, but sometimes our connections can distract us from meaning, that's what happened here. Now I need to go back to where I had that connection and then focus on not thinking too much about it, but rather paying attention to the words in the text.* Reread the paragraph and tell kids you now understand what it says. *I'm going to add this problem to the anchor chart in the first column and what I did to fix it in the second column.*

Keep reading and stop at a confusing part. *I was going to keep reading but I realized that I was not making any sense because I don't understand this word or idea. Since I don't know this word, I am going to have to try to infer the meaning of the word. I need to think about what I know and use clues to make sense. If I read right before and after the word, I might be able to make sense of it.*

③ Guide

Hand out clipboards, think sheets, and pencils. Ask kids to think about times they spaced out when they were reading or times they quit reading because the text was too hard. Have them jot one example in the left-hand column of their think sheet and what they did to fix up the problem in the right-hand column. Then invite volunteers to share some of the problems and fix-up strategies. This is particularly valuable for striving readers, because they see that problems occur not only for you, but also for all their classmates. They are not alone! Jot their responses on the anchor chart and guide a discussion on problems and fix-up strategies.

④ Practice

Now it's time for you to practice in your own reading. Each of you can take this two-column think sheet back to your spots. When meaning does break down, jot the problem with the page number and think about how you can fix it. Check out the anchor chart for some suggestions, but once you have done your reading today, we will probably have more solutions to the problems we have when we read. I will come around and confer with some of you while you are reading.

5 Share

After about 30 minutes practice, invite kids back to the circle and have them turn to a classmate and talk about their reading, since the content of the reading and their thoughts about it are important. You might prompt students by asking, *What surprised you? What do you wonder? What did you learn? What confused you?* (The final question is particularly important to this lesson.) Then invite them to share a problem they had and the fix-up strategy they used. As they share these, jot them on the chart. *Look at this chart! We have all of these problems and useful strategies to fix the problems. We will keep adding to the chart as we discover new problems and ways to solve them.*

Surfacing the Big Ideas

Distinguish what you think is important from what the author most wants you to get out of the text.

Surfacing the big ideas in a text is a perennial problem for striving readers. One reason is that they often have difficulty separating what they think is important from the author's intent. We want them to understand that both matter, their thinking and the author's. The last thing we want is for striving readers to think that their thinking doesn't matter! So, in this lesson, we show them how to distinguish between the two.

Preparation. Choose an engaging one-page nonfiction article from *Scholastic News, Junior Scholastic, Time for Kids*, or any other magazine or Internet source that is aimed at kids. Texts that express a point of view—editorials, opinion pieces, and argument essays—are most effective. Each student needs a pencil, clipboard, and a copy of the article. Have three or four additional articles for independent practice toward the end of the lesson.

1 Connect and Engage

Gather kids on the floor as you model. Engage them by asking them to preview the article and then turn and talk about what they think it is mostly about. Explain that what the reader thinks is the most important information in the text may not be what the writer thinks is the most important information. It's important to ask ourselves, "What is the writer trying to convey?" and "What is his or her big idea(s)?" *When readers read, they often find information that is very interesting and important to them. Sometimes it is the same information the writer wants you to take away from the piece, but other times it is a different idea. And that's okay, because nothing matters more than your thinking when you read. But the writer's thoughts and information matter, too. So, we have to be able to separate what we think is most important and interesting from what the writer most wants us to get out of the text, the writer's big idea(s). Sometimes they are the same thing. Other times they are different. Both matter.*

2 Model

Read through a few paragraphs of the article, identifying what you think is important and distinguishing it from what the piece is mainly about. *Let me show you how it works for me.*

When I read something that I think is important, I am going to underline it, mark it with a star, and maybe jot some thoughts in the margin. When I read something I think the writer thinks is important, I will mark that with a "W" for writer. If I code it with both a star and a "W," that means I agree with what the writer thinks is most important.

To figure out what the writer thinks is most important, I am going to look mainly at two things. First the title—the title is often a clue as to what the writer thinks is a big idea. As I read the text, I am also going to look at how much time the writer spent on that particular idea, the one in the title. But I am going to stop and jot when I come to something that matters to me, because my thinking matters, too. Read through the text and stop to annotate when you come to something that interests you, a detail of sorts. First of all, I am going to put a star where it says _____ because I have a connection to that information and it is interesting to me. But I am quite sure it is not something that the writer cares too much about. It is just a small detail, not a big idea. But it matters to me.

Read the next paragraph. *As I listen to my inner voice, it is easy for me to notice something that is important to me, but I have to remember to read with an eye to what the writer wants me to learn, too. Oh, look here. The writer has written that _____ and she spends quite a bit of time talking about that idea. I also notice that the paragraph relates to the title; I think this might be one of the bigger ideas from the writer's perspective. I'll mark it with a "W."*

③ Guide

Now we can do it together. Hand out the article, pencils, and clipboards. Read the next paragraph, stop, and have students jot something that they think is interesting or important, something they think is important to the writer, or something they think is important to both parties. Have them turn and talk to a partner and share their thinking as you walk around, scanning their work and listening in.

Once they have finished, have students turn their paper over and ask them to jot down three things:

- Something they learned that they think is important to remember
- Something the writer most wants them to get out of the article, a big idea
- One optional response and any questions they have. (Explain that questions the reader has are the most important questions, not the teacher's questions or the textbook's questions.)

From Striving to Thriving © 2017 by Stephanie Harvey & Annie Ward, Scholastic Inc.

Practice

Have three fascinating articles available at different levels. Do an enthusiastic sales pitch on each one and let kids choose. Choice always matters! Kids should have text they can and want to read. If a striving reader chooses an article that is too hard, deal with it quietly in a conference. After kids go off to read, have them turn and talk about what they are supposed to do. When they're finished, choose several students to share out. If they are confused, remind them what you did during the lesson and tell them what you expect. Send them off to read and think. Move around the room, conferring with kids.

 Share

When they come back to the sharing circle, have students turn their paper over and address the same three questions that they did together in the Guide portion of the lesson. Then, invite someone to share either an idea they thought was important to remember or one of the writer's big ideas. Invite a few more students to share with the whole group and then have each student share his or her learning with a classmate. When students are finished, thank them and remind them that the writer worked hard to get his or her ideas out there, so it is important for them to pay attention. But it is important for them to remember that their thinking matters, too.

Shared Reading

❋ WHY

Shared reading mimics the lap book experience by showing print as well as pictures while the teacher's voice leads the reading. During and after the multiple rereadings of text, the teacher can explicitly model the strategies and skills needed to read increasingly complex texts, and students can participate in the rereading for different purposes.

❋ WHAT

Typically, shared reading in classroom instruction uses a short piece or sections of text over several days, with a different instructional focus each day. The most common areas of focus are close reading and comprehension including fluency, vocabulary in context, text structure, and text features. Shared reading works in whole- and small-group classroom instruction for multiple readings of complex text. It is appropriate at all grade levels.

❋ HOW

The teacher and students read together from text that is visible to all; this can be accomplished by using media including a document camera or digital projector. Every student joins the teacher to read at least a portion of the text in unison; the teacher chooses what to emphasize in the choral reading portion for the lesson focus such as determining importance. This enables every student, regardless of ability, to engage in the reading process and scaffolds the access to the text.

The text is usually at grade level or higher and uses a wide range of genres. Shared reading is an effective way to demonstrate how to read all types of text including functional materials; often, students face text types independently that they have never encountered before, including in testing situations. These text types are ideal for shared reading sessions and help students develop a strong mental model for independent reading. Shared reading supports independent reading including transfer and application to new settings and situation.

With the emergent and early reader, a big book or shared digital text is usually read and reread over four or five days.

1. The first day of the reading, or "Text Encounter 1," provides an opportunity for becoming familiar with the overall text for meaning and story elements, characters and setting, beginning-middle-end, and/or problem-solution, depending on genre.

2. "Text Encounter 2" provides opportunities to notice/locate concept of print features.

3. "Text Encounter 3" focuses on retelling and reviewing story elements and reading strategy instruction.

4. "Text Encounter 4" expands work on vocabulary, text features, and structure.

All of these encounters can include writing in response to reading. An additional rereading could involve simple dramatization and further practice of the reading for fluency and independence. After the session, all shared reading material should be available for students to reread independently.

By Dr. Adria Klein, Director of Early Literacy Intervention Center, Saint Mary's College of California.

• • • • •

To learn more:

- Swartz, S. L., Shook, R. E. & A. Klein. (2002). *Shared Reading: Reading With Children.* Carlsbad, CA: Dominie Press.

Write to Read

✻ WHAT

In 1982, Marie Clay, the world-renowned expert in developmental and clinical child psychology who founded Reading Recovery, issued a call for educators to find the writing connection in learning to read (Clay, 1982). Ouellette and Sénéchal have mapped out the way. It turns out that allowing and encouraging children's early "invented spelling" is the key.

✻ WHY

Before children become conventional readers and spellers at the very beginning of learning to read—often in preschool, kindergarten, or the beginning of first grade—they use self-directed and spontaneous attempts to represent words in print. If teachers and parents engage beginners in pencil and paper activity by having them draw their picture and write their story or information, beginners will naturally over time "invent" spellings. The emerging spellings demonstrate what the child knows about the sounds in words, along with how he or she thinks letters represent these sounds. As Richard Gentry has written before, one can literally "see" the child's development—that is, monitor the child's progress in the process of breaking the complex English code—by looking at his or her spelling (Gentry, 2006, 2000). What researchers, including Gentry, and exemplary teachers have found over the last 30+ years of research and practice is that the act of inventing a spelling greatly increases the child's understanding of sound/letter relationships and the role they play in written language and reading. (To learn more, see Feldgus, E., Cardonick, I. & Gentry, R. (2017). *Kid Writing in the 21st Century: A Systematic Approach to Phonics, Spelling, and Writing Workshop*. San Diego, CA: Hameray.)

✹ HOW

When inventing a spelling, the child is engaged in mental reflection and practice with words, not just memorizing. This strategy strengthens neuronal pathways, so as the reader/writer becomes more sophisticated with invented spelling, he or she develops a repertoire of more and more correctly spelled words at the same time. These words are stored in the word form area of the brain where the child can retrieve them automatically as sight words for reading and eventually as correctly spelled words for writing.

By J. Richard Gentry, Ph.D., author, researcher, and educational consultant known for his groundbreaking work on topics such as early literacy; best practices for reading, writing, and spelling; and dyslexia.

• • • • •

To learn more:

- Gentry, J. R. (2008). *Step-by-Step Assessment Guide to Code Breaking*. New York: Scholastic.

- Feldgus, E., Cardonick, I. and Gentry, R. (2017). *Kid Writing in the 21st Century*. Los Angeles: Hameray.

Invested Reading

✸ WHAT

Invested Reading, also known as the subtext strategy, is a versatile, thought-provoking, practical comprehension tool, rooted in dramatic play, that invites readers to imagine others' internal monologues—in other words, what others are thinking. It offers a fresh take on "close reading" by breathing life into ordinary topics and leading readers to sophisticated, fulfilling engagement with a range of texts.

✸ WHY

Fiction. Invested Reading invites all readers, children and adults, to approach fiction in new and deeper ways by studying the text and illustrations and by "stepping inside the story world" to imagine what characters are thinking. It offers many benefits, including helping readers learn to infer, empathize with characters, appreciate multiple perspectives, and comprehend not just deeply, but broadly.

Nonfiction. Readers explore nonfiction texts from outside the text, first capturing their own personal responses to it. Then they each create an imagined reader of their own, whose perspective is different from their own—sketching and creating a backstory for that reader. Next, they revisit the text as their imagined readers, coming up with and recording their responses to the text. Finally, students participate in a "Town Meeting" as their imagined readers, where they discuss the issue under study. These conversations help readers recognize that even "simple" issues are not black and white. As a result, students begin to appreciate not only the complexities surrounding the issue, but the consequences they have as well.

Invested Reading helps striving readers read deeply, think critically, and understand texts and the implications for their characters. Invested readers become more empathetic, less judgmental, and develop a "social imagination" critical to life in our complex times.

✷ HOW

Invested reading:

- provides the scaffolding strivers need to share thoughts, explore issues, and participate in sophisticated discussions.

- integrates speaking, listening, reading, writing, and visual and performing arts, offering different ways for kids of all abilities to enter a text comfortably.

- helps kids develop a powerful capacity to empathize with and appreciate the perspectives of others, creating kinder, gentler citizens committed to fairness and social justice.

- grabs kids' hearts and minds, making literacy learning emotional and memorable; indeed, kids often continue discussions at home with their families.

- helps kids read the socially complex world to make informed, productive life choices.

- helps students develop a sense of agency that positions them not only to approach reading powerfully, but also to live powerfully outside of school, inspiring "make-a-difference-in-your-own-community" social action.

- opens the door to a whole new way of thinking about comprehension and communication.

By Jean Anne Clyde, Distinguished Teaching Professor Emerita at the University of Louisville. (From Stephens, D., Clyde, J.A., Harste, J. (In press). Reading Strategies for Deep Thinking. New York: Scholastic.)

Rime Magic for Word Solving

 WHAT

Written language includes individual words that comprise sound/letter relationships. Some students are able to figure out how this relationship works simply by reading and writing themselves, initially using invented spelling where they work hard to "stretch the word out like a rubber band" and line up letters to go with the sounds they hear. However, other students may need more support with word solving. Sharon Zinke, a 40-year veteran reading specialist, has discovered that the most meaningful way to provide that scaffolding is through Rime Magic, a system she developed as she worked with thousands of struggling readers across the state.

The rime is the key part of a word that makes it easy to see the word's structure (for example, the /ip/ in slippery or the /at/ in splattered). Students quickly learn how to add onsets (i.e., beginnings) and endings to the rimes to combine those parts into words and analyze those words—like magic! They learn to see the natural segmentation patterns of the written word—and "crack the code"—using their ability to hear onsets and rimes to make letter-sound correspondences.

WHY

Rime Magic is a system that focuses on the onset rime patterns that make words comprehensible to students with processing issues. It is not a rule-based approach that leaves challenged decoders scratching their heads at word difficulties trying to recall a rule and apply it. Rather, it's an immersion system that helps students focus on the rime in the middle of the word and build out from there. Students begin to see words as a series of predictable patterns rather than a string of random letters and sounds.

✳ HOW

Intervention and Prevention. The aim is to give kids a quick, targeted strategy for word solving and then move on immediately to fluent, meaningful independent reading. Teachers use rime magic for both prevention, particularly with brand new readers, and for intervention, for kids who got off to a bad start with traditional phonics instruction, which focuses on rules that, given the idiosyncrasies of the English language, often don't work.

To see research about the effectiveness of Rime Magic with older striving students, you can access "Rime Magic: A Breakthrough for Struggling Readers" at Scholastic.com/ThriveResources.

By Sharon Zinke, Reading Intervention Specialist.

• • • • •

To learn more:

- Moustafa, M. (2007). *Beyond Traditional Phonics: Research Discoveries and Reading Instruction.* Portsmouth, NH: Heinemann.

- Zinke, S. (2013). *The Decoding Solution: Rime Magic and Fast Success for Struggling Readers.* New York: Scholastic.

Additional Assessment Forms

You can find these additional forms to use with your striving readers at scholastic.com/ThriveResources.

Independent Reading Observation Guide

Student Name _____ Week _____

Points of Focus	Emerging	Approaching	Achieving
Selects books of appropriate challenge			
Notes			
Sets and meets appropriate reading goals			
Notes			
Reads a variety of genres			
Notes			
Demonstrates engagement with reading			
Notes			
Uses meaning-making strategies to make sense			
Notes			
Reads with fluency and expression			
Notes			
Retellings of text reflect comprehension			
Notes			
Sets and meets appropriate reading goals			
Notes			
Has next reading book in mind			
Notes			

TM ® & © Scholastic Inc. All rights reserved. From Striving to Thriving copyright © 2017 by Stephanie Harvey and Annie Ward. Published by Scholastic Inc.

Monitoring Strategic Reading

Name	Activating Background Knowledge	Predicting	Asking Questions	Monitoring for Meaning	Inferring Meaning	Summarizing and Synthesizing

TM ® & © Scholastic Inc. All rights reserved. From Striving to Thriving copyright © 2017 by Stephanie Harvey and Annie Ward. Published by Scholastic Inc.

Kidwatching In Action

Student Name _____ Observation Dates _____

Settings/Language	Independent	One-to-One or Small Group	Whole Class
READING Behaviors, Attitudes, and Understandings			
WRITING Behaviors, Attitudes, and Understandings			
SPEAKING/ LISTENING Behaviors, Attitudes, and Understandings			

TM ® & © Scholastic Inc. All rights reserved. From Striving to Thriving copyright © 2017 by Stephanie Harvey and Annie Ward. Published by Scholastic Inc.

Burke Reading Interview

by Carolyn Burke (1987)

Name _____ Date _____

1. When you are reading and you come to something you don't know, what do you do?

2. Do you ever do anything else?

3. Who do you know who is a good reader?

4. What makes him/her a good reader?

5. Do you think she/he ever comes to something she/he doesn't know when reading? If your answer is yes, what do you think he/she does about it?

6. What do you think is the best way to help someone who doesn't read well?

7. How did you learn to read? What do you remember? What helped you to learn?

8. What would you like to do better as a reader?

9. Describe yourself as a reader.

TM ® & © Scholastic Inc. All rights reserved. From Reading Miscue Inventory: From Evaluation to Instruction, Second Edition by Yetta M. Goodman, Dorothy J. Watson, and Carolyn L. Burke. Copyright © 2005 by Richard C. Owen Publishers, Inc. Published by Richard C. Owen Publishers, Inc. Used by permission.

304 *From Striving to Thriving* © 2017 by Stephanie Harvey & Annie Ward, Scholastic Inc.

My Reading Log

Name:		Week of	
Day of the Week	Books and Pages Read	Home	School
Monday			
Tuesday			
Wednesday			
Thursday			
Friday			
Saturday			
Sunday			

My Reading Life

Name	What I can do	What I'm working on	What I want to learn next
Choose a book to read that I love			
Explore a range of genres			
Book Talk my book			
Self-monitor my reading for meaning.			
Use fix-up strategies when I lose my way.			
Retell a story I've read and describe the plot, setting, themes, characters, problem and solution.			
Use the features of nonfiction to support my meaning-making.			
Explore the text with others thinking about the text, within the text, and beyond the text.			
Consider, in writing, how a text might have changed me as a human being.			

Reading Conference Tracker

Student _____

What I Know	What I Need to Know	Action Plan: How Will We Solve
Date		
Date		
Date		

Retelling Tracker

Student _____

Date	Title		
		Introduction	
		Setting	
		Main	
		Characters	
		Problem	
		Solution	
		Theme	
Comments			

Date	Title		
		Introduction	
		Setting	
		Main	
		Characters	
		Problem	
		Solution	
		Theme	
Comments			

Acknowledgments

If book writing is a collaborative journey, writing this one was a thrilling roller coaster ride! At every deadline, we found something more that we simply had to include in the book. So, we begin by thanking our passionate, talented, and flexible team at Scholastic. Many thanks to Lois Bridges, our indefatigable editor who offered unwavering encouragement, research, and solutions for every twist and turn; Ray Coutu, simply the best line editor and nicest guy we know; Sarah Longhi, who paid patient attention to detail even as we lurched uphill; and Danny Miller, our over-the-top production editor, Brian LaRossa, our art director, Eliza Hack, our cover designer, and Sarah Morrow, who worked her design magic as we sped toward the finish. This was truly a team effort and we are forever grateful. We are grateful, too, for the warm welcome and kind encouragement we have recieved from Dick Robinson, CEO/President of Scholastic, and Greg Worrell, President of Scholastic Eduction. Thanks also to Pam Parker, Director of Marketing, and her fabulous marketing team.

Also within the Scholastic family, we are deeply indebted to Dav Pilkey for sharing his poignant journey from striving to thriving and for drawing countless striving readers to the reading zone with his mighty pen.

Our thoughts and words stand on the shoulders of many committed researchers and academics who have dedicated their lives to helping kids develop reading proficiency and come to love reading. Dick Allington and Stephen Krashen have been extolling the importance of reading volume for decades, and we are proud to echo their call. Peter Johnston's work on teacher language, the dialogic classroom, and dynamic learning frames is evident throughout. P. D. Pearson's lifelong research on comprehension undergirds our thinking. Ken and Yetta Goodman's work on miscue analysis is especially profound for striving readers. Susan Neuman and Donna Celano's research on children's access to books heightens our determination to eradicate book deserts. Tim Rasinski makes fluency instruction engaging for strivers, and Nell Duke's thinking on early literacy flows throughout. Additionally, we are grateful to Jean Ann Clyde, Richard Gentry, Barbara Gilbert, Adria Klein, Ellen Lewis, and Sharon Zinke for contributing their powerful practices. Many thanks.

We are also grateful to multiple educator/authors, simply too numerous to mention each by name, from whom we have learned over the years. Their work has made an impact on all we do. This book, with its focus on striving readers and the indispensable nature of voluminous reading, has been particularly influenced by Nancie Atwell, Kylene Beers, Katherine and Randy Bomer, Anne Goudvis, Mary Howard, Ellin Keene, Penny Kittle, Teri Lesesne, Debbie Miller, Donalyn Miller, Franki Sibberson, Karen Szymusiak, and Alfred Tatum. We owe them all beyond measure.

We both reserve a special place in our hearts for Shelley Harwayne. It was Shelley who urged Steph to write her first book back in the mid-'90s and then launched her into that world by reading drafts and writing an over-the-top foreword to *Nonfiction Matters*. It was Shelley whose blazing example inspired Annie as a literacy leader and who extended to Annie the formidable opportunity to join her regional team in the New York City Department of Education.

We owe a great debt to Maggie Hoddinott, Mamaroneck Literacy Ambassador, for demonstrating in her work with teachers and librarians the power of classroom library curation, relentless book-matching, and community outreach.

Additionally, Annie would like to thank all of her colleagues in Ridgewood, NJ; New York City; and Mamaroneck, NY, whose love of children, skillful teaching, continual reflection, and sense of humor have been a steady source of camaraderie, energy, and inspiration. The Mamaroneck Board of Education trustees and schools superintendent, Dr. Robert Shaps, have been unflaggingly committed to closing the knowing-doing gaps around book access and voluminous, engaged reading. Annie thanks Steph for inviting her to partner on this project; in fact, she hasn't stopped pinching herself over the thrilling opportunity to collaborate with her longtime mentor. Finally, Annie thanks her entire blended family for their interest and support, especially husband, Bill, and daughter, Mimi, whom she can't wait to join on the sandy beach of Great East Lake with a stack of books.

Steph is most grateful to extraordinary fourth-grade teacher Kai Johnson, who welcomed her into his classroom to work together and do lessons, create source sets, take photos, and any other wacky request that she had. She thanks Annie for doing this book with her. How lucky she has been to have the likes of Anne Goudvis, Smokey Daniels, and now Annie Ward collaborate with her on these amazing projects. She can't forget to thank the "Usual Suspects" after all of these thought-provoking and fun-filled years. And, as always, she thanks Edward, her husband of 42 years, and the rest of her family, which now includes Riley, her precious granddaughter, as well as a grandson coming about the time of this publication. In all things—gratitude.

Of course it is for the kids, particularly the striving readers, who have made us laugh and cry and taught us the most, that we reserve our most profound thanks. With this publication, we hope to "tip the field toward the underdogs" by putting them on reading paths.

References

Allington, R.L. (2014). *What Really Matters for Middle School Readers: From Research to Practice.* Boston: Pearson.

Allington, R.L. (1977). "If They Don't Read Much, How They Ever Gonna Get Good?" *Journal of Reading, 21*, 1, 57–61, Oct.

Allington, R.L. (2009). *What Really Matters in Response to Intervention: Research-Based Designs.* Boston: Pearson.

Allington, R.L. (2012). *What Really Matters for Struggling Readers: Designing Research-Based Programs, Third Edition.* Boston: Pearson.

Allington, R.L. (2013). "What Really Matters When Working with Struggling Readers." *Reading Teacher,* v66, n7, 520–530, Apr.

Allington, R.L. & Gabriel, R.E. (2012). "Every Child, Every Day." *Educational Leadership, 69*, 6, 10–15, Mar.

Allington, R.L. & Johnston, P.H. (2000). "What Do We Know About Effective Fourth Grade Teachers and Their Classrooms?" *Learning to Teach Reading: Setting the Research Agenda,* 150–165. Neward, DE: International Reading Association.

Allington, R.L., & McGill-Franzen, A. (2013). *Summer Reading: Closing the Rich/Poor Reading Achievement Gap.* New York: Teachers College Press.

Allington, R.L. & Woodside-Jiron, H. (2002). Decodable text in beginning reading: Are mandates and policy based on research? In R. Allington (Ed.). *Big Brother and the National Reading Curriculum. How Ideology Trumped Evidence.* Portsmouth, NH: Heinemann, 195–216.

Anderson, C. (2000). *How's It Going? A Practical Guide to Conferring with Student Writers.* Portsmouth, NH: Heinemann.

Anderson, R. C., Wilson P.T. & Fielding, L.G. (1988). "Growth in Reading and How Children Spend Their Time Outside of School." *Reading Research Quarterly,* Vol. 23, No. 3, pp. 285–303.

Atwell, N. & Merkel, A.A. (2016). *The Reading Zone: How to Help Kids Become Skilled, Passionate, Habitual, Critical Readers, Second Edition.* New York: Scholastic.

Balu, R., Zhu, P. Doolittle, F., Schiller, E. Jenkins, J. & Gersten, R. (2015). "Evaluation of Response to Intervention Practices for Elementary School Reading." U.S. Department of Education. ies.ed.gov/ncee/pubs/20164000/pdf/20164000.pdf

Bavishi, A., Slade, M. & Levy, B.R. (2016). "A Chapter a Day: Association of Book Reading With Longevity." *Social Science & Medicine,* Vol. 164, 44–48.

Beers, K. (2002). *When Kids Can't Read.* Portsmouth, NH: Heinemann.

Beers, K. & Probst, R.E. (2017). *Disrupting Thinking: Why How We Read Matters.* New York: Scholastic.

Berns, G.S., Blaine, K., Prietula, M.J. & Pye, B.E. (2013). "Short- and Long-Term Effects of a Novel in the Brain." *Brain Connect, 3*(6) 590–600.

Bomer, K. (2015). "With an Air of Expectancy." *The Teacher You Want to Be: Essays About Children, Learning, and Teaching.* Portsmouth, NH: Heinemann.

Borrero, N. & Bird, S. (2009). *Closing the Achievement Gap: How to Pinpoint Student Strengths to Differentiate Instruction and Help Your Striving Readers Succeed.* New York: Scholastic.

Bridges, L. (1995). *Assessment: Continuous Learning.* Portland, ME: Stenhouse.

Bridges, L. (2010). RTI: The Best Intervention is a Good Book. White Paper. New York: Scholastic.

Bridges, L. (2015). *The Joy and Power of Reading: A Summary of Research and Expert Opinion.* New York: Scholastic.

Britton, J. (1970). *Language and Learning.* Coral Gables, FL: University of Miami Press.

Burkey, M. (2013). *Audiobooks for Youth: A Practical Guide to Sound Literature.* Chicago: ALA Editions.

Burkey, M. (2016). "Voices in My Head." *Booklist,* April 28.

Centre for Longitudinal Studies. "Reading for Pleasure Puts Children Ahead in the Classroom, Study Finds." 11 September 2013. http://www.cls.ioe.ac.uk/news.aspx?itemid=2740&sitesectionid=27

Cervetti, G. (2011). "Comprehension in Science." In *Comprehension Going Forward.* Portsmouth, NH: Heinemann.

Cervetti, G. & Hiebert, E. (2015). "Knowledge Literacy and the Common Core." *Language Arts 92.* (4): 256–259.

Chiarello, E. (2014). The Textual Lineage of a Teacher. In Teaching Tolerance. http://www.tolerance.org/blog/textual-lineage-teacher

Choinard, M. (2007). *Children's Questions: A Mechanism for Cognitive Development.* Monographs of the Society for Research in Child Development. Hoboken, NJ: Wiley-Blackwell.

Clay, M. (1993). *Observation Survey of Early Literacy Achievement.* Portsmouth, NH: Heinemann.

Collins, K. & Bempechat, J. (2017). *No More Mindless Homework.* Portsmouth, NH: Heinemann.

CPE (2014). "Time in School: How Does the US Compare?" Centerforpubliceducation.org

Csikszentmihalyi, M. (2008) *Flow: The Psychology of Optimal Experience.* New York: Harper Perennial Modern Classics.

D'Addario, D. (2015). "17 Famous Writers on Their Favorite Young Adult Books." *Time.* http://time.com/3650304/writers-favorite-ya-books

Daniels, H. & Ahmed, S. (2014). *Upstanders: How to Engage Middle School Minds and Heart With Inquiry.* Portsmouth, NH: Heinemann.

Daniels, H. (2017). *The Curious Classroom: 10 Structures for Teaching With Student-Directed Inquiry.* Portsmouth, NH: Heinemann.

Davenport, R. (2002). *Miscues Not Mistakes: Reading Assessment in the Classroom.* Portsmouth, NH: Heinemann.

Denby, D. (2016). "The Limits of 'Grit.'" *The New Yorker,* June 21. http://www.newyorker.com/culture/culture-desk/the-limits-of-grit

Duckworth, A. (2016). *Grit: The Power and Passion of Perseverance.* New York: Scribner.

Duke, N.K. (2016). "Essential Instructional Practices in Early Literacy, Grades K-3." Lansing, MI: General Education Leadership Network. http://www.gomaisa.org/sites/default/files/K-3%20Literacy%20Essentials%203.2016.pdf

Duke, N.K. (2017). Keynote Speech. Colorado Council of the IRA, Feb 3.

Duke, N.K. & Bennett-Armistead, V.S. (2003). *Reading & Writing Informational Text in the Primary Grades: Research-Based Practices.* New York: Scholastic.

Duke, N. & Pearson, P.D. (2002). "Effective Practices for Developing Reading Comprehension," Farnstrup, A. & Samuels, J. (Eds.) *What Research Has to Say About Reading Instruction, Third Edition,* Newark, DE: International Reading Association.

Dweck, C. (2014). "The Power of Believing That You Can Improve." TED Talk. ted.com/talks/carol_dweck_the_power_of_believing_that_you_can_improve

Dweck, C.S. (2007). *Mindset: The New Psychology of Success.* New York: Ballantine Books.

Engel, S. (2011). "Children's Need to Know: Curiosity in Schools." *Harvard Educational Review 81*(4) 625–645.

Entwistle, D.R., Alexander, K.L. & Olson, L.S. (1997). *Children, Schools, and Inequality.* Boulder, CO: Westiew Press.

EW Staff. "100 Greatest Movies, TV Shows, and More." *Entertainment Weekly.* December 4 (2009). http://ew.com/article/2009/12/04/100-greatest-movies-tv-shows-and-more

Feldgus, E., Cardonick, I. and Gentry, R. (2017). *Kid Writing in the 21st Century.* Los Angeles: Hameray.

Ferlazzo, L. (2016). "Reading Digitally vs. Reading Paper." *Education Week,* May 28.

Flippo, R. (2013). *Assessing Readers: Qualitative Diagnosis and Instruction, Second Edition.* Portsmouth, NH: Heinemann.

Fountas, I. & Pinnell, G.S. (2016). "A Level Is a Teacher's Tool, NOT a Child's Label." Blog post. http://blog.fountasandpinnell.com/post/a-level-is-a-teacher-s-tool-not-a-child-s-label

Fountas, I. & Pinnell, G.S. (2017). *Guided Reading: Responsive Teaching Across the Grades, Second Edition.* Portsmouth, NH: Heinemann.

Fountas, I. and Pinnell, G.S. (2006). *Teaching for Comprehending and Fluency: Thinking, Talking, and Writing About Reading, K–8.* Portsmouth, NH: Heinemann.

Gaiman, N. (2013). "Why Our Future Depends on Libraries, Reading, and Daydreaming." *The Guardian,* October 15.

Gambrell, Linda. (1996). *Lively Discussions! Fostering Engaged Reading.* Newark, DE: International Literacy Association.

Garcia, O. & Wei, L. (2013). *Translanguaging: Language, Bilinguialism, and Education.* London: Palgrave Macmillan.

Gawande, A. (2008). *Better: A Surgeon's Notes on Performance.* New York: Picador.

Gay, G. (2000). *Culturally Responsive Teaching: Theory, Research, and Practice.* New York: Teachers College Press.

Gay, G. (2010). *Culturally Responsive Teaching: Theory, Research, and Practice, Second Edition.* New York: Teachers College Press.

Gentry, J.R. (2008). *Step-by-Step Assessment Guide to Code Breaking.* New York: Scholastic.

Godsey, M. (2016). "Listen to This: Podcasts Can Hook Reluctant Readers While Boosting Critical Thinking and Comprehension." *Literacy Today,* Volume 34 ILA VOL 3 Nov/Dec.

Godsey, M. "The Value of Using Podcasts in Class." *The Atlantic.* 17 March 2016. http://www.theatlantic.com/education/archive/2016/03/the-benefits-of-podcasts-in-class/473925.

Goodman, K., Fries, P., and Strauss, S. (2016). *Reading, the Grand Illusion: How and Why People Make Sense of Print.* New York: Routledge.

Goodman, K. (1996). *On Reading: A Common-sense Look at the Nature of Language and the Science of Reading.* Portsmouth, NH: Heinemann.

Goodman, Y. & Marek, A. (1996). *Retrospective Miscue Analysis: Revaluing Readers and Reading.* Katonah, NY: Richard Owen Publishers.

Graves, D.H. (1983). *Writing: Teachers and Children at Work.* Portsmouth, NH: Heinemann.

Graves, D.H. (1984). *A Researcher Learns to Write.* Portsmouth, NH: Heinemann.

Graves, D.H. (1994). *A Fresh Look at Writing.* Portsmouth, NH: Heinemann.

Graves, D.H. (2001). *The Energy to Teach.* Portsmouth, NH: Heinemann.

Green, R. (2013). *Mastery.* New York: Penguin.

Grosjean, F. (2016). "What Is Translanguaging? An Interview With Ofelia Garcia." *Psychology Today.*

Gross-Loh, C. (2016). "How Praise Became a Consolation Prize." *The Atlantic,* December 16. https://www.theatlantic.com/education/archive/2016/12/how-praise-became-a-consolation-prize/510845/

Guthrie, J.T., Wigfield, A. & Humenick, N.M. (2004). Influences of Stimulating Tasks on Reading Motivation and Comprehension. *The Journal of Educational Research.* http://www.cori.umd.edu/research-publications/2006-guthrie-wigfield-hum.pdf

Halliday, M.A.K. & Hasan, R. (1991). *Language, Context, and Text: Aspects of Language in a Social-Semiotic Perspective.* New York: Oxford University Press.

Halliday, M.A.K. (1973). *Explorations in the Function of Language.* London: Edward Arnold Publishers Ltd.

Harvey, S. (1998). *Nonfiction Matters: Reading, Writing, and Research in Grades 3–8.* Portland, ME: Stenhouse Publishers.

Harvey, S. & Daniels, H. (2015). *Comprehension and Collaboration: Inquiry Circles for Curiosity, Engagement, and Understanding, Revised Edition.* Portsmouth, NH: Heinemann.

Harvey, S. & Goudvis, A. (2016). *Read, Write, and Talk: A Practice to Enhance Comprehension.* Portland, ME: Stenhouse Publishers.

Harvey, S. & Goudvis, A. (2017). *Strategies That Work: Teaching Comprehension for Understanding and Engagement, Third Edition.* Portland, ME: Stenhouse Publishers.

Harwayne, S. (1999). *Going Public: Priorities and Practice at the Manhattan New School.* Portsmouth, NH: Heinemann.

Heard, G. (2016) *Heart Maps: Helping Students Create and Craft Authentic Writing.* Portsmouth, NH: Heinemann.

Hicks, B. (2008). "The Problem With Labeling Children." *The Kid Counselor.* thekidcounselor.com/2008/01/the-problem-with-labeling-children/

Hiebert, E.H. & Martin, L.A. (2015). "Changes in Text of Reading Instruction During the Past 50 Years." In P.D. Pearson and E.H. Hiebert (Eds.) *Research-Based Practices for Teaching Common Core Literacy.* New York: Teachers College Press.

Howard, M. (2009). *RTI From All Sides: What Every Teacher Needs to Know.* Portsmouth, NH: Heinemann.

Howard, M. Tweet from 8/17/17 @DrMaryHoward.

International Reading Association and the National Council of Teachers of English. (2010). Standards for the Assessment of Reading and Writing. Joint Task Force of IRA and NCTE.

Ivey, G. & Johnston, P.H. (2013). Engagement With Young Adult Literature: Outcomes and Processes. *Reading Research Quarterly, 48*(3), 255-275.

Johnston, P.H. (2004). *Choice Words: How Our Language Affects Children's Learning.* Portland, ME: Stenhouse Publishers.

Johnston, P.H. (2012). *Opening Minds: Using Language to Change Lives.* Portland, ME: Stenhouse Publishers.

Keene, E.O. & Glover, M. (2015). *The Teacher You Want to Be: Essays About Children, Learning, and Teaching.* Portsmouth, NH: Heinemann.

Keene, E.O. & Zimmermann, S. (2007). *Mosaic of Thought: The Power of Comprehension Strategy Instruction, Second Edition.* Portsmouth, NH: Heinemann.

Keller, B. (2013). "Toy Story." The Opinion Pages, *New York Times.* http://www.nytimes.com/2013/11/18/opinion/keller-toy-story.html

Kelley, D. & Kelley, T. (2013). *Creative Confidence: Unleashing the Creative Potential Within Us All.* New York: Crown Business.

Kittle, P. (2012). *Book Love: Developing Depth, Stamina, and Passion in Adolescent Readers.* Portsmouth, NH: Heinemann.

Krashen, S.D. (2004). *The Power of Reading: Insights from the Research.* Santa Barbara, CA: Libraries Unlimited.

Krashen, S.D. (2011). *Free Voluntary Reading.* Santa Barbara, CA: Libraries Unlimited.

Krashen, S. & Henkin, V.J. (2015). "The Naruto Breakthrough: The Home Run Book Experience." *Language Magazine.* Vol 15(1): 32–35.

Krashen, S. & Ujiie, J. (1996). "Is Comic Book Reading Harmful?" *CSLA Journal* 19(2): 27–28. http://www.sdkrashen.com/content/articles/1996_is_comic_book_reading_harmful.pdf

Ladson-Billings, G. (1994). *The Dreamkeepers: Successful Teachers of African-American Children.* San Francisco: Jossey-Bass.

Ladson-Billings, G. (1995b). Toward a Theory of Culturally Responsive Pedagogy. American *Educational Research Journal, 32*(3), 465–491.

Lapowsky, I. (October 4, 2013). "Ev Williams on Twitter's Early Years." *Inc.* Retrieved from inc.com/issie-lapowsky/ev-williams-twitter-early-years.html?cid=em01011week40day04b

Larson, J. (2008). CREW: A Weeding Manual for Modern Libraries. Austin, TX: Texas State Library and Archives Commission. tsl.texas.gov/sites/default/files/public/tslac/ld/pubs/crew/crewmethod08.pdf

Lesesne, T. (2003). *Making the Match: The Right Book for the Right Reader at the Right Time, Grades 4–12.* Portland, ME: Stenhouse Publishers.

Lesesne, T. (2010). *Reading Ladders: Leading Students From Where They Are to Where We'd Like Them to Be.* Portsmouth, NH: Heinemann.

Lesesne, T. (2015). Graphic Novels Educators' Guide. New York: Random House Children's Books. randomhousekids.com/media/activities/GraphicNovels_EducatorGd_15_WEB.pdf

Logan, B. (2010). "The Curiosity Coma." Efficacy Institute. www.efficacy.org/Resources/TheEIPointofView/tabid/233/ctl/ArticleView/mid/678/articleId/253/The-Curiosity-Coma.aspx

Manzo, K.K. (2007). Reading Curricula Don't Make Cut for Federal Review. *Education Week.* http://www.edweek.org/ew/articles/2007/08/15/01whatworks_web.h27.html

Mapp, K., Carver, I. & Lander, J. (2017). *Powerful Partnerships: A Teacher's Guide to Engaging Families for Student Success.* New York: Scholastic.

Martin, C. (2013) "Rainbow Loom's Success, From 2,000 Pounds of Rubber Bands." *New York Times.* nytimes.com/2013/09/01/business/rainbow-looms-success-from-2000-pounds-of-rubber-bands.html

McGregor, T. (2007). *Comprehension Connections: Bridges to Strategic Reading, Second Edition.* Portsmouth, NH: Heinemann.

McKearney, M. & Mears, S. (2015). "Lost For Words? How Reading Can Teach Children Empathy." *The Guardian,* May 13. theguardian.com/teacher-network/2015/may/13/reading-teach-children-empathy

McLeod, A. (2013). "Connect Print-Referencing During Read-Aloud With a Children's Book." *Dimensions of Early Childhood,* Vol 41.

Mehta, J. (2015). "The Problem with Grit." Blog post in *Education Week.* http://blogs.edweek.org/edweek/learning_deeply/2015/04/the_problem_with_grit.html

Miller, D. (2008). *Teaching With Intention: Defining Beliefs, Aligning Practice, Taking Action, K–5.* Portland, ME: Stenhouse Publishers.

Miller, D. (2009). *The Book Whisperer: Awakening the Inner Reader in Every Child.* San Francisco: Jossey-Bass.

Miller, D. (2011). "Not So Gradual Release," in *Comprehension Going Forward: Where We Are and What's Next* (Keene et al). Portsmouth, NH: Heinemann.

Miller, D. (2012). *Reading With Meaning: Teaching Comprehension in the Primary Grades, Second Edition.* Portland, ME: Stenhouse Publishers.

Miller, D. (2014). *Reading in the Wild: The Book Whisperer's Keys to Cultivating Lifelong Reading Habits.* San Francisco: Jossey-Bass.

Miller, D. (2015). "I've Got Research. Yes, I Do. I've Got Research. How About You?", The Book Whisperer blog. bookwhisperer.com/2015/02/08/ive-got-research-yes-i-do-ive-got-research-how-about-you/

Moll, L. & González, N. (2004). Engaging Life. In J. Banks & C. Banks (Eds.) *Handbook of Research on Multicultural Education, Second Edition.* (pp. 699–713). San Francisco: Jossey-Bass.

Monáe, J. (2014). "The Power of Yet." Sesame Street YouTube Video with Lyrics by Fanny Wynn. https://www.youtube.com/watch?v=Kd_WENe8H-I

Morehead, J. (2012). "Stanford University's Carol Dweck on Growth Mindset and Education." onedublin.org

Morrow, K. (1977). "Authentic Texts and ESP." In Holden, S. (ed.). *English for Specific Purposes.* Modern English Publications.

National Center for Education Statistics. (2016). Children and Youth With Disabilities. nces.ed.gov/programs/coe/indicator_cgg.asp

National Geographic. (2011). *The Big Idea: How Breakthroughs of Past Shape the Future.* Washington, DC: *National Geographic.*

National Institute of Child Health and Human Development. (2000). *The Report of the National Reading Panel: Report of the Subgroups.* Washington, DC: U.S. Government Printing Office.

Neuman, S.B. (2001). "The Importance of the Classroom Library." *Early Childhood Today*, Vol. 15, Issue 5, p. 12. http://teacher.scholastic.com/products/paperbacks/downloads/library.pdf

Neuman, S.B. & Celano, D.C. (2012). "Worlds Apart: One City, Two Libraries, and Ten Years of Watching Inequality Grow." *American Educator*, v36 n3.

Neuman, S.B. & Celano, D.C. (2012). *Giving Our Children a Fighting Chance: Poverty, Literacy, and the Development of Information Capital.* New York: Teachers College Press.

Nieto, S. (2010). *Language, Culture, and Teaching: Critical Perspectives, Second Edition.* NewYork: Routledge.

Ouelette, G. & Sénéchal, M. (2017). "Invented Spelling in Kindergarten as a Predictor of Reading and Spelling in Grade 1: A New Pathway to Literacy, or Just the Same Road, Less Known?" *Developmental Psychology, 53*(1) 77–88.

Owocki, G. & Goodman, Y. (2003). *Kidwatching: Documenting Children's Literacy Development.* Portsmouth, NH: Heinemann.

Patterson, James (2014). In L. Bridges. *The Lifesaving Power of Reading. Open a World of Possible.* New York: Scholastic.

Pearson, P.D. (2014). Keynote Address, Utah State Reading Association, September 27.

Pearson, P.D., Dole, J.A., Duffy, G.G. & Roehler, A.L. (1992). "Developing Expertise in Reading Comprehension: What Should be Taught and How Should It Be Taught?" in Farstup, J. & and Samuels S.J. (Eds.) *What Research Has to Say to the Teacher of Reading.* Newark, DE: International Reading Association.

Pearson, P.D. & Gallagher, M.C. (1983) "The Instruction of Reading Comprehension." *Contemporary Educational Psychology, 8*(3) 327–324.

Piketty, T. (2015). *Capital in the Twenty-First Century.* Cambridge, MA: Harvard University Press.

Pressley, M. (2003). *Motivating Primary Grade Students.* New York: Guilford Press.

Rasinski, T. (2010). *The Fluent Reader (2nd Ed): Oral Reading Strategies For Building Word Recognition, Fluency, and Comprehension.* New York: Scholastic.

Rasinski, T. & Samuels, S.J. (2011): Reading Fluency; What It Is and What It Is Not." In S. J. Samuels & A. Farstrup (Eds.), *What Research Has to Say About Reading Instruction.* Newark, DE: IRA.

Remenar, K. (2013). "Top Ten Wordless Picture Books." Nerdy Book Club Blog. nerdybookclub.wordpress.com/2013/03/30/top-ten-wordless-picture-books-by-kristen-remenar/

Richardson, J. (2016). *Next Step Forward in Guided Reading: An Assess-Decide-Guide Framework for Supporting Every Reader.* New York: Scholastic.

Robinson, K. (2006). Do Schools Kill Creativity? Ted Talk. ted.com/talks/ken_robinson_says_schools_kill_creativity

Rose, T. (2016). *The End of Average: How We Succeed in a World That Values Sameness.* New York: HarperOne.

Rosenblatt, L. (1938.) *Literature as Exploration.* New York: D. Appleton-Century Co.

Routman, R. (2014.) *Read, Write, Lead: Breakthrough Strategies for Schoolwide Literary Success.* Alexandria, VA: ASCD.

Schmoker, M. (2005). "On Common Ground: The Power of Professional Learning Communities" in R. DuFour & R. DuFour (Eds.), *No Turning Back: The Ironclad Case for Professional Learning Communities* (pp. 135–154). Bloomington, IN: National Educational Service.

Scholastic Kids & Family Reading Report. (2017.) http://www.scholastic.com/readingreport/

Scholastic Teacher & Principal School Report. (2017). http://www.scholastic.com/teacherprincipalreport/

Smith, F. (2011). *Understanding Reading: A Psycholinguistic Analysis of Reading and Learning to Read, Sixth Edition.* London: Routledge Press.

Sparks, S. (2015). "First Graders Who Were Identified for More Help Fell Further Behind." *Education Week.* November 6. http://www.edweek.org/ew/articles/2015/11/11/study-rti-practice-falls-short-of-promise.html

Spiegel, J. (2012). "Teachers Expectations Can Influence How Students Perform." NPR's Morning Edition, September 17, featuring Robert Rosenthal. npr.org/sections/health-shots/2012/09/18/161159263/teachers-expectations-can-influence-how-students-perform

Stephens, D., Clyde, J.A., & Harste, J. (In press). *Reading Strategies for Deep Thinking.* New York: Scholastic.

Strauss, V. (2008). "Author Works to Prevent Reading's 'Death Spiral.'" *Washington Post*, March 24. http://www.washingtonpost.com/wp-dyn/content/article/2008/03/23/AR2008032301754.html

Sung, K. (2016) "Listening Isn't Cheating: How Audio Books Can Help Us Learn." *Mind/Shift*, August 18.

Tatum, A. (2013). *Fearless Voices: Engaging a New Generation of African American Adolescent Male.* New York: Scholastic.

The Telegraph. (2009). "Reading Can Help Reduce Stress." http://www.telegraph.co.uk/news/health/news/5070874/Reading-can-help-reduce-stress.html

Townsend, J.C. (2012) "Why We Should Teach Empathy to Improve Education (And Test Scores)." *Forbes.* forbes.com/sites/ashoka/2012/09/26/why-we-should-teach-empathy-to-improve-education-and-test-scores/#1423577b27c4

Tugend, A. (2012). *Better By Mistake: The Unexpected Benefits of Being Wrong.* New York: Riverhead Books.

Valdés, G. (2001). *Learning and Not Learning English: Latino Students in American Schools.* New York: Teachers College Press.

Vezzali, L., Stathi, S., Giovannini, D., Capozza, D. & Trifiletti, E. (2014). The Greatest Magic of Harry Potter: Reducing Prejudice. *Journal of Applied Social Psychology, 45*(2), 105–121.

Wagner, T. (2012). *Creating Innovators: The Making of Young People Who Will Change the World.* New York: Scribner.

Walsh, R. (2016). "Fluency Instruction: Building Bridges From Decoding to Comprehension." Russ on Reading Blog, Oct 9.

White, M.C. (August 13, 2006). "Here's How Much Your Kid's Teacher Is Shelling Out for School Supplies." *Money.* Retrieved from time.com/money/4392319/teachers-buying-school-supplies/

Wilde, S. (2000). *Miscue Analysis Made Easy: Building on Student Strengths.* Portsmouth, NH: Heinemann.

Wilhelm, J. & Smith, M. (2013). *Reading Unbound: Why Kids Need to Read What They Want—and Why We Should Let Them.* New York: Scholastic.

Willingham, D. (2016). *"Is Listening to an Audiobook Cheating?"* Science and Education. http://www.danielwillingham.com/daniel-willingham-science-and-education-blog/is-listening-to-an-audio-book-cheating

Yuhas, D. (2014). "Curiosity Prepares the Brain for Better Learning." *Scientific American.* www.scientificamerican.com/article/curiosity-prepares-the-brain-for-better-learning

Index

From Striving to Thriving © 2017 by Stephanie Harvey & Annie Ward, Scholastic Inc.